Scottish History

FOR

DUMMIES®

A Wiley Brand

by William Knox, PhD

FOR

DUMMIES®

A Wiley Brand

Scottish History For Dummies®

Published by: **John Wiley & Sons, Ltd.,** The Atrium, Southern Gate, Chichester, www.wiley.com

This edition first published 2014

© 2014 John Wiley & Sons, Ltd, Chichester, West Sussex.

Registered office

John Wiley & Sons Ltd, The Atrium, Southern Gate, Chichester, West Sussex, PO19 8SQ, United Kingdom

For details of our global editorial offices, for customer services and for information about how to apply for permission to reuse the copyright material in this book please see our website at www.wiley.com.

Wiley publishes in a variety of print and electronic formats and by print-on-demand. Some material included with standard print versions of this book may not be included in e-books or in print-on-demand. If this book refers to media such as a CD or DVD that is not included in the version you purchased, you may download this material at http://booksupport.wiley.com. For more information about Wiley products, visit www.wiley.com.

Designations used by companies to distinguish their products are often claimed as trademarks. All brand names and product names used in this book are trade names, service marks, trademarks or registered trademarks of their respective owners. The publisher is not associated with any product or vendor mentioned in this book.

For general information on our other products and services, please contact our Customer Care Department within the U.S. at 877-762-2974, outside the U.S. at (001) 317-572-3993, or fax 317-572-4002. For technical support, please visit www.wiley.com/techsupport.

For technical support, please visit www.wiley.com/techsupport.

A catalogue record for this book is available from the British Library.

ISBN 978-1-118-67615-8 (hardback/paperback) ISBN 978-1-118-67612-7 (ebk) ISBN 978-1-118-67613-4 (ebk)

Printed in Great Britain by TJ International, Padstow, Cornwall

10 9 8 7 6 5 4 3 2 1

Contents at a Glance

Table of Contents

Part V: The Remaking of a Nation (1750–1918) 199

Introduction

●●

*T*his book is about Scotland, a small island nation on the edge of northern Europe. And for 80 per cent of the period covered in this book, Scotland didn't exist (at least not as we think of it today in territorial and political terms). Territorially, Scotland only assumed its current boundaries in 1470, with the acquisition of Orkney and Shetland, and politically it was only a nation-state from 1314 onward before voluntarily giving up its sovereignty in the Union of Parliaments with England in 1707 to create a new nation-state, Great Britain – a move that was deeply unpopular with ordinary Scots.

But in spite of its small size (just under 19 million acres) and several centuries of independence, Scotland has made a massive contribution not only to the history of these islands we call Great Britain but also to the modern world. Indeed, some historians have argued that Scotland – through its thinkers, engineers and scientists – invented the modern world.

Although Scotland has been a unitary state since 1470, it's divided by geography. The Highland Boundary Fault line, which runs from the northeast to the southwest, separates Scotland not just geographically into highlands and lowlands, but also culturally. The lowlands had rich, fertile farming land; the highlands, with its harsher climate, had many more mountains and rivers, but the soil was extremely poor, so rearing animals (especially cattle and, later, sheep) was the main source of income.

Yet for much of our history, more people lived in the north of Scotland than in the south. Such are the many contradictions in the Scottish story. Scotland is also wetter and windier than the rest of Britain, with the Shetland Isles experiencing around 42 days of gales per year. Hearing can be a problem in that part of Scotland!

Scotland also shares a part of a larger island – Britain – with its neighbours, the English and the Welsh. As far the English were concerned, we were 'noisy neighbours' who were there to be subdued. The relationship between the two kingdoms for most of the period covered in this book was, on the whole, fractious and violent. But it was the territorial battles with England that were important in creating a sense of national identity for the Scots – something they have never lost from the Middle Ages to the present day.

About This Book

In this book, I don't give a blow-by-blow account of the history of Scotland from the earliest times to the present. There isn't enough space and, in any case, it would be boring. This isn't a textbook, and it doesn't pretend to be. It reflects my views as a historian (just as most histories reflect their authors' points of view). I leave things out, I skip over things that seem irrelevant and include things that I hope you enjoy.

For any historian, the decision on what to put in and what to leave out is ultimately conditioned by the sources available. So, earlier chapters of the book are concerned with issues surrounding kingship and the relationship between Church and monarch; later chapters discuss elections and party politics.

The information is organised into chapters and parts so that you easily access what you need. Use the book as a reference – you don't need to read the chapters in order from front cover to back, and you aren't expected to remember anything. There won't be a test at the end of the book.

Sidebars (text in grey boxes) and anything marked with the Technical Stuff icon are skippable – the information is interesting but not necessary to your understanding of the topic at hand. Within this book, you may note that some web addresses break across two lines of text. If you're reading this book in print and want to visit one of these web pages, simply key in the web address exactly as it's noted in the text, pretending as though the line break doesn't exist. If you're reading this as an e-book, you've got it easy – just click the web address to be taken directly to the web page.

Finally, as you read this book – and any other history – keep in mind that the wealthy and powerful left more traces of their lives than the poor and the illiterate did. Until relatively recently, 90 per cent of men and all women were denied a political role in Scottish society. So, all history has a certain bias, and the story is never complete. The past is continually being re-invented – that's what makes it so fascinating and something we can all play a part in making!

Foolish Assumptions

In writing this book I've made a few assumptions about you, the reader:

- ✔ You studied some Scottish history at school but were put off by the way it was taught, or maybe you liked it but your memory is a bit hazy about who did what.

✔ You haven't studied Scottish history, but you're interested in doing so and you're not sure where to start.

✔ You enjoy a good story and want to know more about Scotland and its peoples.

Icons Used in This Book

Throughout this book, you see pictures in the margins. These pictures are called *icons,* and they're meant to draw your attention to key pieces of information. Here's a guide to what the icons mean:

The Remember icon alerts you to the most important information – the elements of Scottish history that you don't want to forget.

Sometimes my historian brain likes to go on a bit about details that aren't essential. When this happens, I mark the text with the Technical Stuff icon. If you're pressed for time, you can skip anything marked with this icon. On the other hand, if you read it, you're sure to find fascinating titbits of information.

When I quote famous historical figures or others, I mark the quote with the First Hand icon.

Beyond the Book

In addition to the material in the print or e-book you're reading right now, this product also comes with some access-anywhere goodies on the web. Check out the free Cheat Sheet at www.dummies.com/cheatsheet/scottish history for a guide to the historical periods of Scotland, a list of Scotland's rulers, and the major events and battles in Scottish history.

You can also find online articles that extend the content covered in the book. I provide links to the articles at the beginning of every part. Whether you're looking for information on the Vikings, the Black Douglases or the Treaty of Union, you can find it (and more) at www.dummies.com/extras/scottishhistory.

Where to Go from Here

You're more than welcome to start reading this book at the beginning and work through it until you reach the end, but you don't have to. You decide where you want to go and how far. If you want to know about William Wallace or Robert the Bruce, head to Chapter 10. If you're more interested in Scottish Nationalism, turn to Chapter 16. The choice is yours.

If you're still not sure where to start, have a look at the Table of Contents, or use the Index to look up names or places you're curious about. The story of Scotland is rich in drama and character. All you have to do to discover it is turn the pages!

Part I
Getting Started with Scottish History

In this part . . .

- Find out about the ages – Ice, Stone, Bronze and Iron – as well as some weird and wonderful stuff about prehistoric peoples like the Celts and their world.

- Look at the battles fought by the Romans and the four main peoples of ancient Scotland – the Angles, Britons, Gaels and Picts.

- Discover the origins of kingdoms in the struggles of the ancient Scottish peoples against Roman domination.

- Consider the arrival of Christianity and the saints who spread the Gospel, like Columba and Ninian.

Chapter 1

Welcome to Scotland

In This Chapter

▶ Getting acquainted with the people who make up the land we call Scotland

▶ Seeing how Scotland was formed

▶ Examining how Scotland gained, lost and regained its independence

*W*hen you think about Scottish history, maybe it takes you back to the classroom, where you heard stories from teachers about great heroes and villains. You may have stamped on your brain tales about great men like Robert the Bruce or William Wallace; or women like St Margaret or Mary, Queen of Scots; or maybe the great explorers like David Livingstone or Mungo Park. You would have also heard of villains like Macbeth, or failures such as Bonnie Prince Charlie. These are all wonderful stories in their own right, and they receive their due in this book. But there is more to Scottish history than simply the doings of great men and women, and in these pages you find out more about this nation than a history of the usual suspects can tell you.

The Peoples of Scotland

The history of Scotland is a truly remarkable one. As a nation, Scotland has probably contributed more to world civilisation than any other country of a comparable size. In fact, you could argue that the Scots – through their historians, philosophers, engineers and scientists – invented the modern world. But how did that come to pass? What was it about the people and their history that allowed them to make such a significant contribution to the modern world?

You couldn't put your finger on anything in the Scottish past to answer that question. For many centuries, nothing in particular distinguished the Scots from people from other parts of the globe. Indeed, you could argue that for most of Scotland's history, it has lagged behind other societies, including – wait for it – England!

There aren't any genetic clues either: ancient Scotland was made of at least five different peoples who spoke different languages. At first, they were simply members of tribes searching for food, but later they became farmers and members of small kingdoms. Of course, Scotland didn't exist in their minds: borders and things like national identity were pretty meaningless.

Since ancient times, other people have settled in Scotland. The Romans came, saw and tried to conquer but left empty-handed. Much more successful were the Vikings, who arrived at the start of the ninth century. The Vikings not only raped and pillaged but, in time, also settled on the islands and on the northern coast and became Christians. They were followed by the Anglo-Normans, who arrived in the reign of David I. They were given lands and eventually became successful and powerful members of the Scottish aristocracy. The Bruce and the Stewart families, who were rulers of Scotland at various times, were from this stock.

From the 12th century, we had to wait until the 19th century for the next major influx of people into Scotland. This time it was the Irish, and this influx proved a bit more problematic! The Irish arrived by the thousands in the west of Scotland in the 1840s, fleeing the famine. Their religion made it difficult for them to integrate into Scottish society, which was staunchly Presbyterian. However, they eventually succeeded, only to be replaced by other immigrants from the British Commonwealth in the late 20th century. This last movement of people into Scotland has been on a scale much smaller than experienced in England, but still, one in five children in Glasgow schools is from an Asian background.

So, we are, in a famous Scottish saying, 'aw Jock Tamson's bairns'. There is no such thing as a genetically pure native Scots: we are a hybrid people, and the better for it.

The Formation of Scotland

When it comes to the formation of Scotland, we can start with the Romans. They did little for Scotland except unite the various tribes of the north against them. In fighting the Romans, the tribes realised that bigger was better. When the Romans arrived at the tail end of the third century, there were 17 different tribes; when they left, there were only 4(Angles, Britons, Gaels and Picts).

In the middle of the ninth century, Kenneth MacAlpin united the Picts and the Gaels, and the new territory was named Alba or Scotland. But he didn't control the whole of Scotland – that was not achieved until 1460, when the Norwegians ceded Orkney and Shetland as part of payment of a dowry. So, what we now recognise as the boundaries of Scotland took a long time to be fixed.

Of course, the sovereignty of the kingdom was always contested by our friends in the south. Successive English kings tried to incorporate Scotland into their realm, without much success. The most determined attempt was by Edward I toward the end of the 13th century; that led to a national struggle for independence and made heroes of Robert the Bruce and William Wallace. The result was English recognition of the Scots' claim to be an independent nation. But it didn't end there. The Scots battled the English right up until the Union of Crowns in 1603 when a Scottish king, James VI, became the first king of England and Scotland.

The crowns were united but the nations were not. After about half a century of religious strife and battling the Stewart kings, the parliaments of the two countries were united in 1707 by the Treaty of Union. The Scottish Parliament voted itself out of existence. Why it did so is a matter of debate – people are still arguing over it. However, it meant that a new country called Great Britain was born, and the Scots had to learn to accept that they were British first and Scottish second, which they gladly did.

Scots were happy to accept what is known as a 'dual identity' because they were incorporated into the British Empire. They were quick to recognise a good thing when they saw it. So extensive was Scottish involvement with the empire, as administrators, traders and soldiers, that people have spoken about the 'Scottish Empire'.

Access to new markets and sources of raw materials saw the Scottish economy begin to take off. On the backs of native genius inventors, like James Watt, who invented the steam engine, Scotland became an industrial powerhouse. Scotland led the way in engineering, iron, steel and shipbuilding. Although Scotland beat the world in technology, it was also breaking records for the wrong reasons: the highest rates of squalor, poverty and disease in western Europe.

The late 20th century saw Scotland lose its lead in industry to other countries, like Japan and Korea, and as a result Scotland transformed itself from a maker of ships to a maker of chips (electronic ones, but Scots like the potato ones too!). All the old skills and occupations have gone, and in their place have come new ones associated with what's euphemistically called the 'knowledge economy'. In the past, Scots went down pits; today, they work in brightly lit offices and shops, but in many cases for much less money.

With each successive stage in the country's development, Scotland's sense of identity has undergone change. From a land of a myriad different voices and cultures, it became fiercely nationalistic as a result of the struggles with the English. Then it learned to embrace a new dual identity, which from the 1970s onward became more nationalistic. Unlike the old forms of Nationalism, which were exclusive and masculine, the new identity is inclusive of all Scots, regardless of gender, ethnicity or race.

Identity is never fixed; it's fluid and always in a state of forming and reforming itself. In that respect, Scotland is no different to any other country.

The Union with England and Its Uncertain Future

Scotland and England formed a union in 1707, but because no one was certain it was going to last, it was half-hearted and left the way open for a divorce. The English were in a hurry to get an agreement, so the Scots were able to negotiate a deal that allowed them to retain a separate legal and educational system and secure guarantees regarding the independence of the Church of Scotland – no Anglicanism here, thank you!

So, in spite of it being the beginning of a new country, each of the partners of the union had the building blocks of a nation-state intact in case they wanted to go their different ways in the future. Scotland had become a nation within a nation. The survival of these institutions was of no great importance at the time, but their very existence kept alive the memory of an independent Scotland.

No one doubts the Scottish commitment to Britain and its empire, but even at the high point of imperial pomp and circumstance, there were complaints about the way England had begun to stand for Britain. Instead of the British Empire, it was commonplace throughout the world to talk of the 'English Empire'. As a result, people in Scotland started to demand some form of 'home rule', where the Scots controlled their own affairs but matters of national defence and foreign policy were still the responsibility of the Westminster Parliament.

However, as long as the British Empire stuffed the mouths of the middle class in Scotland with gold, the moaning was confined to a minority. Along came war in 1914, and the moaning became even quieter as the Scots responded more enthusiastically than any other part of Britain to fight for king and country. They also took the biggest hit!

The cause of Nationalism didn't really get going again until the late 1960s, in spite of the formation of the Scottish National Party (SNP) in 1934. Scots were content with their dual identity – after all, they had fought another world war to defend it! But things started to go wrong in the 1970s, and by the end of 1974, the SNP found itself the second largest party in Scotland, with one-third of the vote in the second general election of that year and ten members of Parliament (MPs).

Both the Labour and Tory parties were worried, so they agreed to hold a referendum on devolution in 1978. But they rigged it in such a way that at least 40 per cent of voters would have to be in favour (many general elections have been won with less than that). The Scots were to have their own assembly, but at the last minute, they got cold feet and the dream was over. Things went back to the political status quo – it was once more a two-horse race, Labour versus Tory.

But the genie was out of the bottle. The support for Nationalism declined, but it didn't disappear. All it needed was another spark to ignite it. Step forward the best recruiting sergeant Nationalism ever had – Prime Minister Margaret Hilda Thatcher!

At first, Thatcher's election and the determination to roll back the frontiers of the state (hey, we're subsidy junkies!) saw a massive increase in the Labour vote north of the border. Yes, while England voted for the Tories – even trade unionists – in Scotland it was Labour. It seemed as if the Scots were being governed by an alien government – there was a democratic deficit of enormous proportions. We didn't want the Poll Tax; we didn't want to chant the 'greed is good' mantra; and we didn't want to fight the Argies (Argentinians)!

After a visit by the grey suits, Thatcher was gone by the end of 1990, and the Tories were out on their ear in 1997. By that general election, they had no MPs left in Scotland – it was a Tory-free zone! Teflon Tony Blair became prime minister in 1997 and promised a referendum on a Scottish Parliament. The Scots, in a historic vote, opted to restore their Parliament, which had been in abeyance for more than 300 years, and it sat for the first time in 1999.

The Parliament was set up in such a way that it encouraged power sharing. The first government was a coalition of Labour and Liberal Democrats. However, the tide of opinion in Scotland was flowing toward the SNP and its leader, Alex Salmond. Salmond did the unthinkable at the last general election and won a majority. Immediately, another referendum was on the cards. This time, the stakes were higher – independence would mean the breakup of Britain and an end to a union that had stood the test of time for 300 years.

Whether it will come to pass, who knows? It's still not clear whether the vote for the SNP is a protest vote against the failings of New Labour and the present coalition government, or whether it's representative of a genuine wish of the Scottish people to regain their independence. Only time will tell.

What kind of history?

History depends on documents or texts, which creates a bit of a problem, because for most of human history, people have been illiterate. The creators of documents tended to be the educated elite, and if you go back even further, only clerics. Kings needed clerics and clerics needed kings, so most of the documents that survived from the medieval period concern the church and kingship. The ordinary Scot was more or less invisible – a mere footnote in celebrations of great deeds and daring do.

Following the spread of literacy from the late 16th century onward, other voices began to be heard, although the history of great men still dominated. It was really only from the end of the Second World War that these other voices began to be taken seriously by historians. The Second World War was a people's war, and that led to a people's history. The working class began to appear in history books! From the 1970s on, so did women! History had ceased to be only a story about the rich and powerful. It had become more inclusive, telling the stories of previously marginalised groups and peoples: homosexuals, gypsies, unusual religious sects and many more.

Chapter 2

From Nomads to Farmers: The Earliest Peoples

In this chapter, I cover a greater period of time than the rest of the book put together. We can date settlement of Scotland to some 7,000 to 8,000 years ago, but we don't have much of a clue about the earliest settlers. So much of what is written about them is guesswork, but intelligent guesswork. Because history relies on the written record, which didn't exist during this period, what we know of the lives of the earliest settlers is derived almost solely from archaeology. However, it seems clear that well before the birth of Christ, we moved from being people who only hunted or foraged for food to people who herded animals and grew food – in other words, from nomads to farmers.

We know very little about Scotland's ancient ancestors, but a number of things stand out. They lived through different ages, which lasted much longer than the period of recorded history. These ages were identified by the kind of raw materials (stone, bronze and iron) used and the technologies that developed around them. Perhaps the biggest change in the history of mankind was the transformation of the nomadic lifestyle into settled communities. That laid the basis for the evolution of more complicated societies – as the basic needs were met, the surplus could be used to maintain people (such as artists, kings, priests and warriors) who did not work the land.

In this chapter, I walk you through these earliest days of Scotland's history, before anyone had even heard of 'Scotland'.

Technically, we can't speak about 'Scotland' in prehistory, because boundaries didn't exist. But I use the term *Scotland* throughout this book to refer to the land we think of as Scotland today.

Boundaries and Landscape: The First People to Inhabit Scotland

The first map of Scotland was drawn up by the Roman Ptolemy in his *Geography,* written in the second century AD; the next map was drawn up 11 centuries later by Matthew Paris, a monk of St Albans. But for most of this period, Scotland was uninhabitable – it was too cold! Indeed, most of Scotland remained covered by glaciers when the cave paintings of Lascaux in France were created sometime in the 14th millennium BC.

It was only when the Ice Age began to come to an end in the 11th millennium BC that we have any evidence of human activity in the frozen north. When the ice caps began to melt, they had clearly made their impact on the landscape. Earlier sea levels had been lower, so Orkney and its islands, as well as many of the islands that make up the Inner Hebrides, were attached to the mainland. When the ice melted, they became islands.

The melting of the ice caps allowed for human habitation. As I mention earlier, Scotland was inhabited something like 7,000 to 8,000 years ago. Evidence drawn from archaeological finds shows that from 6,000BC, men from the south travelled up to Scotland and stayed for a few weeks, eating deer, wild boar and fish. Visitors also crossed from Ireland and did pretty much the same thing.

These visitors were *nomads* – people searching for food wherever they could find it. But some of them must have settled – even if for a short time – because the remains of Scotland's first house, from 7,000 years ago, were discovered at Crathes, near Banchory, Aberdeenshire. This circular stone structure measured about 7.6 metres (25 feet) across and housed eight or nine people.

Prior to the Bronze Age, and 1,000 years before the Romans arrived in Scotland, complex societies existed. All we have as reminders of them are the mysterious stone circles, the henge monuments that can be found all over Britain. But there are other structures to consider. Chambered cairns like Maes Howe in Orkney were built to honour the dead, and many were built before the pyramids. At Maes Howe, the stone slabs, some weighing three tons, are so closely fitted together that you can't insert a knife blade between them.

The Ages of Man: The Stone Age, Bronze Age and Iron Age in Scotland

Although it's a bit unscientific, archaeologists and historians tend to think of the transition from nomads to farmers in terms of 'ages'. An *age* is defined by the technology that is used to make tools and other objects. So, the three main ages of man are the Stone Age, the Bronze Age and the Iron Age.

The Stone Age

The first settlers were hunter-gatherers, who were active in what is known as the Middle Stone Age or Mesolithic period. The tools used by people during this period were made of stone, which gave rise to the name Stone Age. The polished stone axe heads that you see displayed in museums are probably the best known Stone Age tools.

During this period, people hunted animals and then processed the hides for clothes and shelter. From around 3,500BC, farming became a way of life. Human beings realised that herding and growing their food would be easier than struggling to find and kill it.

Stone Age people settled by the sea and on the islands. Travelling by land meant having to cope with forests, swamps and wild animals. For this reason, water became the only means of communication between these island communities. Most of these settlements were small in size but not without knowledge of each other. Skara Brae in Orkney, preserved by a freak sandstorm, is the finest example of a New Stone Age (or Neolithic period) village in northern Europe. It housed about 30 people, who shared the accommodation with their animals.

Old traditions of a nomadic life slowly died out, but by 2,000BC, communities in most parts of Scotland had settled on the land.

The Bronze Age

The Bronze Age is thought to have followed the Stone Age and began around 2,000BC. Bronze is made out of an amalgam of copper and tin. It grew in popularity because it was easier to work with and shape than stone. The knowledge of how to make bronze and work with it is thought to have come to Scotland from southern Britain or Ireland. At first, bronze was used only to make decorations such as brooches, but as the tools became more sophisticated, the emphasis was more on making weapons, such as swords and spearheads.

The Bronze Age is considered to have been warmer than the Stone Age, which is borne out by evidence of a fair number of settlements 91.4 metres (300 feet) above sea level. The fact that these settlers lived in timber round-houses with extended families is further proof that the climate was changing for the better.

However, sometime during this period, settlement moved from upland areas to lowland areas. The most plausible explanations for this move are soil erosion and exhaustion. But there was also climatic change to consider. Dust clouds from volcanoes in Iceland floated in and made farming difficult, as did the fact that it was becoming wetter in the latter part of the second millennium.

The Iron Age

From around 800BC, iron technology was imported into Scotland from southern Europe. The advantages of iron over bronze were threefold:

- ✔ It was harder.
- ✔ It was sharper.
- ✔ It lasted longer.

The major invention of the age was the rotary quern for grinding grain. Its invention coincided with a major expansion of arable farming. This tool resulted in another push into the upland areas, as hillsides, such as the Cheviots, were cleared of forests.

The closing of BC also saw construction of large underground grain stores known as *souterrains*. When the Romans arrived, they entered a land largely cleared of forest, but extensive bogs and marshlands remained.

Anybody Out There? The People Who Came to Scotland from Europe

All these ages – particularly the Bronze Age and Iron Age – were identified with people who had come to Scotland from other parts of Europe. The two groups we have the most knowledge of were the Beaker people and the Celts. I fill you in on these groups in this section.

The Beaker people: Let's get hammered!

Remains of the Beaker people – archers and horsemen – who lived at the beginning of the Bronze Age, around 2,000 BC, have been found throughout western Europe. They were given the name by archaeologists because of the distinctive pottery found in their graves. These were small drinking vessels, or beakers, which held mead or beer and were used in religious ceremonies to drink the deceased into the afterlife. In the past, the spread of this kind of pottery was linked to population movement conquest by the Beakers over native inhabitants – but more recent research has shown this to be false. It was more a transfer of a set of religious ideas in which alcohol consumption played a significant part.

The Beaker people didn't just stand around all day drinking beer or making pottery; they were also skilled engineers and surveyors. They may have built the stone circles like the Stones of Stennes and the Ring of Brodgar on Orkney. Thirty stone circles and henges have been discovered in Scotland, but their purpose is a bit of a mystery. Most archaeologists think they were probably linked to the coming of the seasons and equinoxes because they were placed in such a way to observe the movements of the moon.

The most famous stones are at Callinish, Isle of Lewis. Here an avenue of 19 monoliths leads to a circle of 13 stones, which were completed around 1,500 BC. Evidence of this Beaker culture has also been discovered at Stonehenge in England and at Mycenae in Greece.

The Celts: Holding firm

Since the 18th century, it has been common to think of the British Isles, except England, as a Celtic fringe – in other words, the remnants of peoples who once inhabited a 'Celtic Europe' before the expansion of the Roman Empire. But where did these people come from?

The Celts seem to have replaced the Beaker people as the Celts' language and culture spread throughout Europe. How do we know this? Well, because examples of the La Tène style of pottery and ironwork, which is decorated with circles and swirling patterns, turned up all over Britain. La Tène was a village in Switzerland, so how did this Celtic artwork make its way here? Through networks of trade.

People needed a common language that would allow them to communicate with each other. But in the end, how the Celts and their culture found their way to Britain is a still a bit of a mystery. Archaeologists have discounted colonisation because there was little evidence of a large-scale movement of people into Scotland a thousand years before the Romans arrived. So, it seems that the native late Bronze Age inhabitants gradually absorbed European Celtic influences and language.

Although Greek and Roman authors wrote of the Celtae or Keltoi, they never referred to the natives of Britain or Ireland as 'Celts'. The Greek writer Pytheas referred to Britain as the 'Pretanic islands' and Orkney as the 'Orcas' (Orkney is one of the oldest recorded place names still in use).The Roman historian Tacitus described the Scots as 'Britons', but he noted their reddish hair and the fact that they were taller than those of the south. All spoke a variant of Celtic, which we could call British.

The Roman conquest and later exposure to the Roman colony of Gaul changed southern Britain during the first century AD. The British aristocracy in the south adopted Roman names, fashion and architecture. The peoples of the north were less exposed to Roman influence because they proved harder to conquer – a fact borne out by the later building of the Antonine Wall from the Clyde to the Forth and Hadrian's Wall from Solway to the Tyne (see Chapter 3). Thus, Celtic culture continued largely untouched in the north.

What Life Was Like for Scotland's First Settlers

The problem with archaeology is that we can only talk of peoples and rarely individuals. So much of what we know about how these people lived their lives, how they toiled, played and worshipped, we know from archaeology. But archaeology can't tell us anything about what they thought or discussed.

In this section, I give you a composite picture of the economy and culture of these undoubtedly complex worlds.

Tools and toil

Population levels are hard to guess during the ages of man, but there were no concentrations of people in towns – they were far more dispersed. The New Stone Age and Bronze Age populations of the northwest Highlands and islands were potentially larger than in any period before the 18th century.

How did people survive? Hunting had given way to farming, so agriculture was the main occupation. But agriculture wasn't based on private property. The culture was communal – there was little distinction between people based on wealth or birth. A New Stone Age tomb discovered at Isbister, on Orkney, shows that there were no social distinctions in death – there weren't any individual graves.

People probably didn't live long enough to accumulate much in the way of wealth – death rates were high and average life expectancy was only about 30 years. However, there were gender differences: Unlike today, men lived longer than women. But as a whole, it was a young community with very few old people.

Over time, the creation of a food surplus enabled social elites to come to prominence. So, we find prestige goods, such as jewellery, in the Bronze Age, suggesting that not everyone was working the land. The evidence of surplus also suggests that people did more than just survive and that their standard of living was comparable to levels found in northern and western Europe.

Wealth and power

From about 3,000BC, a more elaborate hierarchical social structure began to emerge. We can tell this from examining the contents of graves. During the Bronze Age, the chambered tombs of individuals point to the existence of a heavily armed warrior aristocracy whose power came from their control of the bronze trade.

But this powerful aristocracy seems to have disappeared at the beginning of the Iron Age – there was little inter-communal warfare, so there was no need for them. Land holding, rather than trade or ownership of prestige goods, was the mark of status in the Iron Age, as were the massive hill forts, which were built to emphasise the links of the people to the land and community rather than for the glorification of some individual.

Accommodation was also communal. People lived in what were called *broch towers*. These towers were found in the north and west of Scotland and were round in shape, with cone-like roofs, and capable of housing large numbers of people. In the east and south, the communal roundhouse, which was around 16 metres (52.5 feet) in diameter, was the main type of dwelling.

It was really only when the Romans invaded Britain and tried to extend their rule to northern Scotland that societies emerged that were of the same hierarchical nature as those found in the Bronze Age. Hill forts were built anew, with strictly graded layouts and walled citadels surrounded by terraces and enclosures, with an emphasis on hierarchy, division and exclusion. These forts were monuments to the power of war leaders and dynastic groups. As a result, farmhouses became more modest, and in the first few centuries of the first millennium AD, major social differences were evident. War with the Romans created new power structures based on warrior kings (see Chapter 3).

Death and religion

Iron Age Britain believed in more than 400 gods. Most were of the local variety, and some were animals, such as horses, bulls and deer. Rivers and lakes were considered sacred too. Burial monuments and places of worship dominate the records for the New Stone Age, while graves and grave goods constitute the material culture of the Bronze Age.

Before the adoption of Christianity in the post-Roman period, the detail of religious belief is entirely lost to history. But through archaeology, we can gain some insight into their beliefs. The big bones, like skulls and legs, found in chambered tombs suggest that flesh was allowed to decompose (as opposed to corpses being mummified) to allow the spirit to escape the body. Unlike modern society, the dead were venerated and visited at certain times of the year (for example, the winter solstice). There was also ritual sacrifice – virgins wanted!

Close links between religion and political power were pretty much unknown at this time, and it was only with the spread of Christianity that those links were strengthened. But there is evidence to suggest that organised religion existed. This was more obvious in the later New Stone Age (3,000 to 2,000BC) than before, as evidenced by the construction of hundreds of religious centres throughout Britain. Stone circles and ditched circular enclosures, known as henges (for example, the Ring of Brodgar and the Stones of Stennes, in Orkney), point to a shift in worship from the New Stone Age to the Bronze Age. In the Bronze Age, it was less focused on the sky (that is, the moon, sun and stars) and more focused on the gods of earth.

Chapter 3

Disunited Kingdoms (80–750)

*T*he hunter/gathers (see Chapter 2) gave way to more settled communities. These communities gradually formed alliances with one another, in order to resist the Romans' attempts to conquer the north of Britannia – there was strength in numbers. Under this threat, in time, these tribes morphed into little kingdoms with a recognised ruler or king. The king's standing was enhanced through anointment at the coronation by a representative of the Christian Church. The acceptance of Christianity only served to reinforce the dominant position of the king: one God, one king!

By the time the Romans had given up trying to conquer the north of Britannia, Scotland was divided roughly into four kingdoms, each with its own language. The only common tongue used in this period was the Latin of the Church.

Roamin' in the Gloamin': The Roman Invasion and (Near) Conquest

In 80 AD, Gnaeus Julius Agricola, governor of the province of Britannia, decide to invade the north. The Romans had been in England for 40 years and had been successfully Romanising that part of Britain. But in order to secure a strong northern frontier, Agricola decided to subdue the tribes of Scotland. He reached the River Tay with 20,000 men. A year later, 20 Roman forts had been built across the land between the Forth and Clyde – they were taking conquest seriously! Figure 3-1 shows a map of Scotland during Roman times.

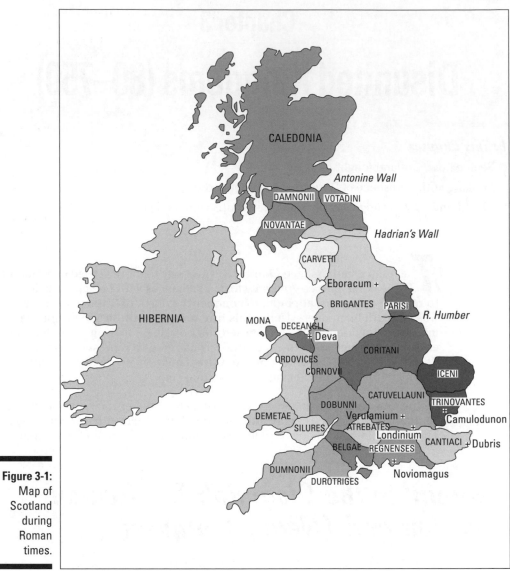

In 83, Agricola took Galloway and then struck north into Morayshire by land, his navy supplying him by sea (a route later followed by Edward I, Oliver Cromwell and the Duke of Cumberland). Agricola built ten more forts and 2,092 kilometres (1,300 miles) of roads north of the Tyne.

According to the Roman historian Tacitus, the Battle of Mons Graupius was fought in 84, possibly at the Pass of Grange, near Huntly. It seems that a Roman army of 15,000 to 30,000 men faced a united force of 30,000 tribesmen of the Caledoni, as the Romans called the northern Scots, led by Calgacus. According to Tacitus, Calgacus lost 10,000 men (killed or wounded), while the Romans lost only 360. As Tacitus wrote,

> men and horses were carried along in confusion together, while chariots, destitute of guidance, and terrified horses without drivers, dashed as panic urged them . . . the earth reeked with blood.

There have been so many fruitless attempts to precisely locate the site of the battle that we can't be sure of the exact location. Some historians have suggested alternative sites, such as Bennachie, in Aberdeenshire, and the Gask Ridge, near Perth. But the truth is, we don't know. A few historians have also questioned Tacitus's account of the battle, arguing that he made it up in order to enhance the reputation of his son-in-law, Agricola.

Another brick in the wall

In the aftermath of battle, Agricola ordered his fleet to sail around the north of Scotland to prove that Britain was, indeed, an island and to receive the surrender of Orkney. He boasted that all the tribes of Britain had been subdued. There is some doubt about this because the bulk of the Caledonian army was still intact, and attacks continued on Roman positions.

One of these attacks, in 117, was supposed to have annihilated the famous Ninth Spanish Legion (Legio Nona Hispana), the cream of the Roman army, but there is little evidence – either archaeological or historical – to support this claim. In spite of it being repeated in a recent film, *The Eagle* (2001), it seems that the Ninth Legion was elsewhere – in fact, on the Rhine – at the time.

After Agricola's departure for Rome, walls became the answer to subduing the northern tribes. In 118, Emperor Hadrian built a wall (still known as Hadrian's Wall) made of stone and turf 6.1 metres (20 feet) high and 3 metres (10 feet) deep, stretching about 117.5 kilometres (73 miles) from the River Tyne to the Solway Firth. In 142, the Antonine Wall, named after Emperor Antoninus Pius, was added; it extended from Bo'ness to Old Kilpatrick, or from the Clyde to the Forth, about 64.4 kilometres (40 miles) long with 18 forts. It took legionnaires from Germany, Gaul, Spain, Egypt and the Middle East three years to build the Antonine Wall, but it lasted only 15 years. The Romans, severely hacked off with repeated attacks from the barbarians in the north, retreated south and abandoned the wall altogether in 185. It was left to the troops stationed at Hadrian's Wall to subdue the northern tribes.

What the Romans did for Scotland

In 208, Septimius Severus was forced to conduct two more Scottish campaigns. During this time, he fought no major battles, and on his death in 211, his son, Caracalla, made peace with the tribes and quit the country. The Roman Empire had bigger troubles further afield.

During the negotiations over the Roman retreat, the first recorded statement by a native of Scotland was made. The wife of a Caledonian chieftain said the following, in response to criticism from Severus's wife, Julia Domma, of the loose sexual morals of Caledonian women:

> We fulfil the demands of nature in a much better way than do you Roman women; for we consort openly with the best men, whereas you let yourselves be debauched in secret by the vilest.

Touché!

South of the border, the impact of the Romans is generally seen as positive, but the impact in the north was piecemeal and very limited. Despite having had a presence for over a century, they left little behind, except a road network. However, their presence did bring the tribes together – before the Romans arrived, there were 17 tribes, and when they left there were only 4. But the most important legacy of the Roman invasion was the introduction of Christianity.

When the Saints Come Marching In

The coming of Christianity to pagan Scotland is, like so much of the history of the country, steeped in myth and personality. The story, as told down the centuries to countless schoolchildren, is the one of Columba, an Irish missionary, who in 563, singlehandedly, from his base in the Hebridean island of Iona, converted the Gaels of Dál Riata to Christianity. It's an often told story, and its appeal lies in the simplistic way it explains the spread of Christianity in Scotland.

However, the truth is, Christianity came to Scotland well before the arrival of Columba. We know this because

- ✔ Archaeological evidence of the Lothians in the post-Roman period shows graves lacking goods, a deviation from pagan practices.
- ✔ Monuments in Galloway and Kirkliston (outside of Edinburgh) bear post-Roman Chi-Rho symbols invoking God and naming priests, deacons and bishops.
- ✔ St Patrick mounted missions to the far west of Scotland in 430 AD.

So, Christianity was already embedded in Scottish society among the northern aristocracy when the following saints arrived:

- **St Ninian:** We know very little about Ninian, except that he was a bishop and a Briton by birth, who studied in Rome and came to Whithorn in 500. But he wasn't sent to announce the Gospel to a pagan southwest; instead, he was sent to govern a Church that already existed. Some people have suggested that Ninian brought Christianity to the southern Picts, but that's doubtful. Some Picts were Christian before Ninian's arrival.

- **St Kentigern:** Later known as St Mungo, Kentigern was raised by monks and established a monastery around which the town of Glasgow eventually grew. He's known as the first bishop of Strathclyde. There's nothing to suggest that Kentigern was a missionary who brought religion to that area.

- **Columba:** Columba was born in Moville in 521 or 522 into the Irish royal clan O'Neil. He began his religious life as a copier of manuscripts, something that got him into deep trouble. His copy of a rare gospel that belonged to his teacher created a scandal over the ownership of the document, which in turn led to a war. For his part in the affair, Columba was excommunicated (which was later reversed), and he was advised to leave the country.

  So, in 563, at the age of 42, Columba arrived in Iona accompanied by 12 followers – Christ and his 12 apostles! But crucially, he did not bring Christianity to the Gaels – the kingdom of Dál Riata was the eastern part of a political and cultural unity whose western part was Ireland. Columba brought his monks to an already Christian society; in fact, he was given Iona by a Christian king. That's why his biographer, Adomnán, described him not as a missionary but an ascetic monk.

The early Christian Church in Scotland, as elsewhere, was monastic – the clergy were monks, not priests. On the whole, it took its lead from Rome, but it differed in some important respects:

- Unlike the Church of Rome, which revered St Peter, the Celtic Church preferred to follow the example of St John – a form of Christianity founded on love, not law. Maybe that's why monastic orders such as the Celi Dei (Clients of God) had a relaxed attitude to celibacy!

- Abbots were generally viewed as more important than bishops. Abbots were the heads of monasteries, and bishops were leading churchmen in a given area or region. One was private; the other, public.

- The Celtic Church calculated the date of the resurrection of Christ earlier in the year than the Church of Rome did. This may seem a bit like splitting hairs, but people tend to take hair splitting very seriously!

Matters came to a head when the Celtic king, Oswald of Northumbria, married an Anglo-Saxon princess who followed the Roman calendar. As the Venerable Bede, the author of *The Ecclesiastical History of the English People* (731), pointed out:

> When the king, having ended his fasting, was keeping the Paschal [end of Lent] feast, the queen and her retainers would be fasting and celebrating Palm Sunday.

To resolve matters, Oswald called a *synod* (a meeting of church leaders) at Whitby in Yorkshire in 664, which after much argument and debate accepted the Roman calendar. As a result, Celtic monasticism was gradually replaced by Roman Catholic orthodoxy. About 710, Abbot Ceolfrith, of the twin monasteries of Monkwearmouth and Jarrow, sent a letter to King Nechtan of the southern Picts and persuaded him to adopt the Roman Church. With his acceptance, the Celtic religious orders, which depended on his protection and goodwill, followed suit. The monks of Iona accepted the Easter ruling in 716; the Scottish Church was no longer Celtic but Roman.

Four Nations and Five Languages

There is no 'original Scot'. There is no common ancestral or genetic heritage that links the peoples of Scotland. The country was a patchwork quilt of various peoples grouped together in tribes who certainly never thought of themselves as Scottish. They owed allegiance only to their kin and king, but in the campaign against Roman imperialism they built federations that laid the basis of kingdoms.

During the period covered in this chapter, Scotland was made up of four separate groups: the Angles, Britons, Picts and Gaels (or Scoti). Each of these groups spoke its own language. The fifth language? Latin, the language of the Church of Rome.

Angles

The Angles, later the Anglo-Saxons, originally settled on the east coast of what we know today as Northumberland and Yorkshire. Their kingdom was known as Bernicia. At the beginning of the seventh century, the two kingdoms of Bernicia and Deira were unified by King Æthelfrith to make Northumbria. These land-hungry people further extended the kingdom: Under King Oswald they incorporated lands northward up to the Firth of Forth by driving the Britons out of the east coast of Scotland. At its greatest extent, the kingdom stretched from just south of the River Humber to the River Mersey, and to the River Forth in the north (roughly, Sheffield to Runcorn to Edinburgh). So, Northumbria became not only part of modern England's far north, but also covered much of what is now the southeast of Scotland.

The Angles spoke a Germanic language. They originally were pagans, but they converted to Christianity in 629, mainly through the efforts of St Aidan of Iona, who founded Lindisfarne.

Britons

By the sixth century, the Britons comprised a series of linked northern kingdoms and lordships covering the northeast of England, the Lothians and Borders of Scotland in the east and Strathclyde in the west. The two main kingdoms were:

- ✔ **The kingdom of Gododdin** (derived from the Latin *Votadini*, the people of Lothian) was centred on Edinburgh (known then as Din Eidyn).

- ✔ **The kingdom of Alt Clut** was centred on Falkirk and Stirling. The fortress on Dumbarton Rock was the stronghold of this kingdom for more than two centuries, until the Vikings destroyed it after a four-month siege in 870.

It was a world of warrior aristocracies motivated by loyalty to the king through the distribution of rewards. Perhaps because of the conquest of this part of Scotland by the Romans, it was also a Christian world: warriors gave alms to the Church before going off to battle, performed penance and were baptised.

In 600, in response to the aggressive bid for territory by the pagan Angles, the king of Gododdin, with 300 men, attacked the Angles' stronghold at Catraeth (perhaps Catterick, North Yorkshire). The battle ended disastrously for the Britons and was memorialised in Aneirin's poem 'Y Gododdin'. The Venerable Bede claimed that the Angles had been sent by God as a scourge to the Britons because they had failed to live up to their Christian ideals.

Defeat at Catraeth effectively drove the Britons out of the east coast of Scotland and led to the disappearance of the kingdom of Gododdin. By the 670s, the Bernicians had captured all the territory of the northern Britons, including the religious centre of Whithorn. From this point forward, the Britons were confined to their stronghold in Strathclyde.

Picts

The name Picts means 'painted people'. The origins of this group are obscure, but they seem to have been a fusion of some of the original Celtic tribes who settled in northeastern Scotland. Picts were closely related to Britons in culture and language, but differences were also evident.

Paganism, particularly among the northern Picts, survived long after the Britons had accepted Christianity. The Picts also accepted *primogeniture* (eldest son inherits), but in cases of dispute, they used the matrilineal pedigree. Although Pict women legally married, they were allowed other sexual partners as well – talk about having your cake and eating it too!

Artistically, the Picts used different symbols from the Britons to decorate their monuments, such as depictions of broken spears, jewellery and animal forms. None of these symbols is entirely understood today.

Archaeological records show that Pictish society hardly differed either culturally or economically from other Gaelic and British societies, and the same applied to the Anglo-Saxons. Indeed, the south Irish poets portrayed their Pictish counterparts as very much like themselves. Although their language didn't survive, we think they spoke some variant of the Celtic tongue of their British neighbours.

The Picts lived in *wheelhouses,* circular buildings divided into ten or so dwellings by stone piers, like the one found at Jarlshof in Shetland. They were farmers who worked their fields systematically, used the quern stone to grind corn, and herded cattle and sheep.

Picts could be found in numbers from Skye to Fife, in the Northern Isles, in the Moray Firth, in Aberdeenshire and in lands either side of the Firth of Tay. By the sixth century, all northern tribes had become known as Picts, with the exception of the Gaels in Argyllshire. The kingdom of the Picts was known as Fortriu.

The Picts were excellent seamen and, as early as the third century, possessed a navy large enough to harass the Romans south of Hadrian's Wall. According to one contemporary source, the *Annals of Tigernach,* in 729 no fewer than 150 Pictish ships were wrecked off a headland called Ross Cuissini. The boats weren't very big, comprising only ten benches with 20 oars (as opposed to the Norse longship of 60 oars).

Politically, the Picts were probably paying tribute to Northumbria, the most powerful of the northern kingdoms, until the reign of King Bridei, who in 685 defeated the Angles or Anglians at the Battle of Dun Nechtain (Nechtansmere), which some historians see as one of the most decisive battles in Scottish history.

Bridei's cousin, King Ecgfrith, was killed in battle, along with the greater part of his army. According to the *Annals of Ulster:*

> The battle of Dún Nechtain was fought on Saturday, May 20th, and Egfrid son of Oswy, king of the Saxons, who had completed the 15th year of his reign, was slain therein with a great body of his soldiers. . . .

Bridei had halted the northward expansion of the Northumbrians, although they continued to dominate much of southern Scotland. From that point onward, Pictavia became the dominant power north of the River Forth and totally independent of Northumbria.

Pictish dominance was evident from the few battles that took place between the separate Scottish kingdoms. In 558, the Pictish king, Brude, defeated the Gaels and their king, Gabran, in battle. Nearly two centuries later, Nechtan's successor, Ungus, occupied Dunadd, the main centre of the Gaels, in the 730s. The Picts may have bossed ancient Scotland, but their dominance was not set to last (see Chapter 4).

Gaels

The Gaels or Goidels are speakers of the Gaelic (or Goidelic) languages. Their origins are in Ireland, and it seems that they made their appearance in Scotland as settlers around 500. Fergus Mor, son of Eric, moved the seat of his kingdom of Dál Riata from his palace in Country Antrim to Dunadd ('fort on the River Add'), near Lochgilphead, Argyllshire. The first settlement only consisted of 150 of Mor's followers, but the numbers quickly grew – so much so that in a fairly short time they were able to colonise the whole of Argyll and the Western Isles.

From before the fourth century, the Gaels were known to the Romans as the Scoti, although the Gaels did not refer to themselves this way. The term *Scoti* had connotations of raiders or pirates. Raiders from Ireland were attacking Britain's west coast during and after the Roman occupation.

The Gaels were, like their neighbours, a warrior society. Their power was drawn from the sea and the land. In Gaeldom, every 20th house was obliged to provide two seven-benched boats. The problem with the Gaels was that their warrior caste wasn't really up to the job! They were no match for the Picts, and when they tried to expand the kingdom in 603 into England, the Gaels were defeated by Æthelfrith at Degsastan.

Under their king, Domnall Brecc, the Gaels fought a number of unsuccessful battles in Ulster; the best documented battle was Mag Rathin in 637. To heap insult upon insult, Owen, king of Alt Clut, killed Domnall in battle in 642 at Strathcarron, Stirlingshire. The Gaels' attempt to burst out of the western Highlands had come to nothing.

Given their weakness in battle, it's strange that the Gaels and their language became dominant after 750, while the Picts and their culture and language disappeared (see Chapter 4). But history is full of odd and unpredictable happenings, which is why we love it so much!

Although the Gaels were a militaristic society, by the beginning of the sixth century, they were also a Christian one. But it wasn't just pray and worship – the Gaels also, when not fighting, enjoyed themselves playing shinty and sharing round their women folk!

Part II
Making the Kingdom (840–1286)

Get to know the Vikings as you've never known them in a free article at www.dummies.com/extras/scottishhistory.

In this part . . .

- ✔ Examine what happened to the Picts and their culture.

- ✔ Look at the formation of the kingdom of Alba and the long reign of the MacAlpin Dynasty.

- ✔ Consider the arrival of the Viking raiders, their bloodthirsty reputation, and their weird love of bling and personal hygiene.

- ✔ Look at the growth of the Christian Church under the direction of our only royal saint, Queen Margaret.

- ✔ Understand how David I introduced feudalism to Scotland.

- ✔ See the arrival of yet another set of peoples, the Anglo-Normans, from whose stock the Scots' greatest hero, Robert the Bruce, came.

Chapter 4

The Kingdom of Alba (840–1040)

*A*lba is an old Gaelic term for 'Britain', but in the period covered in this chapter, it became associated with the territory between the River Forth and the River Spey. This was the former territory of southern Pictavia, which was conquered in the 840s by the king of the Gaels, Cinéad Mac Alpín (Kenneth MacAlpin). The new kingdom formed the basis of what eventually became Alba and later Scotland. But its existence from the outset was fragile and threatened by the presence in the western and northern parts of Pictavia of the Norse invaders, the Vikings. The fact that it survived and became the country we know today as Scotland is a story of epic proportions.

The Disappearance of the Picts

From the end of the Roman period until the 840s, the Picts were the dominant people in Scotland – there were more of them, and they had the best land. But despite their long period of dominance, we know very little about the so-called 'painted people' – no texts have been preserved. Why they disappeared as a people is still a mystery to historians.

However, it seems that in the middle of the ninth century, Pictavia was subjected to a number of devastating attacks from our friends in the north, the Vikings. These attacks not only killed off most of the ruling elite of the Pictish people but also destabilised the whole of Pictavia. In 839, a particularly bad defeat of the Pictish king, Uuen, and his brother Bran in Fortrui opened a window of opportunity for Kenneth MacAlpin, the king of the Gaels of the kingdom of Dál Riata (Argyllshire and the Western Isles), to seize southern Pictavia. The new kingdom of Alba gradually turned its back on its Pictish roots and language. So, what we know of Pictish civilisation is drawn more from archaeological finds than from historical records.

The Picts left behind some impressive examples of metalwork – brooches, dress pins and tableware. Some of the most distinctive examples of Pictish art were the symbol stones, which were decorated with abstract symbols (which, to this day, no one has yet deciphered); realistic depictions of animals, horses and serpents; and everyday items like combs and mirrors. From about the eighth century, Christian symbols were part of the mix.

Geographically speaking, the only surviving evidence of previous Pictish territories is found in place names that begin with *Pit* or *Pett,* such as Pitlochry, Pittodrie or Pitlessie.

Kenneth MacAlpin: King of the Scots?

Kenneth MacAlpin succeeded to the kingship of Dál Riata after the death of his father, Alpin, at the hands of the Picts around 834. As king of the Gaels, MacAlpin came to Pictavia in 842 and 'destroyed' the Picts, reigning until his death from a tumour in 858 at Forteviot.

Historians vigorously debate whether MacAlpin can be considered the father of the nation. He was never referred to as 'King of the Scots'– he was 'King of the Picts'. The title King of the Picts was conferred on him at his coronation in 843 on Moot Hill at Scone in Perthshire. Indeed, it was not until the reign of Donald II (889–900) that the monarch became known as *ri Alban* (King of Alba).

The location of MacAlpin's coronation was the stone seat of the coronation of succeeding monarchs until it was removed by Edward I of England in 1296 and lodged in Westminster Abbey, where it remained until its return in 1996.

Historians are also less inclined to view the merging of the two kingdoms – Gaels and Picts – as an act of conquest as earlier accounts would have it. Instead, they stress the fact that the Gaels and the Picts had a shared culture and had become bonded through intermarriage (see the nearby sidebar). So, the process of merging these two kingdoms was achieved less through violence and more by assimilation over a long period of time. Indeed, Kenneth MacAlpin's mother was thought to have been a Pictish princess, giving him a strong claim to the throne of Pictavia.

But there were also good practical reasons other than blood ties to merge the kingdoms:

- ✔ They were both Christian kingdoms.
- ✔ They needed strong leadership, which only dynastic authority could give, in order to combat the aggression of the Norse invaders.

If you can't beat 'em, marry 'em

Marriage was another way of dealing with the Viking threat – it became the cement that held a number of peace treaties together. There was just one stumbling block: the Vikings were pagans and the Scots were Christians. This difficulty could be ignored from time to time. One of Kenneth I's daughters was married to a pagan Norse king of Dublin sometime during the reign of Constantine I. However, the use of marriage as a form of appeasement reached its apex in the reign of Constantine II. The fact that he was named, like his uncle, after the first Roman emperor, and that he ended his days in a monastery, didn't appear to give him much angst when he married his daughter off to the heathen king of Dublin, Olaf III!

However, things became a little easier in 995, when King Olaf Tryggvason of Norway visited Orkney and ordered the earl and his people to adopt Christianity. This was an acknowledgement that a great deal of integration had taken place between the Norse and the indigenous population of the Northern and Western Isles. Indeed, by the time of Somerled, lord of the Isles (see Chapter 5), the one-time Vikings in the Isles were indigenous by both intermarriage with the local population and by adoption of some of the language and customs.

We know little about MacAlpin, except that he invaded Lothian (or Saxonia as it became known) six times, burning Dunbar and Melrose, and that he oversaw the removal of the relics of St Columba, patron saint of Dál Riata, to Dunkeld. However, the main achievement of his reign was to produce a dynasty that aspired to rule the whole of Scotland for most of the medieval period. But it was left to his descendants to do the conquering.

The tanistry system

In MacAlpin's time, kings were appointed by a system known as *tanistry;* a *tanist,* or successor to the king or chief, was designated from among a kindred group. So, he could be an uncle, a brother, a grandson, a cousin – there was no right of the eldest son to succeed his father. The test was, 'Who is the best man for the job? 'So, Kenneth was succeeded by his brother Donald I rather than by any of his sons.

However, there was a major flaw in the tanistry system: it created multiple rivals for the throne and that led to instability, mayhem and murder.

Of the 14 kings who reigned between 943 and 1097, ten were murdered. Here's a handy guide to the infamous killings:

- ✔ **954:** The men of Moray murder Malcolm I. He is succeeded by his cousin Indulf.

- ✔ **962:** The Daes kill Indulf. He is succeeded by Malcolm's son Dubh.

- ✔ **966:** Indulf's son Culen kidnaps and kills Dubh. Culen becomes king.

(continued)

(continued)

✏ **971:** The king of Strathclyde kills Culen for raping his daughter. Culen is succeeded by Kenneth II.

✏ **995:** Kenneth II is murdered, allegedly by a booby-trapped statue! Constantine III becomes king.

✏ **997:** Constantine III is killed in battle against his cousin Kenneth and his own illegitimate son. Long live Kenneth III!

✏ **1005:** Kenneth III is killed by his cousin, who becomes Malcolm II.

But it wasn't just murder that made the throne of Alba a merry-go-round. There were other reasons:

✏ A king might have been killed in battle.

✏ A king might have died of natural causes, a strong possibility because most of the kings of Alba were middle-aged.

✏ A king might have been driven out by his people because he was incompetent (as happened to King Aed in 878).

However, whatever the cause of a king's death, it was a miracle that Alba survived and grew – and that any claimants to the throne were left! Of the 14 kings who ruled during the period 858 to 1034, five reigned for five or fewer years, and

another four ruled for ten or fewer years. The only reigns of any duration were Constantine II (900–943), the longest-reigning king until William the Lion; Kenneth II (971–995); and Malcolm II (1005–1034). Here's a full list of the monarchs and the years they ruled:

✏ **Kenneth I:** 843–858

✏ **Donald I:** 858–862

✏ **Constantine I:** 862–877

✏ **Aed:** 877–878

✏ **Giric:** 878–889

✏ **Donald II:** 889–900

✏ **Constantine II:** 900–943

✏ **Malcolm I:** 943–954

✏ **Indulf:** 954–962

✏ **Dubh or Duff:** 962–966

✏ **Culen:** 966–971

✏ **Kenneth II:** 971–995

✏ **Constantine III:** 995–997

✏ **Kenneth III:** 997–1005

✏ **Malcolm II:** 1005–1034

The Viking Invasion

The Vikings are probably, outside the Romans, the most distinctive set of invaders ever to step on the soil of what is known today as Britain. The long-haired and bearded blond warriors with their horned helmets and fearsome weaponry and long ships are easily recognised in caricatures even today. From about 750, the Vikings were forced to look for new sources of support because there wasn't enough land available to satisfy their rising population. Using their advanced seamanship skills, roving groups of Norse, Swedes and Danes set out to look for new territories to exploit.

Their reputation has undergone a bit of a makeover depending on where you live. In Anglo-Saxon England, they're usually looked on as a positive force, but the same can't be said for Scotland. The first Viking attacks were on the religious community of Iona, which suffered more than most –it was sacked four times between 795 and 825. On the last occasion, at Martyrs' Bay, every single member of the monastic community was murdered trying to defend their relics.

This is where the image of the plundering, pillaging and raping Viking warrior originates. Most of the chronicles on which historians base their understanding of the early medieval past were compiled in churches or monasteries, so it's little wonder that the Vikings were depicted in this way. That was the experience of clerics and monks.

But why did the Vikings choose the churches? The answer is simple:

- ✔ Churches were sanctuaries during war and were considered safe places by laymen and ecclesiastics alike to deposit gold and silver.
- ✔ Churches were the site of fairs that drew in large numbers of the native population.
- ✔ Churches were undefended – no Christian would violate these sanctuaries.

But the Vikings weren't Christians – they were heathens! So, with gold and silver available and a ready source of slaves to capture and sell, attacking churches was a no-brainer! Let's go a' raiding!

The Vikings were a bit preoccupied with booty and slaves, and they mounted serious attacks on Alba and beyond in pursuit of them. In the 860s, they plundered the kingdom during the reign of Constantine I and took many slaves, along with Angles and Britons, to Ireland. In 875, the Vikings inflicted a massive defeat on the men of Alba at Dollar, near Stirling. Constantine was forced to retreat north, where he was finally slain at the battle of Inverdufatha (at the mouth of the Firth of Tay) in 877.

One interesting aspect of the battle of Dollar was the use, for the first time, of the term *Scotti* in the *Chronicle of the Kings of Alba* to describe the defeated forces of Constantine.

Putting down roots

Generally, the Vikings weren't looking to settle in any of the lands they attacked; instead, they wanted to establish a system of control, better known today as a protection racket! They sought *tribute* – in other words, if you pay us enough money, we won't attack you. If that didn't work, they installed puppet rulers to collect the tribute for them. But where they had the manpower available, they established settlements.

The Vikings spread from Orkney and Shetland into the northern and western parts of Scotland – they constituted the last population movement of outsiders into the north of Scotland. Archaeological excavations at the Brough of

Birsay, a small island off Orkney, reveal that although the Picts were very active there in the seventh century, by the ninth century the Vikings had completely taken over.

The Vikings also settled in the Western Isles where even today four-fifths of the villages in the Isle of Lewis have names that are Norse in origin. Viking settlement displaced Gaelic culture and language in these places, as well as the people's connection with Ireland. Indeed, by 1200, most of Scotland north of the Dornoch Firth was entirely Norse-speaking.

From studying the chronicles produced by the Viking invaders and their descendants, some historians have painted a picture of near genocide of the Pictish population of Orkney and Shetland and the enslavement of those who survived. Indeed, 30 per cent of the present indigenous Orcadian population can show Scandinavian ancestry on both their paternal and maternal sides. The overwhelming number of place names on the islands would tend to point to the obliteration of a once-thriving Pictish culture as well.

Other historians argue that it wasn't all rape, pillage and plunder. There is evidence that an equal number of Viking women and men were settling in that part of Scotland, suggesting stable agricultural communities peacefully co-existing with the native population and, through intermarriage, furthering integration. So, rather than a violent obliteration of Pictish culture, it seems that the process was one of gradual dominance of one over the other. But in truth, no historian can say for sure.

What we can say with certainty is that from the middle of the ninth century, the invaders were settlers with their own royal dynasty no longer directly connected to Norway, and by the end of the century, this dynasty controlled all of the north and west of Scotland from the Northern and Western Isles to Caithness, Sutherland and Inverness.

That's not to say the declaration of independence from Norway went uncontested. In 872, Harald Fairhair became king of a united Norway, and his grab for power led to an exodus of his enemies to the Scottish Isles. Harald didn't give up on them. He followed them to Scotland and, in the process, declared the Northern Isles part of his kingdom in 875. A decade later, he added the Hebrides. Sometime around 886, the local Viking chiefs rebelled, and he sent in his enforcer, Kentil Flatnose, to quiet them. Instead of restoring the rule of his king, Kentil declared himself 'King of the Isles'.

Harald gave the Northern Isles to Rognvald as an earldom in reparation for the death of his son in battle in Scotland. Then he passed the earldom on to his brother Sigurd the Mighty. Sigurd's line barely survived him. Torf-Einarr, Rognvald's son by a slave, founded a dynasty that controlled the Northern Isles for centuries after his death.

Strangely, there are no Viking settlements in eastern lowland Scotland. This area was much richer in resources and land than the more inhospitable parts of Northern Scotland and the Isles. That doesn't mean that eastern Scotland was never raided and laid waste by the Vikings – it was devastated on a few occasions – but no permanent settlements were established. The Vikings came, plundered, accepted tribute and left. There are two possible explanations for this:

- ✔ There were fewer religious centres in the east, so they looked elsewhere.
- ✔ The territory of Alba was well defended.

Regardless of the reason that there were no Norse communities in eastern Scotland, it was a geographical and military fact that Alba was under threat. It was confronted on its northern and western borders, and it was facing further problems from the Danes and Anglo-Saxons on its southern front. Clearly, something had to be done about the Vikings, but what? Well, you could fight them or marry them! And that's what happened.

Battling the Vikings: The North

The beginning of the tenth century was not a very happy period for the Vikings – they suffered setback after setback on the battlefield. In 902, they lost control of Dublin, their base for attacks on the British mainland, but that loss only increased their resolve to attack Alba. In 903, Dunkeld and 'all Albania' was sacked, but the Viking charge was halted by Constantine II, son of Aed. Constantine led his men into battle behind the *crozier* (pastoral staff) of St Columba at Strathearn the next year.

According to the *Chronicle of the Kings of Alba* (circa 995), this was the first occasion the word *Albania* had been used to describe the lands held by descendants of Kenneth I. Before then, they were described as Pictavia.

That victory marked the last of the northern Scandinavian invasions of the MacAlpin kingdom. However, it didn't mean stability. The Norse presence in the west and north meant that, from time to time, the leading nobles, or *jarl-sas* they were known, tried to expand their territories south into Moray.

These attacks continued well into the second half of the tenth century. In 962, King Indulf was killed fighting the Norse near Cullen, Moray, at the Battle of Bauds. All the Scottish kings who followed him in this period failed to subdue the various Norwegian earls of Orkney (jarls given 'dominion' over Orkney and Shetland by the Norwegian king). Kenneth II (971–995) failed to check the ambitions of Sigurd the Stout, who annexed Caithness and extended his control into Moray. He also controlled the Hebrides and the Isle of Man.

The successors of Kenneth II –Kenneth III (997–1005) and Malcolm II (1005–1034) – also had to accept that they had neither the means nor the authority to rein in the earls of Orkney. The marriage of Malcolm's daughter to Sigurd – by then a Christian convert – in 1008 was an acknowledgement of this fact. By the time of Sigurd's death in Ireland in 1014 at the Battle of Clontarf, the boundary between Alba and the earls of Orkney lay as far south as the Moray Firth.

Battling the Vikings and Saxons: The south

In order to understand Scottish involvement in England, you have to know something about the history of English power struggles in the tenth century.

In 917, the Vikings under Sihtric and Ragnall had retaken Dublin. The following year, Ragnall turned his attention toward the kingdom of York. He invaded Northumbria, which at that time was ruled by Ealdred, son of Eadulf. Ealdred sought the help of the Scottish king, Constantine II (900–943), to repel the Viking invaders. This conflict climaxed in the Battle of Corbridge in 918. The men of Albanaich again rallied behind the crozier of Columba, although this time the battle proved indecisive. However, it did force Ragnall to take a detour and head south to York, where he proclaimed himself king in 919.

In 920, in true *Godfather* style, the kings of England and Scotland came together under Edward the Elder, grandson of Alfred the Great, and king of West Saxon or Wessex. At the meeting, Edward was declared 'father and lord' by all present, including Ragnall and Constantine II, as recorded in the *Anglo-Saxon Chronicle*.

The word *scottas,* from which *Scots* derives, was used in the *Chronicle* for the first time to describe the inhabitants of Constantine's kingdom.

Ragnall died a year later and was replaced by Sihtric as king of York. Edward the Elder followed him, dying in 924. Edward's lands were divided between his sons Æthelstan and Ælfweard. However, Ælfweard died a few weeks after his father, so Æthelstan inherited all of Edward's territories. He added to them by occupying Northumbria in 927, becoming king of a realm that stretched all the way from the south of England to the Firth of Forth.

Æthelstan's power didn't go uncontested. An opposition formed, made up of Constantine II, Owen (king of the Britons of Strathclyde) and the Welsh kings. In open defiance of Æthelstan, the Scots gave sanctuary to Gofraid, deposed brother of Sihtric, who had died in 927, and Sihtric's son, Olaf Cuaran. However, an English invasion of Scotland in 934 secured the submission of the Scottish king by laying waste to the east coast as far north as Dunnottar, the gateway to the Mounth. Constantine recognised the overlordship of Æthelstan, as had Owen and the Welsh kings before him, and one of his sons was given as a hostage. After this, Constantine appeared from time to time at the English court, where a document described him as *subregulus* (an under-king).

But acceptance of Æthelstan's overlordship didn't last long. Within three years, the 'hoary' (grey) old warrior Constantine and Owen rebelled. In the company of the pagan king, Olaf Guthfrithson of Dublin invaded England. A 'Great Battle' ensued at Brunanburh, somewhere near the River Mersey in the Wirral. It was a bloodbath and, by all accounts, a disaster for the invaders. As a contemporary chronicle makes clear,

> a great battle, lamentable and terrible was cruelly fought . . . in which fell uncounted thousands of the Northmen . . . . And on the other side, a multitude of Saxons fell; but Æthelstan, the king of the Saxons, obtained a great victory.

But Brunanburh proved to be a pyrrhic victory: four years later, Æthelstan was dead. Within a year of that, his successor, the 18-year-old Edmund, had witnessed the virtual collapse of the empire built by his older brother. He spent the rest of his reign trying to reconquer the lost territories, and he pretty much managed to do so by 945. In that year, he conquered Strathclyde but ceded the territory to the new Scottish king, Malcolm I (943–954), in return for a treaty of mutual military support. So, the boundaries of Alba now stretched to the west and, during the rest of the period, extended south to include Edinburgh.

However, before this, in 943, Constantine, at the age of 70, abdicated and entered the Culdee monastery at Cennrígmonaid/Kinrimund (St Andrews). This is the first indication of St Andrews as a royal centre – one of the few power-centres in this period set in a coastal location. It was also recognition of the extent to which the church and Scottish culture had become Gaelicised (because the Culdees, the most powerful religious body in Alba, were of Irish origin). In the sixth year of his reign, Constantine met with Bishop Cellach on the Hill of Belief next to the royal stone of Scone. There, he pledged to keep the laws and disciplines of the faith and the rights of the church and the gospels.

Malcolm's accession to the throne of Alba saw renewed raids deep into Northumbria in 949 and again in the 970s during Kenneth II's reign. The goal was to extend the boundaries of Alba as far south as the River Tees. The raids met with some enduring success – Scottish occupation of Lothian was accepted in 973 by Edgar, king of Wessex.

Mapping the kingdom

Further clarification of the boundary between England and Scotland was decided by the Battle of Carham in 1016 or 1018. Before this, in 1006, Malcolm II (1005–1034) invaded Northumbria and besieged the new episcopal city of Durham. However, the Scots were defeated by an army drawn from Bernicia and York, led by Uhtred the Bold.

Local women were said to have washed the severed heads of the Scots, receiving a payment of a cow for each head. The heads were fixed on stakes at Durham's walls.

Uhtred was rewarded by King Ethelred II with the ealdormanry of Bamburgh even though his father was still alive. In the meantime, Ethelred had Earl Ælfhelm of York murdered, and he allowed Uhtred to succeed Ælfhelm as ealdorman of York, uniting northern and southern Northumbria under the house of Bamburgh. Things were definitely looking up for Uhtred, but it didn't last.

An *ealdormanry* is basically governorship of a shire or region.

Symeon of Durham in his *Historia Regum* (History of the Kings) wrote that in 1018,

> A great battle between the Scots and Angles was fought at Carrum [Carham] between Huctred [Uhtred], son of Waldef [Waltheof], earl of the Northumbrians, and Malcolm [Malcolm II], son of Cyneth [Kenneth II], king of the Scots, with whom there was in the battle Eugenius [Owen] the Bald, king of the men of Clyde [Strathclyde].

There is a little confusion regarding the date of the battle. Some historians have argued that because the earl of Northumberland was listed in the *Anglo-Saxon Chronicle* as murdered along with 40 of his men by King Cnut in 1016, the battle must have taken place in that year. However, other historians have more convincingly suggested that it took place in 1018 and that it was Uhtred's brother, Eadulf Cudel, 'a very lazy and cowardly man', who engaged the Scots in battle and lost.

There is also the problem of whether the victory of the Scots led to Lothian being ceded to them. Again, some historians have argued that, from 973, Lothian was in the hands of the Scots, so the battle was less about that than the Scottish king's desire to achieve control of Bernicia. That goal was never realised, but the defeated Eadulf formally recognised Malcolm's possession of all of Northumbria as far as the Tweed. As a result, the southern boundary of Alba was set at the River Tweed, where it remains today.

Chapter 5

Good Kings, Bad Kings and a Saintly Queen (1034–1153)

*I*n this chapter, I explain the shifting nature of kingship, from one based on the blood ties of the old Celtic society, to one based on landownership. In this new society, kings ruled in a different way. Men were tied to the king through the granting of land; in return, they pledged to serve the king and no other. The new system of rule was called *feudalism,* and it spread throughout the southern half of Scotland and into parts of the north. Feudalism was a top-down process, led by the monarch, and it affected all aspects of society, which became far more hierarchical and authoritarian. Nowhere were these changes more evident than in the Church, which became the agent of royal authority in Scotland. This led to the gradual decline of the world of the Gael and Gaelic as the language of the Scots.

Enter Macbeth, Stage Right: The End of the MacAlpin Dynasty?

The MacAlpin kings had ruled Scotland for more than 200 years, but all that came to an end through the actions of Mac Bethad mac Findláich of Moray (known as Macbeth). Macbeth defeated Duncan I, king of the Scots, in a battle at Pitgaveny, near Elgin in Moray, on 14 August 1040.

Before his defeat and death, Duncan had ruled the kingdom of Alba (as Scotland was known at the time) as the nominated heir of his grandfather, Malcolm II. Duncan's reign was not a happy or long one. Crowned king on 30 November 1034, Duncan was never popular, and a number of poor decisions added to his troubles.

In 1038, Earl Eadulf of Northumbria raided Strathclyde. In 1039, in retaliation, Duncan embarked on a reckless invasion of the north of England. He laid siege to Durham but suffered a comprehensive defeat at the hands of the besieged and suffered a humiliating retreat.

Duncan also had his problems in the north of Scotland. Scottish kings were surrounded by a group of regional rulers, known as *mormaers* (earls). There was no system of *primogeniture* (eldest son inherits the throne); instead, it was a system of *tanistry,* in which the best person was selected to rule, regardless of where he stood in relation to the deceased king. The point is that tanistry created many potential candidates for the throne. Macbeth, as king of Moray, was one of them, and Duncan thought it would be a good idea to put an end to Macbeth's claim by engaging in battle with him in 1040. It didn't go so well for Duncan.

Shakespeare, in his play *Macbeth,* paints a picture of murder and treason, but I have to make a number of corrections to the Bard's version of events:

- Duncan was not murdered; he was killed in battle.
- Duncan was not the old man depicted in the play; he was a young man of 25.

Far from being a murderer, Macbeth had equally strong claims to the throne of Alba as Duncan had:

- Macbeth was of royal blood – a grandson of Kenneth II.
- Macbeth was married to Gruoch, daughter of Boite, son of Kenneth II, whose only brother was murdered by Malcolm II, so it was expected he would carry on the blood feud with the royal line.
- Duncan was a discredited warrior king.
- Duncan's sons went into exile when he was killed in battle – Malcolm to Northumbria and Domnall to the Hebrides. Macbeth was left without a rival.

Our views of Macbeth are highly coloured by Shakespeare's play, in which he's depicted as a man tormented by his demons and guilt over the murder of Duncan; manipulated by his ruthless consort, Lady Macbeth; and drawn to witchcraft and other dark arts. In Shakespeare's eyes, Macbeth was a tyrant and a bully in public, but essentially a weak and vain individual in private.

Macbeth's contemporaries never would have recognised this depiction of him. His rule lasted 17 years and was remembered by some as a time of peace and plenty for a number of reasons:

✔ Macbeth brought peace by concluding a treaty with the Norse warrior king of Orkney and Caithness, Thorfinn, which allowed him to focus on Alba without the distractions of war in the north. In 1045, he defeated and killed his only other rival, Duncan I's father, Crinian, abbot of Dunkeld.

✔ Macbeth was so secure in his kingship that in 1050 he made a pilgrimage to Rome (the only reigning Scottish king to do so), a journey that took many months.

✔ Macbeth gave generously to the Church. He was recorded as a benefactor of the monastic order the *Céli Dei* (Clients of God) of Loch Leven. He and his wife, Gruoch, granted estates in west Fife to the monastic order.

✔ Macbeth was aware of developments in the wider world. In 1052, he took two Norman knights into his service – the first Scottish king to take such men.

But Macbeth's line did not displace the MacAlpin Dynasty permanently. Duncan's eldest son, Mael Coluim 'Cean Mór' (Great Chief), better known as Malcolm Canmore, backed by a powerful Northumbrian army, engaged Macbeth in a bloody battle on 27 July 1054 at Dunsinane, Perthshire (the only thing that Shakespeare got right!). Victory put Malcolm in control of Scotland south of the River Tay, which he used as a base to mount another challenge for power at Lumphanan, in Aberdeenshire, in August 1057. This time it proved fatal for Macbeth who was killed in battle.

Strangely enough, it wasn't Malcolm who assumed the throne, but Macbeth's stepson, Lulach, known variously as the 'stupid' or 'unlucky' one. But sadly for him, his reign lasted only eight months. Lulach was ambushed and killed by Malcolm on 17 March 1058 in Strathbogie, Aberdeenshire.

Malcolm and Margaret: The Ideal Couple?

The MacAlpins were back on the throne, but it was a different form of kingship, based less on an allegiance to the Celtic past and more inclined to look to England and France for political and cultural influences. This shouldn't come as a surprise: Malcolm spent 14 years in exile at the court of Edward the Confessor, so something must have rubbed off on him.

Making Scotland more English

During Macbeth's time on the throne, two Norman knights sought sanctuary in Scotland, but that trickle became a flood under Malcolm, helped by the Norman conquest of England in 1066. Malcolm provided lands and positions for his newfound Anglo-Norman friends. The Flemings (from Flanders), the Sinclairs (originally from Saint-Clair-sur-Epte in Normandy) and others were invited north of the border. But this wasn't simply a process of resettling elite families; these groups spearheaded the introduction of feudalism in Scotland under Malcolm and his successors.

So, what was feudalism? In a *feudal* state, all the land is owned by the king, who has supreme authority. He delegates the land (a *fief*) and the authority that goes with it to a lesser person (the *vassal*). The vassal agrees to provide military service to the lord, and in return the lord provides protection to the vassal. In other words, you scratch my back, and I'll scratch yours. Feudalism may have been a simple concept, but it was crucial in transforming tribal Celtic society into one that more closely resembled European culture.

Feudalism spread more easily in Lowland Scotland. In the remote western Highlands and islands, the old Celtic traditions based on bonds of kinship survived for many hundreds of years and were only gradually transformed under force of arms. In these areas, allegiance was to the clan chief and not to the king.

Making England more Scottish

Malcolm had military and territorial ambitions that lasted throughout his reign. His main desire was to annex Northumbria between the River Tweed and the River Tees. The first of his five raids into northern England took place in 1061, when Holy Island was plundered.

A better opportunity came in 1066. Malcolm, along with Tostig, earl of Northumbria, the count of Flanders and the king of Norway, plotted to overthrow King Harold Godwinson of England and partition the country between them. Tostig and the king of Norway invaded, but they were defeated at the Battle of Stamford Bridge. Malcolm had no part in it. Meanwhile, a more successful invasion was mounted by William the Conqueror, who defeated Harold at the Battle of Hastings.

Malcolm got caught up in the English resistance. In 1068, he gave sanctuary to Edgar Ætheling (who was leading the English opposition to William) and his mother and two sisters, Margaret and Christina. Little did he know that encounter would prove to be momentous, not only for him personally but also for his kingdom (see the next section).

By Easter 1070, the English resistance was effectively broken. This allowed William the Conqueror to turn his attention to the Scottish king in a bid to halt Malcolm's frequent raids into Northumbria. In 1072, an English army reached the Firth of Tay where Malcolm paid homage to William at Abernethy, near Dundee.

In medieval society, *homage* involved the vassal (in this case, Malcolm) pledging submission to his feudal lord (in this case, William). Symbolically, it was saying that Malcolm was William's man and no other's.

But Malcolm's paying homage to William didn't stop the raiding. By 1079, Malcolm was at it again, although this time he spared the land around Hexham out of reverence for local saints. William the Conqueror was getting more than a little annoyed with Malcolm. He sent an army north, led by his eldest son, Robert – the first full-scale English invasion of Scotland. However, it achieved nothing except the building of a castle at Falkirk!

There was a period of calm, but Malcolm's obsession with Northumbria continued. In 1091, another raid was launched as far south as Durham. This action led to a series of tit-for-tat skirmishes and the illegal English takeover of Carlisle in 1092. To resolve their differences, a meeting was arranged between the two kings at Gloucester in August 1093. But when Malcolm arrived, the English king, William Rufus, refused to meet with him – it was a wasted journey.

Infuriated by this major insult, Malcolm immediately sought revenge. He raised an army with the intention of inflicting maximum damage on the north of England. But his actions were too impulsive. His fifth raid into England proved to be his last. North of Alnwick, Malcolm and his son Edward were ambushed by the earl of Northumbria, Robert de Mowbray, and killed on 13 November 1093. Malcolm was buried later that month at Tynemouth Priory.

Malcolm wasn't a great innovator, but his rule is widely remembered for its vigour and its remarkable stability. However, it could be argued that his reign wouldn't have been as memorable without his queen and Scotland's only royal saint, Margaret.

Margaret and the soul of Scotland

Margaret was not Malcolm's first wife; she was his second. His first wife was Ingibjorg, the daughter of Thorfinn, the earl of Orkney, whom he married in 1060, but she died in 1067 after producing three sons. Malcolm's first marriage was a marriage of convenience; it helped establish friendly relations between Malcolm and the Scandinavian rulers of the Northern Isles. In contrast, his second marriage, to Margaret, seems to have been a genuine love match, at least on Malcolm's part – it was guaranteed to annoy William of England, because Margaret was the sister of his sworn enemy, Edgar Ætheling.

Scotland's first royal saint, Margaret, was not born in Scotland; in fact, she had spent most of her formative years in exile in Hungary. While taking refuge with her family in Scotland, she married Malcolm at Dunfermline sometime in 1069 or 1070. Margaret didn't really want to marry Malcolm. She would've preferred to have entered a religious life, but given the circumstances, she had little choice but to agree to the arrangement. The marriage lasted 23 years and produced six sons and two daughters, all of whom survived to adulthood. The offspring didn't do too badly for themselves: three of the sons became king of Scotland, and her daughter Maud or maybe Matilda (historians aren't sure of her name) married Henry I of England in 1100.

From an early age, Margaret had established a reputation for devotion and piety, as is evident in her youthful desire to become a nun. Her biography (written around 1100 by her former chaplain, Turgot) is full of references to Margaret's compassion toward children (especially orphans) and the poor, as well as the severity of her self-denial, including a lot of fasting. According to Turgot, Margaret supported 24 poor people year-round, washed the feet of 6 of them during Lent and Advent, and had 300 people fed before her in the royal hall.

But Margaret was not just a devoted disciple of God; she was also an innovator, who did a lot to bring the Church in Scotland into line with Western doctrine and practices. In particular, Margaret urged the clergy and people of her adopted kingdom to

- ✔ Receive communion more frequently than once a year at Easter.
- ✔ Abstain from ordinary labour on Sundays.
- ✔ Observe the Lent fast from Ash Wednesday instead of the Monday following.
- ✔ Forbid marriage between a man and his stepmother or sister-in-law.
- ✔ Celebrate the Mass with a universally accepted ritual.
- ✔ Replace Celtic dialects with Latin as the language of the Mass.

Of course, none of these reforms would've been possible without the support and goodwill of her husband. Turgot stresses the extent to which Malcolm was a helpmate to her in dealing with the clergy and her charitable work. He also acted as an interpreter in clerical conferences for her because her first tongue was English, not French, as was the custom at the time.

Margaret was also a benefactor of various monastic orders. She had the church in which she was married in Dunfermline converted into a Benedictine priory. More famously, there was the construction of the chapel of St Margaret at Edinburgh Castle – the first building in Scotland to be built in the Norman style. She persuaded Malcolm to abolish the charges on the crossing over the Firth of Forth to Fife (later known in her honour as Queensferry) for genuine pilgrims heading for St Andrews, a shrine she greatly venerated. The Céli Dei at Loch Leven also benefited from her generosity.

Margaret established a reputation for her religious work, a reputation that went well beyond Scotland. She was the subject of many eulogies from chroniclers who praised her 'virtue and holy life'. She died of a broken heart on 16 November 1093 at Edinburgh Castle a few days after hearing of the death of Malcolm III. She was buried in the monastic church she had founded at Dunfermline where, in the reign of her son Alexander I (1107–1124), she was joined by her husband's body. Strangely enough, that was not the end of the story. During the Reformation, Philip II of Spain had the remains of Malcolm and Margaret transferred to a chapel in the Escorial (royal residence) at Madrid.

In spite of her reputation for devotion and piety and a cult that developed around her in Scotland, it took more than 150 years for Margaret to be recognised as a saint by the papacy, and that was only after a sustained campaign by Scotland's most senior clergy.

There is no doubt that Malcolm and Margaret were the greatest husband-and-wife team to rule Scotland. Through their efforts, Scotland became a very different kingdom to what it had been before 1050:

✔ It was more clearly defined territorially.

✔ It was more Anglo-Norman than Celtic.

✔ It was more firmly positioned within western European Catholicism.

They were modernisers who literally put Alba or Scotland on the European map.

The Four Stooges: Donald, Duncan, Edgar and Alexander

There was a series of short-lived kingships between the death of Malcolm III and the assumption of David I to the throne of Scotland. Indeed, the typically medieval scramble for power took place with its recurring stories of betrayal and bloodshed.

On Malcolm's death, his brother, Donald Bane, pushed his nephews aside and claimed the throne for himself as Donald III. It didn't last long. Malcolm's son by his first marriage, Duncan, with the support of Norman knights from England, mounted a successful invasion of Scotland to depose Donald. But

Duncan had little support in the country, particularly among the old Celtic aristocracy; in any case, Duncan was soon murdered by the mormaer of Moray, one of the descendants of Macbeth, and the mormaer's son Lulach. Donald III was back on the throne by the end of 1094. Three years later, his other nephew, Edgar, Malcolm's fourth son, with the help of the English king, invaded and Donald was quickly eliminated. Long live King Edgar of the Scots!

Edgar's reign was uneventful but lasted only ten years; when he died in 1107, unmarried and childless, he was succeeded by his brother Alexander I. As decreed in Edgar's will, the kingdom of Alba was virtually split in two, with David controlling the lands south of the Forth and Alexander the lands north of the Forth. Alexander died in 1124 a widower. With no legitimate heirs, the crown fell to David, something that did not go uncontested (see 'David I: The Revolutionary King', later in this chapter).

The minor kings were deeply religious and carried on their mother's tradition as benefactors of religious establishments. Edgar founded the Benedictine priory at Coldingham, Berwickshire; his brother Alexander went even further. Monastic communities were founded at Scone in Perthshire and at Inchcolm in the Firth of Forth. The most fashionable of Continental religious orders were brought to Scotland – for example, the Tironensians, a mainly French order, arrived in Selkirk in 1113. But their achievements pale in comparison to the reign of arguably Scotland's greatest king, David I, the youngest son of Malcolm and Margaret.

The Englishing of Scotland

Despite being rather undistinguished Scottish kings, these monarchs – Donald, Duncan, Edgar and Alexander – advanced the process of Anglicising Scotland begun in Malcolm's reign. Here are some examples:

✔ Donald III was the last king to be buried in Iona. From that point onward, monarchs were buried on the Scottish mainland in churches or monasteries based on the Norman model laid down by Margaret.

✔ The names of the descendant kings of Malcolm and Margaret were close to those of English and European rulers. For example, David was not only the greatest king in the Bible but also the name of a recent Hungarian ruler; Alexander was named after Pope Alexander II; and Edgar was as English as you can get.

✔ These kings spent a good portion of their lives at the English court and, thus, could not help but be influenced by their time there.

✔ Intermarriage did a lot to strengthen ties between the Scots and the English. Alexander I was married to Henry I's illegitimate daughter, Sybilla, and in 1113, David married Matilda, the widowed daughter of the earl of Northumbria, who at 40 was 10 years his senior.

David I: The Revolutionary King

David had a difficult start to kingship because a number of the Celtic Scottish nobility felt the sons of Donald, especially Alexander, had superior claims. David had to fight his way to the throne. But he had one advantage the others didn't – the support of Henry I of England! Not only had David spent his adolescence at the English court, but he'd also become a member of the royal household when his sister married Henry I in 1100.

Malcolm chose to fight for his crown, but he was in no position to defeat David and his retinue of heavily armoured Norman knights. Outnumbered and outfought in two battles, Malcolm escaped into parts of Scotland that weren't yet under the rule of the king to fight another day.

Like all Scottish kings, David's kingship was inaugurated at Scone, although as a foretaste of what was to come, he nearly didn't go through with it. He was deeply religious and showed no desire to take part in what was essentially a pagan ceremony. However, once possessed of the rod or wand of kingship, David went about his task of changing the face of Scotland – both religiously and politically – with gusto.

The governance of Scotland

While ruling southern Scotland, David I showed that his time at the court of Henry I had left its mark. David perceived lordship solely in feudal terms and invited followers from Normandy and England into Scotland – for example, Robert de Brus (Bruce) and the Fitzalans, who in time became the house of Stewart! They had extensive tracts of land or *fiefs* settled on them in return for military service. De Brus was settled in Annandale in southwest Scotland and Fitzalan was settled in Strathclyde.

But David was a pragmatist – he realised that if he tried to impose feudalism on the hereditary Celtic and Norse dynasties of Scotland, he would face revolt. So, he allowed older governing arrangements to stand in those areas, which created the basis for peaceful relations between himself and the Celtic and Norse aristocracies.

The only exception to peaceful co-existence was the revolt by Malcolm and his ally Angus, Mormaer of Moray, and a descendant of Lulach, Macbeth's son, in 1130. Sneakily taking advantage of David's absence in England, Angus landed an army near the River North Esk, Brechin, in Angus, but it was decimated by royal troops, with the mormaer himself being killed along with 4,000 of his men. David annexed Moray and put in place Flemish followers.

It didn't end there. Another four years of civil war continued until, in 1134, Malcolm was captured and imprisoned in Roxburgh Castle. From that point onward, nothing more is heard of him. You can probably guess what happened!

To consolidate his rule, David introduced sweeping reforms in government. These reforms were based on those in place in Anglo-Norman England. New sheriffdoms were created to administer royal lands at Berwick, Perth, Scone, Roxburgh and Stirling; they were also responsible for collecting the king's taxes. *Justiciars* (judges), who were also barons, travelled the country administering the king's justice. The administration of the royal household was also overhauled. New offices created included those of constable, chancellor, chamberlain, marshal and steward. By the end of David's reign, a national system of administration and justice was established in Scotland.

It didn't end there. David also began building towns, or *burghs* as they were known in Scotland. The first of these were Berwick and Roxburgh. A *burgh* was a settlement with marked-out boundaries, with guaranteed trading rights, and where the king could collect and sell the product of his *cain* (rent in kind – for example, sheep and poultry).

David went on to found 15 burghs, which were immensely important in reshaping the long-term economic and ethnic makeup of Scotland. These planned towns were or became English in culture and language and did a lot to create the idea of the Lowland/Highland divide in Scotland. However, to make sure his presence was felt in the Highlands, two royal burghs were founded at Elgin and Forres.

The transformation of the Scottish Church

The most powerful instrument in helping David to transform Scotland or Alba was the Church. Indeed, David was one of medieval Scotland's greatest monastic patrons. He founded monasteries all over the country, and the latest monastic orders were invited in even before he was crowned king – the Augustinians to Jedburgh, the Cistercians to Melrose and the Tironensians to Kelso. After 1124, these monastic orders spread to Scone, St Andrews and Holyrood, as well as enlarging the Benedictine monastery at Dunfermline.

The clergy didn't just look after the spiritual needs of the community; they became the king's closest advisors. The monks formed an educated bureaucracy, managing the king's records and that of his government. On top of this, the massive grants of land given to them by David (much regretted by later monarchs) boosted the economy through encouraging more trade with Europe. The Cistercian monasteries introduced new agricultural practices to Scotland, which transformed the southern part of the country into one of northern Europe's most important sources of wool.

But how did all these developments affect the local population? The answer is: in many ways. The Church increased its pastoral activities by establishing a parish system of more than 1,000 parishes by 1200, based on the local priest, who blessed crops and tended to the spiritual needs of his flock. This was important because if Catholicism as a religious system had been based simply on monasteries, it would've become a closed and hierarchical system only for rich patrons. The parish system brought Catholicism to the Scottish people.

To ensure that all parts of the kingdom were singing from the same hymn sheet of David's reforms, the Church was placed under the control of the bishops of the two largest dioceses – St Andrews and Glasgow. David also used his bishops to rebuff any claims by York or Canterbury to ecclesiastical authority over the Scottish Church.

Anglo–Scottish relations

Even before he became king of Alba, David was a major player in English court politics. Through his marriage to Matilda, he owned land stretching from south Yorkshire to Middlesex, although most of it was concentrated in four English counties – Northampton, Huntingdon, Cambridge and Bedford. Collectively, the lands formed the 'honour of Huntingdon'.

Such was David's influence that he presided over a treason trial of Henry I's chamberlain, Geoffrey Clinton. As long as Henry I was living, relations between the two kingdoms seemed friendly enough. In fact, in 1127, David agreed to recognise and swear fealty to Henry's heir and successor, his daughter Matilda, the former empress of the Holy Roman Empire.

However, Henry died in December 1135, and a succession crisis erupted because the English barons didn't want to be ruled by a woman, far less one who was married to a member of the Angevins of France. The barons and the Church rallied behind the banner of her cousin, Stephen of Bois, and Matilda's claims were thrown aside.

Never one to miss an opportunity, David invaded and took possession of Carlisle and Cumbria, something he would never have attempted while Henry I was alive. But in a subsequent treaty with the English in February 1136, he recognised Stephen's authority in return for keeping Cumbria and having his son Henry recognised as lord of the honour of Huntingdon, but giving up Northumbria.

Having sworn an oath of fealty to his niece Matilda, David was pulled into the civil war in England in early 1138, when Matilda's half-brother, Robert, Earl of Gloucester, took up arms on her behalf. In that year, the Scots were invading Northumbria and pushing on toward Yorkshire. David's army came in for severe criticism due to the brutality of their actions. One of the English chroniclers, Richard of Hexham, wrote:

> an execrable army, more atrocious than the pagans, neither fearing God nor regarding man, spread desolation over the whole province and slaughtered everywhere people of either sex, of every age and rank, destroying, pillaging and burning towns, churches and houses.

However, the brutal conquest came to a sudden halt on 22 August of that year when David's army of 26,000 men engaged in battle with the English at Cowton Moor, near Northallerton. This became known as the Battle of the Standard. The fighting began at 6 a.m. and was went on for more than three hours. The English archers inflicted huge casualties on the Scots, who were reckoned to have lost around 10,000 men, many of them cut down as they fled the battlefield.

But oddly enough, the Scots snatched victory out of the jaws of defeat! Due to his troubles in the south, the English king failed to press home his advantage. In April 1139, another peace treaty was agreed between David's son Henry and Matilda of Boulogne, Stephen's wife, at Durham. The terms of the treaty gave David all he had hoped for: his son was made earl of Northumbria and restored to the honour of Huntingdon; the Scots king kept Carlisle and Cumbria. In return, Henry paid homage to Stephen for his English lands and David swore to remain loyal to him – he didn't.

Empress Matilda's last bid for power came in 1141, when she captured Stephen at the Battle of Lincoln and tried to launch herself on the English throne but was thwarted by a rebellion in London. David and his son joined forces with Matilda but failed to support her when she was defeated later that year at Winchester. The civil war in England continued until the signing of the Treaty of Winchester in November 1153. This treaty recognised Matilda's eldest son, Henry of Anjou, as the next king of England. In return, Matilda agreed that Stephen's son, William, would be allowed to keep his family lands in France.

The shifting power balance adversely affected David and his son's holdings in England. David lost the honour of Huntingdon, but more importantly, he held on to lands between the River Tweed and the River Tyne. He was even able to extract a promise from Empress Matilda's son (whom he knighted at an elaborate ceremony in Carlisle in 1149) that, after his accession to the English throne, the Scots would be left undisturbed rulers of the English northern counties. In fact, Carlisle became David's regular seat of government. Of course, like most promises made during these years, it was broken; in this case, as soon as David's 12-year-old son, Malcolm IV, came to the throne.

In 1157, Malcolm IV travelled to Chester to pay homage to Henry, who declared that "the king of England ought not to be defrauded of so great a part of his kingdom, nor could he patiently be deprived of it."

That was it. Or was it? Read on in Chapter 6.

David I: The greatest of Scottish kings?

You could make a strong case suggesting that David I was the greatest and most revolutionary of Scottish kings. The only two who come close – Robert I and James IV – were not game changers in the way that he was. David transformed Scotland from a Celtic society to an Anglo-Norman one, although admittedly parts of the Highlands and islands clung to their traditional ways. He did this in five ways:

- **Religion:** Under David's leadership, the Scottish Church conformed more closely to the doctrines and practices of western Catholicism, but at the same time, he guarded its independence from Canterbury and York.

- **Political:** David introduced feudalism as the basis of government.

- **Cultural:** David's openness to outside influences of all sorts served to strengthen Scotland not only artistically but also economically.

- **Administration:** Royal justice, through the introduction of justiciars, was more thoroughly established under David. Those mormaers who had their own courts were informed that if they failed to provide justice, the king would intervene.

- **Territory:** David restored the southern border of the kingdom to what it had been prior to 1092.

The achievements don't end there. David was the first king to have a silver coin struck in his name at the royal mints established at Berwick, Carlisle and Edinburgh. He also held what was reckoned to be Scotland's first Parliament in 1140 at Edinburgh Castle.

But although far-reaching in their impact, the changes brought about by David built on foundations laid by those monarchs who had gone before him. In that sense, he was no innovator, but more of a synthesiser. However, he pushed the changes further and faster than any monarch before him, and in that sense, he can be seen as revolutionary.

David died on 24 May 1153 at Carlisle Castle, about a year after his son Henry. He was buried in early June before the high altar of the church of Dunfermline Abbey.

Chapter 6

Peace and Plenty? (1153–1286)

In This Chapter

▶ Considering the very short reign of Malcolm IV

▶ Looking at the very long reign of William I

▶ Focusing on the middling reign of Alexander II

▶ Studying the golden age of Alexander III

The century or more covered in this chapter has been regarded by some as a 'golden age' in which disentanglement from damaging wars with Scotland's noisy neighbour brought a period of sustained prosperity. It also witnessed the shift from a kingship to a kingdom.

The four Scottish kings between David I and John Balliol extended royal authority much further than their predecessors, bringing rebellious parts of the north and west of the country under their control. Increasingly, from 1153 onward, charters issued by the monarch referred to 'the kingdom of Scotland' or 'the kingdom of Scots'.

This period also witnessed the establishment of *primogeniture* (in which the eldest inherits the throne) as the basis on which new monarchs assumed the throne. Primogeniture also extended to females – the period ended with the infant granddaughter of Alexander III, Margaret, the Maid of Norway, inheriting the Scottish throne on Alexander's death (see Chapter 7).

The Very Short Reign of Malcolm IV (1153–1165)

Malcolm was never intended to become king – that was his father, Henry's, destiny – but unfortunately Henry died in June 1152. When David I died on 24 May 1153, Malcolm was crowned king at Scone three days later, before the late monarch was even buried. Malcolm was only 12 years old when he assumed the throne; he was nicknamed Virgo (The Maiden), owing to his age and lack of experience. And as with all minority monarchs, there were challenges from rivals from the outset of his reign.

Almost as soon as Malcolm was installed as king, three challengers emerged:

✔ Somerled, Viking king of Argyll and the Hebrides

✔ Henry II of England

✔ Fergus, lord of Galloway

The first challenge came six months into his reign, from Somerled and his allies in the north. Somerled never posed a serious threat because he was fighting a war at the same time with Godred Olafsson, king of the Isles (the islands of the Firth of Clyde and the Isle of Man), which lasted until 1156.

A more difficult situation was young Malcolm's relationship with King Henry II. At the outset of Malcolm's reign, the Scots had possession of much of the north of England, and Malcolm granted Northumbria to his brother (and, later, king) William, while keeping Cumbria for himself. Within four years, Northumbria and Cumbria were back in the possession of the English king.

In return for losing these important territories, in 1157, Malcolm was given the earldom of Huntingdon for which he paid homage to Henry at Peveril Castle in Derbyshire. Malcolm also accompanied Henry to France, taking part in the siege of Toulouse in 1160.He was knighted for this, which didn't go down very well in Scotland.

In capitulating to the English king, Malcolm was seen as weak by his earls. His perceived feebleness sparked off a rebellion on Malcolm's return from France in 1160. Six of his earls, led by Ferchar, Mormaer of Strathearn, besieged Malcolm in his own castle in Perth. The course of events is obscure, but the revolt led to a punitive assault by the king on Fergus, Lord of Galloway. Fergus was replaced by his sons and ended his days as a monk in Holyrood Abbey. That left only one challenger to deal with – Somerled.

In 1164, Malcolm, although only 23 years old, was suffering from a bone disease. His frail condition provoked some of his enemies within the Scottish nobility to recruit Somerled to overthrow the king and replace him with William FitzWilliam, grandson of Duncan II of Scotland. To side-foot the opposition, Malcolm demanded that Somerled pay him homage and turn over his lands to the crown, although he could still run them as a tenant or vassal of the monarch.

Somerled refused Malcolm's demand and instead assembled an army of 15,000 men, whom he transported in 160 ships to the shores of the Firth of Clyde to engage with the king's army at Renfrew. It turned out to be a disaster for Somerled – his Gaelic and Norse warriors were no match for the knights and men-at-arms of the royal army led by Herbert, Bishop of Glasgow, and Baldwin of Biggar, Sheriff of Lanark. Somerled was wounded by a spear in the leg and then killed by an opponent's sword along with his eldest son. With his death, the Celtic/Viking army disintegrated, and Somerled's severed head was delivered by a priest to the good bishop Herbert.

After defeat at Renfrew and Somerled's death, the Kingdom of the Isles was broken up and redistributed among various nobles. Shortly after the battle, Malcolm himself died, childless, at Jedburgh on 9 December 1165. Although his reign was short, it wasn't uneventful, and neither was it short on religious and administrative achievements. Malcolm founded the Cistercian monastery at Coupar Angus and introduced the office of sheriff – an official who represented the monarch – in places such as Crail, Dunfermline, Edinburgh, Forfar, Lanark and Linlithgow.

Contemporary chroniclers drew attention to his piety, but few could forgive Malcolm for ceding the lands of the north of England to Henry II. They were much relieved when his brother, William, replaced him as king.

The Very Long Reign of William I 'the Lion' (1165–1214)

From the start, I need to put a few things straight about William:

- ✔ He was never called 'the Lion' during his lifetime; that came later.
- ✔ He was given the title not because of feats of bravery on the battlefield but because he put a lion on the royal flag of Scotland.

However, compared to his frail brother, from whom he inherited the throne in December 1165, William must have *seemed* like a lion. He was red-headed and red-blooded, a fiery, dynamic, headstrong character who became Scotland's second-longest-ruling monarch, after James VI.

War and its consequences

From the moment he became king, William had one overriding ambition: to recover the earldom of Northumberland, which his brother had turned over to Henry II in 1157. His obsession prompted him to take part in the 'great' revolt against Henry II, led by his eldest sons and rebellious barons, supported by France and Flanders in 1173–1174. He made two attacks on Northumbria: the first attack floundered because of the Scottish army's inability to take Newcastle; the second attack was larger and more serious, but it had terrible consequences for the Lion.

In the summer of 1174, William again invaded Northumbria, avoiding Newcastle, but besieging Prudhoe Castle. After three days, he gave up and moved on to Alnwick. William was never a great military tactician, and he made a mistake in splitting his army into three columns – one to lay waste to surrounding territories, one to carry on with the siege and one to protect the king. A group of 400 English knights, led by Ralf de Glanvil, the illegitimate son of Henry II, was apparently lost and stumbled upon the king's encampment in the fog. William only had the protection of 60 or so fighting men, but nevertheless he charged the greater English force, allegedly shouting, 'Now it appears who knows how to be a knight.'

It was quickly all over – the king's horse was felled by a spear and William was taken prisoner, first to Newcastle, and then in chains to Northampton. Neither of these fortresses was considered secure enough to hold the Scottish king, so he was put on a ship to Henry II's castle in Normandy, Falaise, where he was thrown into a dungeon. Meanwhile the avenging English army took the castles of Berwick, Edinburgh, Jedburgh, Roxburgh and Stirling, and as medieval armies were wont to do, they laid waste to the surrounding lands.

To win his release from prison, the Scottish king was forced to pay homage to Henry II and sign the Treaty of Falaise in December 1174. Under the terms of the treaty, William had to agree that

- ✔ He held Scotland only with the permission of the English king.
- ✔ Scottish soldiers were to evacuate castles and garrisons and be replaced by English soldiers.
- ✔ The expenses of the English garrisons were to be met by the Scots – paying for their own subjugation.
- ✔ The Scottish Church would be placed under the authority of the Archbishop of York.

The Treaty of Falaise lasted for 15 years. And if all this was not humiliating enough, in 1175 William declared fealty to the king and future kings of England at York. Later, in 1186, the English king chose a bride for William, Ermengarde de Beaumont, granddaughter of Henry I. As her dowry, she received Edinburgh Castle. This only served to reinforce William's subservience to the English king.

Fortunately, Henry died on 11 July 1189 and was replaced by Richard I, the *Coeur de Lion* (Heart of the Lion, or Lionheart), who was in need of cash to finance his participation in the Third Crusade to the Holy Land. For the sum of 10,000 silver merks, he was prepared to release William from the Treaty of Falaise through the Quitclaim of Canterbury and return to him all the castles in Scotland still held by the English crown. It was an offer the Scots could not refuse. The money was paid, and the English left.

Scotland had avoided becoming a northern province of England, but the price it paid was a heavy one. The country was nearly bankrupt from 15 years of high taxation, which was compounded by the cost of repurchasing the castles from the English. Many people were unhappy, and unhappy people tend to get angry.

Challenges to royal authority

The embarrassing capture of William at Alnwick in 1174 was the signal for the first revolt of his reign in Galloway, which lasted until 1186 and prompted the building of the castle at Dumfries. In 1179, the king and his brother David led a royal army north to deal with expansionist threats posed by the Norse earls of Orkney and Caithness into Ross-shire. More expeditions would be necessary in 1197 and 1202.

A more serious threat was posed in 1181 by Donald Meic Uilleim, a direct descendant of Duncan II, who took control of Ross-shire and only relinquished his control when he died in 1187. But it took another ten years before the boundaries of William's kingdom could be established north of that county. Even then, there were further rebellions in Ross-shire in 1211 and again shortly after William's death in 1214.

It was clear that royal authority had to be extended, and William threw himself into this task with enthusiasm. New royal burghs were created, such as Ayr, Dumfries and Perth, and the office of high sheriff was expanded over the non-Highland part of Scotland. There was also a formidable programme of castle building in order to shore up royal power in Ayrshire, Berwickshire and Dumfries-shire in the south, and in Moray and Ross-shire in the north. New sources of support were found by advancing families like the Bruce and Stewart families, whose rise made them the aggressive agents of royal authority in the southwest and north of Scotland.

These changes didn't pacify the country – revolts continued – but they helped ensure that royal power would ultimately prevail. No previous Scottish king had ever exercised the apparatus of military power that William had available to him, but then you could argue he needed it more than they did!

Big Bad John

Richard the Lionheart's reign lasted only ten years, and he was replaced by King John I, which was bad not only for the English but also for the Scots. The two kings initially were on friendly terms, meeting amicably in 1206 and 1207 – however, not *that* amicably: John turned down William's request for the earldom of Northumbria to be restored to him. Things began to change due to William's repeated raids into the disputed territories, especially when John got wind of information that he was seeking an alliance with Phillip II of France.

The pious king

In line with other kings of the MacMalcolm Dynasty, William sought to advertise his piety through the building of churches and the founding of monasteries. He founded the Tironensian Abbey at Arbroath in 1178, where he was eventually laid to rest, and established the bishopric of Argyll in 1192 in the same year as papal confirmation of the independence of the Scottish Church was declared by Pope Celestine III.

In 1209, John marched a large army to Norham, near Berwick, to reassert his sovereignty over the disputed territories of the northern counties of England and to demand the homage of the king of Scotland. Again humiliated, William was force to sign the Treaty of Norham, which gave the English king control of his daughters and a payment of 10,000 merks. The treaty was renewed three years later.

Lamb or lion?

By the turn of the century, William's powers were beginning to wane. By the time of King John's invasion, he was a spent force. William died in Stirling at the age of 71, apparently senile, on 4 December 1214. From around 1300, he became known as William the Lion, but was the title deserved? Although he was by reputation strong-headed and courageous, never was a Scottish king so humiliated on so many occasions as William was. Indeed, his frail brother, Malcolm IV, never underwent anything like the treatment experienced by William. So, the accolade of the 'Lion' derives mostly from his contribution to heraldry. He bequeathed to future Scots the Lion rampant as a source of inspiration for the continuing fight for independence that would dominate the 14th century.

The Middling Reign of Alexander II (1214–1249)

Alexander was only 16 when he inherited the throne of Scotland, and no sooner had he been crowned at Scone on 6 December 1214 than he faced a rebellion from the north. Yes, Donald Meic Uilleim was at it again, this time in league with the MacHeth clan. Fortunately for Alexander, the revolt was speedily put down by loyalist forces, which allowed the young Scottish king to look southward. Indeed, Alexander has the honour of having taken an invasion force farther south into England than any other Scottish monarch – all the way to Dover.

Troubles with John

What caused Alexander to go all the way to Dover? On the face of it, his actions were rather ungracious. He had lived in England as a boy, and John had previously knighted him at Clerkenwell Priory in 1213. But Alexander coveted the areas of Cumbria and Northumbria, and by aligning himself with the rebel English barons against the king, he felt he would be rewarded by having his claims to the disputed territories recognised. However, the first Scottish invasion was repelled by John in 1215, and in consequence Berwick was sacked (yes, again!), as were Roxburgh, Haddington and Dunbar. With the Scottish threat seemingly neutered, John headed south to deal with the English rebels, who by this time had chosen Prince Louis of France as his replacement.

Alexander led a second invasion force south in September 1216.They reached the southeast coast of England. Entering Dover, Alexander paid homage to the French pretender for his lands in England. However, the death of King John on 18 October ended the rebellion. Alexander's hopes of taking Cumbria and Northumbria as a reward for supporting the rebels were dashed.

The English aristocracy and the pope threw their support behind Henry III, the 9-year-old son of John. This forced the French and Scottish armies homeward. But Henry's accession to the English crown ushered in a period of peace between these warring nations. By the Treaty of Kingston of 12 September 1217, peace was declared; this was further strengthened in June 1221 with the marriage of the English king's 10-year-old sister, Joan, to Alexander. She died in 1238, childless. Alexander's sister, Margaret, was in turn married off to a former regent of Henry's.

The Treaty of York

After Alexander's marriage to Joan, relations between Scotland and England were fairly amicable. In this new era of mutual understanding, the Treaty of York was signed with Henry III in 1237. This treaty was very important because for the first time the border between England and Scotland was officially defined. The border was to run from the Solway Firth (in the west) to the mouth of the River Tweed (in the east). However, by signing the treaty Alexander abandoned his forefathers' claims to Northumbria and Cumbria.

Expansion of the kingdom

The settled state of his relations with England allowed Alexander to look inward and deal with the questions of expanding royal power and the boundaries of his realm. His main interest was the Western Isles, which had long been controlled by Norse rulers. Alexander made a number of attempts to purchase the islands from Hakon IV of Norway, but the offers were rejected. When diplomacy and bribery failed, Alexander opted for a new strategy.

First, he tried to persuade Ewen, Lord of Argyll, to renounce his allegiance to the Norwegian king. When Ewen rebuffed the overtures, he turned to force. In July 1249, Alexander assembled a fleet and army to compel Hakon and his ally Argyll to agree to his offers. However, on the way to battle, he suffered a fever and, while resting on the Isle of Kerrera, across the bay from what is now the town of Oban, he died at the age of 50.

Alexander had successfully subdued Argyll, but the Isles would have to wait for another time and another king. But at least for the first time during his reign, Scotland as a territorial unit had been officially defined and recognised by the English. This was not Alexander's only achievement. There were others of a religious and political nature:

✔ In 1227, Alexander founded a number of religious establishments, such as the Cistercian abbey at Balmerino in Fife.

✔ The first Scottish Parliament of barons and bishops for which there is a surviving record was held at Kirkliston, near Edinburgh, in 1235.

✔ Alexander encouraged leading English families such as the Balliols to marry into the Scottish aristocracy.

The Golden Age of Alexander III (1249–1286)

The reputation of Alexander III as one of Scotland's greatest monarchs is founded on the twin pillars of peace and plenty. But unlike his ancestor David I, Alexander III was never seen as a legend in his own lifetime. His legendary status was conferred by later generations of chroniclers, the first of whom was John of Fordun, writing in the 1380s, nearly a hundred years after Alexander III's death.

However, such high esteem was as much a matter of timing as anything else. Alexander's demise in 1286 plunged the country into a succession crisis (see Chapter 7), which marked the beginning of 300 years of continuous warfare and internal strife. Given all this, it's hardly surprising that his reign is often referred to as a 'golden age' by poets and historians alike.

The boy king

Alexander was only 7 when his father died and he assumed the throne of Scotland – the first boy king in more than a hundred years. But his reign lasted 36 years – only William the Lion reigned longer in the 12th and 13th centuries. As with all minorities, a power vacuum developed, with ambitious noble families only too happy to act as regents for the young king. Scotland was no different to other societies. Two rival families – the Comyns and the Durwards – vied with each other for control over the affairs of state.

The Comyns were widely regarded as Scotland's most powerful family, while the Durwards, who had little influence among the Scottish aristocracy, sought English support to advance their interests. With the approval of the mother of the boy king, Marie de Coucy, Alan Durward was initially in control of the government of Scotland. To shore up his position, he arranged a marriage between Alexander, at the age of 10, and Margaret, the 11-year-old daughter of Henry III, on Boxing Day in 1251.

The marriage was a mistake because it allowed the English to interfere, once again, in Scottish affairs. After the wedding ceremony, Henry III demanded homage from Alexander for the lands he held in England. The latter demand was refused and no further discussion of the matter took place. End of story? No. The English king couldn't stop interfering in matters not of his concern.

As a result, the balance of power in Scotland began to shift toward the Comyns. Henry engineered the resignation of all the main officials of the Scottish household and the appointment of a new royal council dominated by the Comyn family and their allies. The plan was a cunning one, but it never delivered the outcomes desired by Henry – the new government became even more difficult than the one it had replaced.

The Scots nobles showed little respect for the interfering English king. In Gascony in 1253, his demands for military assistance fell on deaf ears; only the ousted Alan Durward, who had made his peace with Henry, went on campaign with the English magnates. Another source of contention was the money ordered to be levied by the papacy in Scotland to support an English crusade. Not surprisingly, the Scots refused to pay because the enterprise was only intended to win the throne of Sicily for Henry III's second son, Edmund.

By the summer of 1255, the situation had become intolerable to Henry. His solution: remove the Comyn party from office. But neither the English king nor the Scottish king realised the amount of power enjoyed by the Comyns. In 1257, negotiations were held aimed at ensuring peace, but they broke down without an agreement. In retaliation, Walter Comyn, Earl of Menteith, and his followers kidnapped Alexander and his queen at Kinross in October that year. Henry III threatened invasion to put down the rebellion, but it seems to have been an empty bluff. By this time, the warring factions realised that the only hope for stability was to unite behind the king. So, a compromise was reached in September 1258, in which the regency was to be representative of both parties.

Coming of age

Henry III realised that he had little influence left in Scotland now that Alexander was coming of age and clearly in personal control of the Scottish government. So, Henry requested a visit of the Scottish king and queen to England, which took place in November 1260. The visit marked the end of faction and signalled the beginning of steady growth of the country both politically and economically.

However, there was still the issue of the Western Isles to be resolved. On attaining his majority at the age of 21 in 1262, Alexander declared his intention to resume his late father's policy of claiming the disputed territories as Scottish, a decision that did not go down well with the king of Norway, Hakon IV. Another thing that did not go down well was the attack on the Isle of Skye by the earl of Ross, which led to tales of church burning and the killing of women and children. The Scots were clearly the aggressors, and an outraged Hakon assembled a fleet to avenge the attacks and put paid to the demands of the Scottish king.

The Battle of Largs

The invasion fleet arrived on the west coast of Scotland in the late summer of 1263, occupying the Firth of Forth. Negotiations began, but they got nowhere. Alexander was buying time for the weather to worsen, which meant bad news for the Norwegian fleet. Storms drove some of Hakon's ships ashore, and with things deteriorating, he decided to engage the Scots in battle in early October.

The Battle of Largs has been mythologised in terms of its importance and size. Chronicles talked of the Norse force of a thousand men, when in reality both sides probably comprised only several hundred. The battle itself was indecisive, although it didn't stop each side from claiming a great victory over the other.

What is beyond dispute is that the Scots repelled the invasion force, and Hakon and his men were forced to retreat homeward. Hakon sailed northward, exacting tribute from the Islands as he went, and arrived in Orkney in October. While wintering there, he fell ill and died two months later.

Hakon's death signalled further aggressive action by Alexander in Caithness, Skye and other parts of the Western Isles in 1264, which intimidated many of the Scottish nobles formerly loyal to Hakon into accepting the king's 'peace'. The king's surrender of the Isle of Man to the Scots brought the Norwegians to the negotiating table. The new king of Norway, Magnus IV the Law-mender, made an agreement in July 1266 at Perth, in which the Western Isles were ceded to Scotland in return for a lump sum of 4,000 merks and an annual payment in perpetuity of 100 merks. The northern islands of Orkney and Shetland were to remain in Norwegian hands, something that remained unaltered for another 200 years.

What we know as the boundaries of Scotland today were beginning to take a firm shape in the south by the Treaty of York and in the west by the Treaty of Perth. Relations between the two countries were further cemented by the marriage of Alexander's only daughter, Margaret, to Magnus's successor, King Eric II, in 1281.

Finding an heir

The peace and tranquillity of the later years of Alexander's reign were overshadowed by problems relating to who was to succeed him. His queen, Margaret, had died in early 1275, leaving behind a daughter, also known as Margaret, and two sons, Alexander and David. The problem was that they all died during the last five years of Alexander's life: David in 1281, Margaret in 1283 and Alexander (married but without an heir) in 1284. The only direct descendant to Alexander left was his half-Norwegian granddaughter, Margaret, Maid of Norway.

In 1284, at Scone, Alexander took the precaution of having the Scottish Parliament recognise his granddaughter as heir presumptive should he fail to produce another heir. However, help was at hand in this matter, or least so it appeared. On 14 October 1285, Alexander married Yolande, daughter of Robert, Count of Dreux. His second wife became pregnant shortly after the marriage, but the baby was stillborn. The following year, on a stormy night in March, Alexander himself, only 44 years old, and on his way to his wife in Kinghorn, Fife, died after his horse stumbled and threw him.

His death had been prophesied the previous evening by Thomas of Erchildoun, better known as Thomas the Rhymert:

> Alas for the morrow, day of misery and calamity! Before the hour of noon there will assuredly be felt such a mighty storm in Scotland that its like has not been known for long ages past. The blast of it will cause nations to tremble, will make those who hear it dumb, and will humble the high, and lay the strong level with the ground.

A golden age?

The view that Alexander's reign constituted a 'golden age' was in many ways an invention of the chroniclers of the 14th and 15th centuries. Writing in the midst of war and upheaval, it was understandable that they would look to the past for some comfort. So, the golden age metaphor is perhaps an exaggeration. Nevertheless, it does have a measure of truth about it.

Due to the prolonged peace, the economy was beginning to grow, as did the population. Favourable climatic conditions saw agriculture production increase. Indeed, Berwick alone, the main Scottish burgh of Alexander's day, had customs revenues equal to a quarter of all the customs of England, and the money from export duties significantly boosted royal income. The wool trade also grew significantly during Alexander's reign.

The growing prosperity of the country was also reflected in its architecture. Work on some of Scotland's more important religious buildings was begun in this period, including the cathedrals of Dunblane, Dunfermline, Glasgow and St Andrews.

But let's not get carried away. Overseas trade was growing, but it was based on primitive primary products, such as coarse wool and hides. Sophisticated goods, such as wine, silks and metal goods, had to be imported. The burghs were expanding their economies, but in terms of size, they were distinctly modest. There were more coins in circulation, but the supply of money was never in danger of increasing dramatically.

The absence of war greatly helped in creating the conditions for such economic improvement as there was. Alexander was known as the 'Peaceable', and not for nothing was this title conferred upon him. He avoided war with Scotland's neighbour during his rule, accepting homage for his lands in England but never for Scotland, in spite of the demands made on him by his father-in-law, Henry III, and his brother-in-law, Edward I. Perhaps his greatest achievement was the completion of the project begun by his father, Alexander II, to claim the Western Isles for Scotland.

Through this endeavour and the policies he pursued to create consensus and stability in society, as well as his sturdy defence of Scottish independence, Alexander III was able to unite the people of Scotland behind his rule.

A fairer assessment may be that Alexander's reign was marked by relative peace and moderate but growing prosperity, in addition to being politically stable and (outside of his minority) free from internal strife. Although not appreciated at the time, when Alexander went over the edge in 1286, it was more than a personal tragedy; it was a national one.

Part III
Making the Nation (1286–1542)

Sir W. Wallace.

© Classic Image/Alamy

 Consider the case of the Black Douglases in an article at www.dummies.com/extras/scottishhistory.

In this part . . .

✔ Examine the problems created by the premature death of Alexander III for the throne of Scotland and how this allowed Edward I of England to invade Scotland.

✔ Understand the resistance by William Wallace and, later, Robert the Bruce.

✔ Appreciate the artistic achievements of the Stewart kings during the Renaissance.

✔ Consider the Reformation and the struggles between Mary, Queen of Scots, and the Protestant reformers like John Knox.

Chapter 7

The Wars of Independence (1286–1371)

*T*he years 1286 to 1357 are perhaps the most decisive in Scotland's history. The danger of being forcibly incorporated into a greater Britain was never more real than during this period. The existence of an independent Scottish kingdom was under serious attack, and it was never really guaranteed until 1357. More than 60 years of continuous warfare between Scotland and England created within the Scots a strong sense of national identity among all social groupings – from the elite to the peasantry – and linked the Church with the cause of national independence. Resistance to English aggression helped forge the nation. The campaigns of William Wallace and, later, Robert the Bruce galvanised the Scottish people in an epic struggle for independence. That story is so powerful, it resonates even today, and it's incorporated in the country's unofficial national anthem, 'Flower of Scotland'. It has made national heroes of Wallace and Bruce, the superstars of Scottish history.

From 1357 onward, England would no longer forcibly try to incorporate Scotland as a province under its control. This did not mean the end of Anglo–Scottish wars, but the wars were of a different nature and fought for different reasons.

The Auld Alliance

A good way of thinking about Scotland's alliance with France is to imagine a school playground where a smaller kid is being bullied by a bigger one. The smart smaller kid will seek to befriend another big bully, which will make the other one think twice before trying it on. This is exactly what drove Scotland into the French embrace, and it proved a smart move on more than one occasion.

The Maid of Norway

Strange as it may seem, the Anglo–Scottish conflict began as an accident. In 1286, the Scottish king Alexander III was travelling in darkness on horse-back, on his way to visit his second wife, Yolande, when he fell from his horse at Kinghorn, Fife. The problem (besides the fact that he died):Alexander had lost his son and heir two years before. Cue power struggle and civil war.

There were a number of claimants to the vacant Scottish throne – some genu-ine and some bogus. The Scottish Parliament offered the crown to Margaret, the Maid of Norway, infant granddaughter of Alexander III. Given the fact that she was a minor, a committee of 'guardians' was set up to run the country; the committee included four barons and the archbishops of St Andrews and Glasgow.

The first challenge to the committee's authority came from the southwest of Scotland and was led, ironically enough, by the Bruce family – the two Roberts, father and son. The father was the great-great-grandson of David I (see Chapter 5) and the closest male relative to the late king. In fact, he had been named successor by Alexander before Margaret was born. So, you could argue that he had a genuine claim to the throne. The Bruce rising, however, was put down by the guardians, who ran the country for the next three years.

Most people thought it was inconceivable that Margaret could rule in her own right as a female – a husband had to be found for her. The king of Norway's choice was Edward, infant son and heir to Edward I of England. The proposal was formalised by the Treaty of Birgham in 1290. Under the terms of the treaty, the English would acknowledge Margaret's right to the Scottish throne, but children of the marriage would inherit both thrones. In addition, Scotland would remain a separate kingdom with its own government and not subject to English jurisdiction. One problem: the Maid of Norway died in the autumn of 1290 in Orkney while making the journey from Norway to Scotland, appar-ently from seasickness. Bring forward a new cast of claimants –14 in all!

Finding a king

These 14 contenders for the throne of Scotland staked a claim in what was known as the 'Great Cause', in which they put forward legal arguments in favour of their credentials. The king of Norway even staked a claim on the basis that he was the Maid's father and son-in-law to the late king! But there were more credible candidates. John 'the Black' Comyn was not only a guardian but head of one of the most powerful baronial families in Scotland as lord of Badenoch. He also could trace his lineage back to a former Scottish king, Donald III.

Despite his qualifications, Comyn chose to stand aside in favour of his brother-in-law, John Balliol, who had a stronger claim than Bruce's on the basis that Balliol's mother was older than Bruce's mother and so by the law of primogeniture (in which the oldest inherits) the titles fell to her and her offspring.

With civil war looming, the bishop of St Andrews suggested that Edward I be invited to adjudicate on the various claims, and his suggestion was accepted by the Scottish Parliament. However, Edward had his own agenda:

✔ The guardians would accept him as lord paramount of Scotland.

✔ The leading Scottish nobles would swear allegiance to him as lord paramount.

✔ Every royal Scottish castle would be placed temporarily under his control.

✔ Every Scottish official would resign and be reappointed by him.

✔ He would preside over the court held in the Great Hall of Berwick Castle.

The convention was made up of 24 English bishops and barons hand-picked by Edward, together with 80 representatives from Scotland –40 picked by Bruce and 40 by Balliol – and lasted six months. After all the submissions and investigations into the rival claims had taken place, Edward chose John Balliol to be Scotland's new king, and he was duly crowned at Scone with the support of the Scottish nobility on St Andrews Day in 1292.

The trouble with John

From the beginning, it was clear that King John was a puppet king. The real power in Scotland was being exercised by Edward I. Even before John's death in 1313, his nickname was 'Toom Tabard' (Empty Jacket), symbolic of the fact that he was king in name only. Indeed, Edward, in his desire to unify the whole of the land mass known as Britain under his rule, seriously undermined the reign of King John in three ways:

✔ By forcing John to pay homage to Edward at Newcastle in December 1292 as king of Scots

✔ By encouraging appeals to Edward's court, undermining the Scottish king's position as the fount of justice

✔ By demanding in September 1294 that John and his barons perform military service against the French king

The last demand was untenable – the king of Scotland couldn't force nobles to take up arms for another monarch abroad. Plus, France controlled Flanders, the chief source of Scottish revenue for wool sales. It was also a repudiation of the Treaty of Birgham.

The only road was open defiance. In 1295, John made overtures to Philip IV of France for a treaty of mutual aid, which was to be formalised through the marriage of John's son and heir, Edward, to the niece of the French king, Jeanne de Valois. This was the beginning of what became known as the Auld Alliance, as John allied himself with England's fiercest rival. The Alliance became the lynchpin of Scottish foreign policy down to the Treaty of Edinburgh in 1560. It was reciprocal – Scots fought with Joan of Arc in 1429 to relieve Orleans. The kings of France established the Scottish Guard – the Garde Ecossaise – which existed until the French Revolution.

However, there was a price: as a condition of the Alliance, Scotland was to invade England in the spring of 1296. When news of the Franco–Scottish Treaty reached him, Edward had only one thing on his mind after this show of disobedience: give them a lesson they will never forget. He met with a band of 80 Scottish nobles at Wark Castle, 24.1 kilometres (15 miles) south of the River Tweed, all of whom held lands on both sides of the border and had agreed to pay homage to the English king. Those present included the 7th Robert Bruce and his son, the future king. In retaliation, King John confiscated all Bruce's lands in Annandale and gave them to John Comyn, his brother-in-law. From that point, the struggle for mastery in Scotland was between three families: the Comyns, the Balliols and the Bruces. But for now, the king of England held all the aces.

If you hate the English, clap your hands

After the meeting at Wark Castle in Northumberland, Edward took Berwick and, in the process, slaughtered hundreds of its inhabitants, including 30 Flemish artisans who had established themselves in the town. Every building was sacked, and it was rebuilt as an English garrison town. In April 1296, the Scots were defeated at the Battle of Dunbar by an English army that include Robert the Bruce on its side.

Scotland was rapidly conquered in 1296 as first Roxburgh Castle fell, then Edinburgh, then Stirling, and finally Perth, in fairly rapid succession. Brutality at Berwick was not an isolated event – the English showed no respect for the chivalric code of honouring your enemy. The garrison holding Stirling Castle under Sir William Oliphant finally succumbed in 1304. They were paraded with ropes around their necks like traitors.

It was only due to repeated requests that Edward I spared them execution and disembowelling. Contrast this kind of barbarism with the Scottish treatment of the starving English garrison of Stirling Castle, which was successfully besieged in 1299; there, the garrison was given a safe conduct and left unharmed for England.

At Montrose on 8 July, the formal surrender of King John and his abdication was completed when the bishop of Durham in a humiliating gesture ripped the Scottish arms from his jacket. The symbolism was clear: the king was king no more. He died in obscurity in 1313 on his estate in Picardy, France.

Exalting in his triumph, Edward, as the Malleus Scottorum (Hammer of the Scots), returned to England with the Black Rood of St Margaret and the Stone of Scone to lie in Westminster Abbey beneath the throne of England. The official records of Scotland were burnt or taken to London. John Balliol was locked up in the Tower of London for three years.

In August 1296, Edward convened a Scottish Parliament at Berwick, in which he received the homage of most of the Scottish nobility, including the Bruces. Scotland was under direct control of England and no longer a kingdom. The victorious commander at Dunbar, the earl of Surrey, was made governor, and Sir Hugh de Cressingham was appointed treasurer.

The arrogance and brutality shown by the English toward their 'subjects' didn't just create a feeling of animosity among the Scots toward them; it generated a burning hatred.

The First War of Independence (1296–1328)

Resistance was the only thing left for the Scots. First, through William Wallace and Andrew de Moray, and then through Robert the Bruce, the Scots took the struggle to the English, inflicting heavy defeats on them. Eventually, Scotland forced the English to agree to recognise the integrity of the Scottish realm.

William Wallace and the Scottish resistance

'Cometh the hour cometh the man': step forward, William Wallace (see Figure 7-1). But who was he, and where did he come from? The origins of the Wallace family are a bit hazy, but it seems that they were Welsh and had come to Scotland sometime in the 12th century. Wallace himself was born at Paisley in 1270, or was it Eldersie, Renfrewshire? No one really knows. However, we do know that he was the second son of Sir Malcolm Wallace. Malcolm was chief vassal of the steward of Scotland and one of a small number of Scottish nobles who had refused to pay homage to Edward in 1296.

Figure 7-1:
William
Wallace.

© Classic Image/Alamy

In May 1297, at the age of 26, Wallace made his entrance onto the national stage when he murdered the English high sheriff of Lanark, William de Heselrig, for allegedly murdering Wallace's wife, Marion. Wallace chopped Heselrig into little pieces and then carried out a series of guerrilla raids against the English, most notably at Scone with Sir William Douglas.

But Wallace's rebellion was only one of a series of rebellions taking place across Scotland. In the north, Andrew de Moray captured the castles of Aberdeen, where he burned English ships at anchor in the harbour of the town, Inverness, Montrose, Brechin and Forfar. In his campaign, de Moray was supported by the burgesses, while the barons and earls stood aside. The nobility, including Robert the Bruce (shown in Figure 7-2) and James the Steward, had reaffirmed their allegiance to Edward at Irvine in July of that year.

Figure 7-2:
Robert the
Bruce.

With the nobility compromised, Moray and Wallace joined forces and became, as they said, 'leaders of the army of Scotland'. On 11 September 1297, they achieved a stunning success with an army drawn from all over Scotland against the English at the Battle of Stirling Bridge. Although vastly outnumbering the Scots, the English army, under the command of the governor of Scotland, the earl of Surrey, was routed.

The English had been trapped on Stirling Bridge as they tried to cross over to the north side of the river. The narrowness of the bridge prevented many soldiers from crossing together – maybe as few as three abreast. The Scots held back until half of them had passed and then killed the English as quickly as they crossed. One of Wallace's captains charged the English, causing some of them to retreat as others pushed forward. Under the overwhelming weight, the bridge collapsed, and many enemy soldiers were drowned.

The victory was won by lesser knights, peasants and *freeholders* (tenant farmers) because the aristocracy were not prepared to defend them or the nation. The opportunistic tactics used by Wallace at Stirling and elsewhere were a reflection of those who supported him. He had to make use of what he had. But these tactics were unappreciated by the English because they went against the standard rules of accepted medieval combat, which were based on strength of arms and elaborate rituals bound up with knightly warfare. The English also didn't appreciate that Wallace had the skin of one of their fallen commanders, Hugh de Cressingham, the English treasurer, flayed to make a belt for his sword.

After Stirling Bridge, Moray and Wallace assumed the title of guardians of the kingdom of Scotland on behalf of King John Balliol. Soon after this, in late 1297, Moray died of wounds suffered on the battlefield. As guardian of Scotland, Wallace ruled for only a year. During that time, he made repeated attacks on the English in their own backyard and laid waste to parts of Northumberland. But Wallace lacked royal authority, and the nobility refused him support.

Edward made peace with France and moved his seat of government from London to York. In April 1298, at the head of 12,500 footmen and 2,000 cavalry, he led a second invasion of Scotland. The English plundered the Lothians and recaptured some castles, but they failed to engage with Wallace's army. Wallace had decided to play a waiting game with the English: wait till they ran out of money and supplies; then harass them when they retreated south. But in July, Edward, facing near mutiny in his army, received news that the Scottish army was at Falkirk.

On 22 July, Edward engaged the Scots in battle. This time, history didn't repeat itself – he proved victorious. Edward's Welsh bowmen proved to be the undoing of the Scots, and their casualties were high (although Wallace escaped unharmed). By September 1298, Wallace had resigned as guardian of Scotland in favour of Robert the Bruce, Earl of Carrick and future king, and John Comyn, lord of Badenoch and King John Balliol's nephew.

Where Wallace went next is a bit of a mystery, but the likeliest explanation is that he was in France trying to get Philip the Fair to agree to support the struggle for Scottish independence. If he was, then he came back empty-handed.

By 1303, Wallace was back in Scotland, and involved in skirmishes:

- At Happrew, near Peebles, in February 1304, with English knights, whose numbers included Robert the Bruce. The English knights had been sent south from Dunfermline under Sir John Segreve to locate and capture Wallace.

- At Earnside, Perthshire, in September 1304, the last action known to be fought by Wallace. Wallace was hunted down and ultimately betrayed by Sir John Menteith, a Scottish knight loyal to Edward, who turned Wallace over to English soldiers at Robroyston near Glasgow on 5 August 1305.

Wallace was brought to trial in Westminster's Great Hall, accused of atrocities against civilians in war ('sparing neither age nor sex, monk nor nun') and of treason. His response to the charge of treason was pointed: 'I could not be a traitor to Edward, for I never was his subject.'

While true, his response fell on deaf ears. He was crowned with a garland of oak to suggest he was the king of outlaws. But the humiliation and the suffering did not end there. Found guilty of treason, Wallace was dragged naked on a two-wheeled cart from Westminster to the Tower of London, and then taken to Smithfield, where he was hanged, drawn and emasculated, and his bowels were burnt before him. His head was cut off and dipped in tar to preserve it; then it was piked above London Bridge. His severed head was later joined by those of his comrades in arms, the Fraser brothers, John and Simon. Wallace's severed limbs were displayed separately in Newcastle, Berwick, Stirling and Perth, as a warning to others.

While undeniably a charismatic figure, and the subject of a great deal of romantic fiction, did Wallace achieve anything of lasting significance for the cause of Scottish independence? Historians would argue that from his brief appearance on the national stage, three developments of lasting benefit emerge:

- ✔ Wallace's repeated raids on Northumberland provided a blueprint for the 30 years of guerrilla warfare used by Robert I against the English.

- ✔ By engineering the appointment of William Lamberton to the bishopric of St Andrews in 1297, Wallace ensured the commitment of the Church to the national struggle.

- ✔ Wallace restored the guardianship as representative of the community of the realm.

Robert the Bruce

After the demise of Wallace, it seemed as if Scotland had been finally conquered and beaten into submission by the English king. In May 1305, the Scottish Parliament had gone as far as to agree to appoint commissioners to negotiate Scotland's absorption into the English state. But Edward never truly recognised the extent of Bruce's determination to become king of Scotland, or the lengths he would go to in achieving that goal. In fact, despite the fact that he was governor of Carlisle and sheriff of Lanark in the service of Edward I, Bruce had been plotting since 1304 with the bishop of St Andrews, William Lamberton, to become the next king of an independent Scotland.

There were a number of obstacles in Bruce's way, not the least of which was his rival in Scotland, John Comyn, Lord of Badenoch. At the time, Comyn, who was related to many of the most important noble families in Scotland and England, was the most powerful nobleman in Scotland. He also had vacillated less than Bruce had done in his relations with the English king.

On 10 February 1306, the two rivals met at Greyfriars Church, Dumfries, and they got into an argument over the issue of conspiring with the English. Bruce was convinced that Comyn had informed Edward I of Bruce's plans. In the course of the argument, Bruce lost his temper and stabbed his rival in the neck in front of the altar. His *retainer* (a kind of family servant), Roger de Kirkpatrick, finished him off.

Murder before the altar was the highest form of sacrilege, and Bruce was later excommunicated by the pope, but on making his confession to Robert Wishart, Bishop of Glasgow, he received absolution. Five weeks later, Bruce was crowned king of Scotland at Scone on 25 March.

Bruce's coronation was a rather strange, low-key affair. Because her brother was being held captive in an English prison, Isabella MacDuff, Countess of Buchan, was the only available representative of the family of the earls of Fife who had the immemorial right of seating the king on the stone of inauguration. So she was the one to crown Bruce. In attendance at the coronation were only Bruce's four brothers, along with his wife, two abbots and the earls of Atholl and Menteith.

The reaction from Edward was brutal. A petition was sent to the pope for permission to raze Scone Abbey to the ground. Three of Bruce's brothers were executed, along with the earl of Atholl; Bruce's wife, Elizabeth, his sisters Mary and Christina, and the countess were imprisoned. Mary and Isabella were particularly harshly treated – they were kept in wooden cages exposed to the elements for four years! Bruce didn't see his wife again for eight years. Plus, his estates were given to supporters of Edward I.

A spider's tale

Things were getting worse for Bruce. Not only was he excommunicated for killing Comyn, but at the Battle of Methven, Perthshire, on 19 June, his army was defeated by the earl of Pembroke. Bruce and his army were forced to take to the hills of Kintail and Kintyre in the southern Highlands. He suffered another defeat at the hands of the MacDougall clan, who were closely tied to the Comyn family, at Dalrigh (the field of the king), and fled Scotland with his small band of supporters.

At his lowest point, holed up in a cave in Rathlin Island, off the coast of County Antrim, Northern Ireland, an outlaw and a fugitive, Bruce is said to have been inspired by a spider trying to spin a web across a gap in the roof. Despite repeated failures, the spider persisted and its struggle became a metaphor for Bruce's struggle – if you don't succeed, try and try again. However, the story – no matter how inspiring – was based entirely on fiction invented by Sir Walter Scott some five centuries later.

In February 1307, Bruce and his followers returned to Scotland in two groups. Robert and his brother Edward landed at Turnberry Castle and began a guerrilla war in the southwest of Scotland. Two other brothers landed farther south at Loch Ryan, but they were soon in English hands and executed. In April 1307, Bruce and his men made a military breakthrough, slaughtering a small English cavalry force at Glentrool in Dumfries-shire. On 10 May, he won another victory at Loudon Hill, where he defeated Aymer de Valence, the 2nd Earl of Pembroke. Revenge is sweet!

To Bruce's great fortune, Edward I died after an attack of dysentery at Lanercost Priory near Solway on 7 July 1307. The new king, Edward II, was not as interested in holding Scotland as his father had been. Bruce took advantage of this situation, and gradually reduced the English presence in Scotland. He captured castles and destroyed them so that the English couldn't use them again. By the summer of 1309, Banff and Dundee were the only strongholds in English hands north of the River Tay. Comyn's old supporters, the earls of Buchan and Ross, attempted to hinder Bruce's progress, and they were systematically destroyed. By 1309, Bruce was sufficiently confident that he controlled enough of Scotland to hold his first parliament at St Andrews.

Two years later, he had finally pushed the English out of Galloway and Lothian. In 1313, Perth, Roxburgh and Edinburgh were taken; Bruce was now acknowledged king of northern Scotland and the southwest. He even made forays into England, capturing the Isle of Man in June 1313. He held parliaments, issued charters and, through loyal bishops, opened diplomatic contacts with Europe.

Only Stirling Castle, the most strategic of all, as the gateway to the north and south, held out against Bruce. As he besieged the castle, Edward II, with an army of 20,000 men and 3,000 cavalry, moved north. The English army included Bruce's old enemy Aymer de Valence, Sir John Comyn of Badenoch (looking to avenge his father's murder), the earl of Angus and several MacDougalls.

The Battle of Bannockburn

Robert's brother Edward had secured an agreement with Sir Philip Mowbray, English commander of the castle, that if Edward II's army did not show themselves by midsummer 1314, Mowbray would surrender. The English king arrived at Falkirk on 23 June, but the conditions were such that cavalry got bogged down and the English archers were dispersed by Scottish light cavalry. Even though the English force was three times the size of the Scottish one, the English were badly defeated at Bannockburn. They were so humiliated that Edward II lost his shield, privy seal and court poet, who subsequently was forced to compose verse celebrating the Scottish victory! The booty plundered on the battlefield and from the English baggage train amounted to an estimated £200,000. There were also lucrative ransoms from English captives to be had – a good day's work.

Edward II fled the field and made for Dunbar where his fleet lay at anchor. Of the 16,000 English foot soldiers who had made the journey north, only 5,000 returned. Among the dead were John Comyn, the would-be avenger, and the earl of Gloucester. David had slain Goliath. The Scots army was drawn from all ranks across Scotland; the nation had acted as one.

John Barbour, in his epic poem, 'The Bruce', gave a clue as to why the Scots had prevailed over such a superior force:

> We for our lyvis [lives],
>
> And for our children and our wifis [wives]
>
> And for the freedom of our land
>
> Ar strenyeit [forced] in battle for to stand

Perhaps the outcome was in some ways predictable after Bruce's personal combat with Henry de Bohun, nephew of the earl of Hereford. Bohun charged at Bruce with his lance just prior to the battle, only to be killed by a blow to the head from Bruce's battleaxe. It was a sign of things to come. Chided by his commanders for the huge risk he had taken, the king only expressed regret that he had broken the shaft of his axe!

After Bannockburn, Bruce held a parliament at Cambuskenneth, near Stirling, which confiscated the lands of the Balliols, the Comyns and the earl of Atholl who had deserted him on the eve of battle. It was a historic occasion –the first parliament to include representatives of the burghs. The mood of celebration was so great that they agreed that a tenth of all rents were to be paid directly to the king to help defray the cost of his expenses.

Bruce may have won the battle, but the war was not over. Buoyed by his military successes, Robert I launched repeated raids against northern England, reaching as far as Yorkshire and Lancashire. Under the pretext of freeing the Irish from English domination, and at the invitation of the king of Tyrone, he invaded Ireland in 1315. More cynically, this action was designed to weaken the position of Edward II even further and, at the same time, protect the southwest of Scotland from invasion from the English army in Ireland.

Bruce used his notion of 'Pan-Gaelic Greater Scotia' to further justify his incursion into Irish territory. As a king descended from a line of Scottish and Irish Gaelic monarchs (or so he claimed), Robert I saw himself ruling as king of both Ireland and Scotland. Indeed, his brother Edward was crowned as high king of Ireland in 1316. But the truth was, Robert had little support in Ireland outside of the power base of his father-in-law in Ulster.

The Irish saw little difference in Scottish rule, particularly as it coincided with a large-scale famine; Scottish troops were fed at the expense of locals. It became an army of occupation so loathed by the Irish that the people of Dublin burnt the town down rather than allow the Scots to take it over. The occupation came to an end with the defeat and death of Edward Bruce at the Battle of Faughart, near Dundalk, on 14 October 1318. His head was cut off, packed in salt and sent as a gift to Edward II.

The Declaration of Arbroath

Robert I's military adventure produced nothing tangible. The idea of a Pan-Gaelic kingdom was in shreds, but his forays into diplomacy proved to be more successful. What he needed was not only complete control of Scotland, free from English interference, but recognition of his position as the rightful monarch of an independent realm. The Declaration of Arbroath of 1320 launched a diplomatic offensive aimed at achieving this goal.

The declaration was written in Latin by a cleric on behalf of the Scottish nobility. It was intended to justify Scotland's and Robert I's fight for independence to Pope John XXII in the hope that the pope might lift the excommunication order on the Scottish king.

The declaration contained the lines that have proved enduring in the ongoing struggle for independence from England:

> For as long as one hundred men remain alive, we shall never under any conditions submit to the domination of the English. It is not for glory or riches or honours that we fight, but only for liberty, which no good man will consent to lose but with his life.

The declaration succeeded in winning papal recognition of Bruce's kingship in 1324 and lifting his excommunication ban in 1328. The English, however, remained unimpressed.

The war continued and on the day of the coronation of Edward III in February 1327, the Scots launched an attacked on Norham, the first site of Edward I's hearings on the Great Cause in 1291. The following year, the English retaliated with an invasion, but this time it ended in farce. A Scottish raid on the English camp in Weardale nearly led to the capture of the English king, a boy of 15, who apparently burst into tears.

A peace treaty was signed between the two sides in May 1328, recognising Scottish independence and Robert I's kingly status. To set the seal on it, David II was married to Edward III's sister, Joan of the Tower, at Berwick on Tweed on 17 July 1328.

A year later, the king was dead from unknown causes. His heart was famously extracted and placed in a silver casket to be taken by Sir James Douglas on Crusade to the Holy Land. The casket never reached its destination and ended up in Spain with Douglas at Grenada, fighting with the king of Spain against the Moors. Douglas lost his life at the Battle of Teba in 1330, but the casket was recovered and returned to Scotland were it was interred at Melrose Abbey. Robert I's body was buried at Dunfermline Abbey. He was succeeded by his 5-year-old son, David II, who was crowned with his queen at Scone in 1331.

The Second War of Independence (1332–1357)

The Northampton/Edinburgh Treaty created a breathing space, and hostilities resumed soon after the signing. The English became obsessed by the threat that the renewed Scottish/French alliance of 1327 posed to its national security. This fear was used to justify a final settlement of the Scottish situation. The plan was to place Edward, son of John Balliol, on the throne as king of a truncated Scotland. The English king would control the southern counties; the Scottish king, the northern.

The choice of Balliol's son was a shrewd one – there were still people in Scotland who thought of Robert I as a murderer and not the rightful king. Plus, a number of unhappy campers were among the disinherited nobility who were only too keen to reclaim their estates on both sides of the border. With the not-too-secret approval of Edward III, Balliol's army landed in Fife in July 1332 and defeated a much larger Scottish army, led by the guardian of the realm, the earl of Mar, at Dupplin Moor near Perth on 10 and 11August. Mar was killed in battle only ten days after his appointment, as was Lord Robert Bruce, illegitimate son of Robert I. Balliol was crowned king at Scone on 24 September; two months later, he paid homage to the English king as his overlord at Roxburgh.

Balliol was feeling secure, so he dismissed his English troops and retired to rule from his stronghold in Galloway. He arrogantly issued two letters for general circulation in Scotland. The first letter thanked the English king for helping him reclaim his throne; the second letter claimed Scotland had always been a fief of England and he would remain loyal all his reign to Edward III.

Writing these letters was a very bad idea. In December at Annan, Dumfriesshire, Balliol was surprised by a night-time attack by a party of Bruce loyalists, led by Sir Archibald Douglas, the half-brother of Bruce's trusted ally James Douglas. Although most of his men were killed, Balliol escaped through a hole in a wall, after which he was chased (humiliatingly) half-naked across the English border to Carlisle.

The Scottish resistance

Balliol had genuine support in his Galloway heartland, as well as in Fife and Lothian. But in other parts of Scotland, he was seen as the English puppet king, and his authority was ignored. The new guardian, Sir Andrew Moray of

Bothwell, whose father fought at Stirling Bridge with Wallace, led the resistance, but he was captured in April 1333 while attacking Balliol's supporters at Roxburgh. Moray was replaced as guardian by Sir Archibald Douglas, but he died along with other nobles loyal to the Bruce cause at the Battle of Halidon Hill, near Berwick, on 19 July as English archers decimated the Scottish army. Thousands were killed, while the English lost only 14 soldiers. Bannockburn had been avenged.

By now, much of Scotland was under English occupation, with Balliol ceding to England eight of the Scottish lowland counties from Dumfries to Haddington. Indeed, at a meeting of the Scottish Parliament in February 1334, Balliol acknowledge his fealty and subjection to the English king. As a precaution, David II and his queen were sent to France for their own safety in May 1334, where they were to remain for seven years.

But while England was dominant, the Bruce loyalists kept up the struggle. They targeted Balliol's three main allies in Scotland – Richard Talbot, Henry de Beaumont and David of Strathbogie. Talbot was taken prisoner by Sir William Keith of Galston, de Beaumont was forced to flee to England and Strathbogie, under threat of his life, joined the loyalists. The loyalists were successfully using the guerrilla war tactics perfected by the Bruce nearly 20 years before.

Three cheers for the Auld Alliance!

In November 1334, the Scottish guardian made an appeal for assistance from France under the terms of the Auld Alliance. As a result, Philip VI sent his ambassador, the bishop of Avranches, to England to ask why Edward III was acting against David II and his own sister, Queen Joan. A temporary truce was declared while the English king dodged the question. But really all the truce did was to allow him to organise for another invasion of Scotland – this time with a much larger army of 13,000 men. In a three-pronged attack, Edward established control of Scotland in July 1335, first taking Glasgow and then Perth, and generally turning the country into a wasteland. The ball was back in the French court.

The French king announced that unless the English accepted the offer to put the dispute between the two countries to papal arbitration, he was going to aid the Scots by every means in his power. And by the way, he had a large fleet and an army of 6,000 men preparing to invade both countries. Edward III called the French bluff and ignored the ultimatum. The ball was still in the French court.

In desperation, the Scottish guardian, Sir Andrew Moray, now released from captivity in England, tried to find a path toward peace by agreeing to recognise Edward Balliol as monarch in return for naming David II as his heir. It was a way out, but there was a major stumbling block: the young exiled king refused to agree to the terms of the treaty. However, it did bring a truce of sorts between October and December 1336, which gave Murray time to defeat the turncoat Strathbogie's troops at the Battle of Culblean, killing him in the process.

English concerns were growing regarding a French invasion. In May 1336, Edward sent Henry of Lancaster to Scotland to deal with the loyalists who had been laying siege to Cupar, Fife and Lochindorb, Aberdeenshire. By June, the siege at Lochindorb had been lifted and the English troops laid waste to everything in their path, culminating in the burning of Aberdeen. Later that month, the Clyde valley and Carrick were subjected to the same brutal treatment by English troops under the earl of Cornwall.

In August 1336, Philip VI declared war on England and attacked English ports: Scotland was being downgraded in Edward III's strategic plan. With the English king so preoccupied with France and his plans to invade Gascony in the spring of 1337, the Scots made hay. The resistance adopted a scorched-earth policy. They attacked, captured and destroyed castles; they laid to waste land; and they harassed English troops. The ruthless policy of Guardian Moray to leave the English nothing – nothing to eat, nowhere to rest – hurt the Scottish people as much as it did the invaders because famine and disease spread. However, it did not diminish their appetite for battle against the Auld Enemy.

The Scottish spring

Moray and Douglas mounted attacks on English strongholds in Fife and Perth and were met with surprisingly little resistance. By the end of March 1337, Scottish troops had reclaimed most of the country north of the Forth and inflicted serious damage on Balliol's lands in Dumfries-shire.

Successes bred confidence and what seemed unthinkable just a few years ago happened: the Scots entered the north of England and laid waste to Cumberland. In 1338, Edward III sent the earl of Salisbury north to deal with the situation, but it was too little too late. He couldn't even take Dunbar Castle after six months laying siege to it!

That same year, Moray died of an illness at the age of 40 and the guardianship passed to Robert Stewart (later the first Stewart king). By this time, Balliol had lost most of his main supporters to the Bruce cause, and the English garrisons tumbled under Scottish attack. Cupar fell in the summer of 1339, then Perth, and finally Edinburgh, which was taken audaciously by William, Earl of Douglas, in April 1341.

The Return of the Boy King

With control established throughout the country and the English repelled, the Bruce loyalists felt confident enough to invite David II to return to Scotland, which he did in June 1341. He was only 18 years old and totally inexperienced in the art of government when he resumed ruling Scotland. After years of civil war, the country was exhausted, divided and impoverished. There was little in the way of crown revenue because taxes weren't collected during the war-torn years of the 1330s. So, David had his work cut out for him.

His main task was to force the English king to recognise him as the rightful monarch of Scotland and to end, once and for all, Balliol's claim on the throne. Using the tactic of harassing the north of England in 1342, 1345 and 1346, David II hoped that if he proved a big enough nuisance, Edward III, who was fighting against France, would recognise his claim as a price worth paying for calling off these raids. After all, English troops were being diverted from the main struggle against France to deal with the Scottish intruders.

But the Scottish king was also an ally of the king of France, Philip VI. And the king of France, under the terms of the Auld Alliance, appealed to David in June 1346 to carry out a full-scale invasion of the north of England. This would force the English to fight on two fronts: one in France and the other in England. David reluctantly accepted the request of Philip VI to open up a second front. This was a big mistake.

An army of 12,000 men was raised under the personal command of King David II, with the objective of taking Durham. The Scots never expected to face any difficulty in taking the town, because most of the English troops were at Calais fighting the French. David's army left Scotland on 7 October and ambled through the north, sacking Hexham Priory on the way, forcing Carlisle to pay protection money. However, ten days later, the army was in tatters. The English had expected an invasion from the north, and they were prepared for it.

Under the supervision of the archbishop of York, a smaller force of around half the size of the Scottish army confronted the Scots on 17 October at Neville's Cross, near Durham, and routed it. The Scottish king himself was wounded by an arrow in the face, captured and taken off to England, where he remained in captivity at Odiham Castle, in Hampshire, for 11 years.

He's back, but not for long!

After the defeat at Neville's Cross, the English army overran much of southern Scotland. Balliol, with a small force, reached Glasgow and reasserted his claim to the Scottish throne. But the Scots were in no more a mood to recognise him now than they had been in the past.

What added to Balliol's problems was the ransom the Scots were prepared to pay Edward III in return for their king and recognition that he was the rightful monarch of Scotland. The lure of the ransom was too much for the English king to refuse, and he waved Balliol a not-so-fond farewell.

Left to sink or swim, Balliol retreated to his heartland in Galloway, where he finally gave up his claim to the Scottish throne on 20 January 1356 in exchange for an English pension of £2,000 a year. The last 11 years of Balliol's life were spent in obscurity near Doncaster, Yorkshire, where he is buried, allegedly under a post office there!

Balliol left no heirs, so David II was now the recognised sole king of Scotland. In October 1357, he was released from captivity under the Treaty of Berwick. The Scots agreed to pay a huge ransom of 100,000 merks (£66,666) over ten years. The second War of Independence was over.

The second reign of David II

David II was 33 years of age when he set foot in Scotland once more; he had spent two-thirds of his life in France and England. During what might be called his 'second reign', he had two tremendously difficult tasks:

- Restore the royal finances.
- Restore royal authority.

Restoring the royal finances

The huge ransom – amounting to almost seven years' total royal income – agreed for his release placed enormous burdens on an economy that had been practically ruined by almost 50 years of continuous warfare. However, David set about the task of restoring the royal finances with enthusiasm. Within two years of his return to power, custom duties on exports had tripled. Furthermore, a new system of direct taxation was introduced to pay for his ransom. But David realised that there was never any possibility of being able to pay the debt off in ten years. The first instalment was paid on time, the second was late and the third never arrived!

What David tried to do was to renegotiate the ransom with Edward III by offering him or one of his sons the throne of Scotland if he died childless. In return, Edward would cancel the payments. This was a shrewd move given David's age – time was on his side to produce an heir. But the offer would never be acceptable to the Scottish elite; led by Robert the Steward, they revolted.

The proposal to make Lionel, Duke of Clarence, the next king of Scotland was rejected by the Scottish Parliament in 1364. David continued to negotiate with Edward in secret and managed, in 1369, to get the ransom payment down to 56,000 merks. It was never paid in full.

Restoring royal authority

David also faced the problem of curbing noble power, which had grown in strength during the long absences of the monarch. When he returned to Scotland in 1357, he rewarded the men who had done most to rule Scotland while he was in captivity. He rewarded with earldoms his cousin and heir (should he remain childless), Robert the Steward, as well as William Douglas and the earl of March.

But David realised that he also had to create alternative sources of support instead of relying on those three. Besides, he didn't exactly trust them.(As the old saying goes, 'Keep your friends close, but your enemies closer'!)

Queen Joan died in August 1362, so David took the opportunity to build an alliance with the powerful Drummond family through marrying Margaret Drummond, the widow of Sir John Logie. This decision, as much as the agreement with Edward III over the issue of succession, sparked a rebellion in 1363. However, the alliance David was after floundered, because Margaret failed to produce an heir. David divorced Margaret in 1370 in spite of her appealing to the papacy at Avignon for a reversal of the sentence of divorce.

David was lining up a third wife – his mistress, Agnes Dunbar, niece of Agnes Randolph, also known as 'Black Agnes of Dunbar', who had held Dunbar Castle in 1338 against the English. But David died unexpectedly at the age of 47 at Edinburgh Castle on 22 February 1371.

David II has had a mixed reception from historians: some see him as a weak and incapable ruler who betrayed the patriotic ideals of his father; others see him as visionary who foresaw the later union of the two countries in 1603 and did a lot to improve the economic position of the country and the monarchy. Although David nominally reigned for 42 years, he was actually only an active monarch for 19 of them. He also faced revolts from within and invasions from without and led a country that was exhausted and impoverished as a result. Maybe given the hand he had to play, he didn't do too badly. After all, he died in his bed with no serious rivals to his throne. Not many Scottish kings can say that!

The Black Death

One of the reasons people didn't look too fondly on the reign of David II was the outbreak of plague, known as the 'Black Death' (so called because of the black spots it left on victims' skin). Scottish soldiers engaged in border warfare in 1349 praised God that many of their English opponents were being felled by a new and terrifying affliction. However, unwittingly, they became carriers of the deadly disease themselves.

There were two forms of the disease:

- **Bubonic plague,** which was deadlier in the summer when fleas are more evident.
- **Pneumonic plague,** which was deadlier in the winter and spread through coughing, sneezing and speaking.

Scotland's colder and wetter climate favoured the pneumonic strain of the deadly disease. Within months of it arriving, Scots had begun falling victim to what they described as 'the foul death of the English'; according to some estimates, a year later more than a quarter of the population was dead. One local example was St Andrews where two-thirds of the canons of the cathedral perished in 1349.

John of Fordun, in his *Chronicle,* described the impact and nature of the disease:

> In 1350, there was a great pestilence and mortality of men in the kingdom of Scotland, and this pestilence also raged for many years before and after in various parts of the world. So great a plague has never been heard of from the beginning of the world to the present day, or been recorded in books. For this plague vented its spite so thoroughly that fully a third of the human race was killed. At God's command, moreover, the damage was done by an extraordinary and novel form of death. Those who fell sick of a kind of gross swelling of the flesh lasted barely two days. This sickness befell people everywhere, but especially the middling and lower classes, rarely the great. It generated such horror that children did not dare to visit their dying parents, nor parents their children, but fled for fear of contagion as if from leprosy or a serpent.

The strain died out after 1350, but it returned again in 1361, this time striking more at children. The Black Death forced Scots to reconsider their relationship with God. Perhaps they weren't, as Robert the Bruce had suggested, God's chosen people.

It wasn't all bad. The death of so many people relieved pressure on food supplies and saw an increase in the standard of the Scottish peasantry. It's an ill wind!

Chapter 8

The Foundations of the Stewart Dynasty (1371–1460)

In This Chapter

▶ Looking at the reigns of the first four Stewart kings

▶ Considering the social and economic life in Scotland during the Stewart Dynasty

*E*xamining the foundations of the Stewart Dynasty is not only important in understanding the rise of absolute monarchy in Scotland, but also for the light it sheds on the Stewarts as future kings of Britain. These hundred or so years marked a fierce struggle for control between the monarchy and ambitious nobles, in particular the Albany Stewarts and the Black Douglases, and were marked by lawlessness, feuds, murder and rebellions.

As one contemporary source put it:

> In those days there was no law in Scotland, but the strong oppressed the weak, and the whole kingdom was one den of thieves. Homicides, robberies, fire-raisings and other misdeeds remained unpunished, and justice seemed banished beyond the kingdom's bounds.

To impose order on the lawlessness of the nobility was the huge task faced by the early Stewart kings. As you see in this chapter, some were up to the task and others were not.

The Reign of Robert II

Many historians think of Robert II as a lame-duck king who gave away too much power to the nobility and, thus, created the basis for a great deal of instability in his realm. With the crown politically and militarily paralysed, the members of the Scottish nobility wreaked havoc on each other as they fought for land and power.

However, you could argue that Robert was a bit savvier than many historians give him credit for. Sure, the nobility increased in power under Robert II, but so did the influence of the crown through his astute policy of marrying his many offspring to the major noble houses, thus creating a series of alliances that shored up the crown rather than weakened it.

The fact that Robert became the first Stewart king was a bit of a fluke. He had the lineage as son of Marjorie, daughter of Robert the Bruce, but his fortune came when David II, last of the Bruce kings (see Chapter 7), died unexpectedly without an heir in 1371.

Robert II was 54 years old when he was crowned king in 1371. By that time, he had sired 22 children; of these, 9 were by his mistress, Elizabeth Mure (whom he later married in 1348), and 4 (2 boys and 2 girls) were by his second wife, Euphemia de Ross (whom he married in 1355, the same year as Elizabeth's death). Succession was never going to be a problem, especially because he had five sons.

Don't worry about keeping track of all these people – the main point is that Robert II had a lot of children by a variety of women, and he didn't have to worry about finding someone to succeed him.

Jobs for the boys

Robert used his family to extend his authority by promoting them to influential positions within the government and as major regional *magnates* (great landholders). Here are some examples:

- ✔ His heir presumptive, John, was earl of Carrick and keeper of Edinburgh Castle.

- ✔ His second surviving son, Robert, was granted the earldoms of Fife and Menteith and was keeper of Stirling Castle.

- ✔ His fourth son, Alexander, was made earl of Buchan and the king's lieutenant for the north and west of Inverness.

- ✔ The earldoms of Strathearn and Caithness went to David, his eldest son by Euphemia.

Robert also married off his daughters to powerful rivals, such as John, lord of the Isles, and James, the heir to the earls of Douglas. By the mid-1390s, only four of the 15 Scottish earldoms were outside the direct control or influence of the Stewart family.

A little family difficulty

Robert's strategy was to delegate authority to his powerful sons and earls. This plan generally worked for the first decade of his reign, but from 1380, it began to unravel.

One serious drawback affected Robert's ability to reign: he couldn't ride a horse. Because of this, he found travelling difficult, which caused him to fail one of the key functions of medieval kingship: the dispensation of justice. Plus, his failure or unwillingness to deal with his rebellious son Alexander, now styling himself as the Wolf of Badenoch in the north, and to consider mobilising for a war against the 'auld enemy' led to political upheaval in November 1384. The council, in a *coup d'état,* removed Robert's authority to govern and appointed his son, the earl of Carrick, as lieutenant of the kingdom.

With Robert sidelined, there was now no impediment in the way of war with England. In June 1385, a force of 1,200 French soldiers joined the Scots in a campaign that involved the earl of Douglas, the earl of Carrick and the king's other son, Robert, Earl of Fife. The 'war' was really a series of border skirmishes with the English that led to small territorial gains, but a quarrel between the French and Scottish commanders saw the abandonment of an attack by the Scots on the English-held Roxburgh castle.

However, better things were to come in August 1488, when the Scots defeated a superior English force at the Battle of Otterburn, Northumberland. (We're much better underdogs!) According to contemporary sources, around 2,000 English were killed and more than 1,000 were captured (compared to only 100 Scots dead and 200 taken prisoner). One notable casualty was Carrick's ally, James, Earl of Douglas; his death had unintended results for the lord lieutenant.

Douglas died without an heir, and various candidates came forward to claim the title. Carrick supported the claim of Malcolm Drummond, the husband of the late earl's sister, while his brother Robert championed the claim of Sir Archibald Douglas, lord of Galloway. With the support of his new ally, Robert was able to engineer a second coup d'état in December, when the guardianship moved from Carrick to Fife.

This move was popular with the leading nobles because Fife proposed to deal with the lawlessness in the north of Scotland largely provoked by his younger brother, Alexander, Earl of Buchan and Wolf of Badenoch. In 1389,Alexander had taken revenge on the bishops of Moray and Ross, who had excommunicated him for deserting his wife, by burning down the town of Forres and the magnificent Elgin Cathedral. Fife stripped Buchan of his office of king's lieutenant and justiciar in the north and gave them to his son, Murdoch Stewart.

The transfer of power from one branch of the Stewart family to the other seemed complete when the king toured the north in late January 1390 and gave his blessing to the new balance of power. However, within two months, Robert II was lying dead in Dundonald Castle in Ayrshire, and a new monarch was on the throne.

The Reign of Robert III

In 1390, the Scottish Parliament granted John, Earl of Carrick, permission to change his regnal name to Robert III, mainly because it suggested a direct line to Robert I, but also because it distanced him from a connection to John Balliol (see Chapter 7). By the time he had assumed the throne, Carrick was disabled through a kick by a horse and spent much of his reign unable to assert royal control of the affairs of state. His weakness was the signal for a massive push by ambitious nobles for power, which created a period of instability and law-lessness, in which violence was the chosen method of negotiation.

Within nine years of acceding to the throne, Robert III had been largely side-lined and made irrelevant to the business of government. At a meeting in November 1389 held in Falkland Castle and attended by the leading magnates and churchmen, a decision was taken over the king's future. That decision was made clear when, at a council meeting, it was declared that, owing to the king's 'sickness of his person', his 21-year-old son and first Scot to hold the title of duke, David of Rothesay, was to be made lord lieutenant of the kingdom for three years, although subject to supervision by a parliamentary group dominated by his uncle, Robert, Earl of Fife, now also Duke of Albany.

The rise of the Albany Stewarts

With Robert III out of the way, Rothesay began to act with little regard to the best interests of the kingdom, using his office to enrich himself and appearing to be high-handed and callous in his dealings with his peers. His efforts were beginning to create deep divisions in Scotland.

He reneged on a promise to marry Elizabeth, the daughter of George Dunbar, Earl of March, and instead married Marjorie, the daughter of the earl of Douglas. Dunbar was so angry with the duke that he wrote to Henry IV and entered the English king's service in July 1400. Rothesay was also plundering the public purse by appropriating the customs revenues of the east coast burghs, which were intended for the crown. Talk about robber barons!

Rothesay, in alliance with his disgraced uncle, Alexander, Wolf of Badenoch, began to confront the influence of Albany in central Scotland – a big mistake. He had clearly got above himself, and he had to go. In late February 1402, as soon as his three years were up, Rothesay was arrested on his way to St Andrews and imprisoned in Albany's residence, Falkland Castle. It was not going to end well!

In fact, Rothesay died on 26 March 1402 in suspicious circumstances, appearing to have been starved to death. In May of that year, a public inquiry exonerated Albany of any blame and reappointed him as lord lieutenant. The duke of Albany was now Scotland's most powerful man and had designs on the throne itself.

The English and Scottish battle in Northumberland

Shortly after Rothesay's death, Albany's regime was drawn into the fierce and seemingly endless conflicts around the border of the two kingdoms, which threatened to destroy all he was working to achieve. In June 1402, a small government-backed force returning from a border raid was intercepted by the son of George Dunbar (revenge time) and defeated at the 'battle' of Nesbit Moor. This incident was used as a pretext for Archibald Douglas, 4th Earl of Douglas, to lead a punitive expedition in September into England. At the head of 10,000 men and with Murdoch Stewart at his side, they laid waste to the whole of Northumberland, reaching as far as Newcastle.

The Scots were decimated. Archibald Douglas was captured, along with George Douglas, 1st Earl of Angus; Thomas Dunbar, 5th Earl of Moray; and Murdoch Stewart. It was really only Henry IV's internal problems, particularly in Wales, that prevented the English from mounting a full-scale invasion of Scotland. But with so many of the Scottish nobles in English custody, it cleared the stage of rivals for Albany.

The Albany Governorship (1406–1424)

Robert III may have been weak in body, but he wasn't weak in the head. Reading the cards, he saw that the next victim of Albany would be his son James, now heir presumptive. To escape the 'guardianship' of Albany, in 1406 Robert arranged for his son to be sent to France for safekeeping. But Stewart plans almost always ended in farce or tragedy, and this was no different.

The young prince had to hide out in Bass Rock before boarding the *Maryenknyght,* a Danzig-bound ship out of Leith with a cargo of hides and wool. But the vessel was attacked on 14 March by English pirates, and James was handed over to Henry IV of England, where he would remain for the next 18 years.

The news of the capture of his son was the final straw for Robert III. He died on 4 April 1406 and was laid to rest in the Abbey of Paisley. He supplied his own epitaph: 'Here lies the worst of kings and the most wretched man in the whole realm.'

When confirmed as governor in June 1406, Albany was in his mid-60s. Scotland was a kingless kingdom – James had never been crowned, although he was still referred to as 'our king'. Although undoubtedly a king in all but name, Albany didn't have it all his own way.

Serious opposition remained from the lord of the Isles, Donald, who confronted Albany with a force of 10,000 clansmen at the Battle of Harlaw, near Inverurie, Aberdeenshire, in July 1411. The cause of the hostilities was the attempt by Albany to secure the earldom of Ross for his second son, John, in spite of the fact that MacDonald had a better claim on the title. The battle was known as 'Red' Harlaw, due to the savagery with which it was fought. Although the battle was indecisive, the Stewarts claimed a victory because MacDonald withdrew from the field. Within a year, Albany had recaptured Ross and forced Donald to surrender.

Given his position in Scotland, Albany, who relished the trappings of power, was not in any hurry to secure the release of his nephew James from the English king, now Henry V – something he and his family were not forgiven for. He died in 1420 at more than 80 years old, and was buried at Dunfermline. Who says crime doesn't pay?

Albany's son Murdoch succeeded him as 2nd duke of Albany. He was responsible for negotiating the release of James from English custody in 1423 for a ransom of £40,000 to be paid over six years.

The Reign of James I

During his captivity in England, James was treated more as a guest than a prisoner. He received an education in the arts of kingship and formed a close bond with Henry V, who had come to the throne of England in 1413.

The presence of the uncrowned Scottish king at the side of the English king was of immense propaganda value during England's wars in 1420 with France. The success of the English in these struggles saw James rise in English society. He was allowed to attend the coronation of Queen Catherine in February 1421 as an honoured guest; the next month, he was knighted on St George's Day.

James backed Henry's ambition to become king of France and was joint commander with the duke of Bedford at the successful siege of Dreux in July 1421. When Henry died of dysentery at the age of 35, James was part of the escort, taking the English king's body back to London.

The icing on the cake was the marriage between James and Joan Beaufort, the niece of Henry IV, on 12 February 1424. They had eight children together, including the future James III. No bastards this time – how very un-Stewart-like! At his coronation at Scone, when James received the allegiance of his nobles, he had them swear their allegiance to Joan as well, as if she was a co-monarch.

The fall of the Albany Stewarts

While under the tutelage (some might say 'spell') of Henry V, James learnt a great about the business of governing a kingdom. His arrival back in Scotland signalled a shift away from the weak, laissez-faire government of the first two Stewart kings. Instead, he introduced a much more vigorous monarchy in which the rights and privileges of the crown were ruthlessly enforced. Bad news for the Albany Stewarts!

Despite the fact that from 1413 until Murdoch's release in 1415 they were together in the Tower of London and at Windsor Castle, James never forgave Murdoch for the part his family played in the death of his brother, duke of Rothesay, and for dragging his heels in negotiating James's release from captivity. In 1425, James had the leading Albany Stewarts, including Murdoch and two of his sons, as well as the 80-year-old earl of Lennox, executed in front of Stirling Castle for treason – the first state executions since 1320.

In retrospect, the conviction was made easier because Murdoch's youngest son, James the Fat, in retaliation, led a rebellion with the men of Lennox and Argyll against the crown. They burned Dumbarton and killed the keeper of Dumbarton Castle, the king's uncle. James the Fat's success was short-lived, and he soon fled to Antrim, Ireland, where he spent the rest of his life in exile. As a result, the earldoms of Lennox, Fife and Menteith were forfeited to the crown, which brought in an extra £1,000 a year to the royal coffers.

The early Renaissance prince

Not only had James learned the act of governance in England, but he returned a gifted writer, poet and musician. His *The Kingis Quair,* a semi-autobiographical piece, is considered one of the finest works of medieval Scottish literature and shows the influence of Geoffrey Chaucer. He also began the building of Linlithgow as an unfortified residence, something that later Stewarts would add to (see Chapter 9).

The Church also came under closer royal control. James appointed his own men to important *bishoprics* (dioceses) such as Dunblane and Glasgow. At his say-so, in 1425 the Scottish Parliament instructed clergy to say prayers for the monarch and his family. A year later, fines were introduced for those clerics failing in this duty.

The king also had a more cosmopolitan outlook than his predecessors, perhaps as a result of his English upbringing and his time in France. Unlike the two Roberts, who had married their daughters off to the leading nobility of Scotland, James looked farther afield for marriage partners among Europe's elite. His 12-year-old daughter, Margaret, was betrothed to the dauphin of France in 1436, which drew him into the orbit of French influence (see 'The French connection', later in this chapter).

James was building a cult of the monarchy, but it was costly, and the means to achieve it created a great deal of resentment.

Money, money, money

Marriages cost money. A dowry was expected – the greater the catch, the bigger the down payment. Inevitably, taxes had to be raised to finance James's ambitious foreign policy.

At the first meeting of the Scottish Parliament after his coronation, James persuaded it to introduce a general tax to pay for his ransom. Within a year, he had raised £26,000, but only half of that went to the English – he spent the rest supporting his lifestyle, including refurbishing Linlithgow.

To raise income, James reclaimed customs revenues that had, in the past, been used to provide pensions and annuities for the nobility. This did not go down well. But James failed to raise enough to match his ambitions – in fact, the income of the crown didn't reach levels enjoyed during the 'weak' kingship of Robert II.

The lord of the Isles

The governorship of Albany had failed to deal with the threat posed by the lord of the Isles to internal stability in spite of the bloody Battle of Harlaw. James was determined to bring the lord of Isles to heel.

In August 1429, James summoned the clan chiefs in the north and west to a sitting of Parliament in Inverness. As each of the 50 or so chiefs appeared before the king, they were seized and thrown into a dungeon, including Alexander, 3rd Lord of the Isles and his mother, Mary, Countess of Ross. Three of the chiefs were hanged, but the remainder, with the exception of Alexander and his mother, were quickly released.

When James and his Parliament left Inverness, Alexander sacked the town. The king immediately retaliated and confronted him at Lochaber, where he demanded that Alexander pay homage to him in Edinburgh. Wearing only a shirt and drawers and holding his claymore by the blade, the lord of the Isles knelt before the high altar at Holyrood and offered the king his weapon – a humiliating experience for someone who considered himself the monarch of the Highlands.

But the problem was never resolved. You could argue that James's humiliation of Alexander only intensified Alexander's desire for revenge. In September 1431, the Islesmen rose again and won two important victories over the king's men. The earl of Mar's army was beaten at Inverlochy, Inverness-shire, as was Angus Moray in a fierce battle near Tongue, Caithness. These defeats seriously dented the reputation of the king and his credibility as a warrior king.

The French connection

The marriage of Princess Margaret to the French dauphin brought Scotland into the sphere of French influence, something that James had tried to avoid – he preferred a neutral stance between France and England. However, the collapse of talks between these two rivals led to an alliance between France and Burgundy against England. As part of the marriage agreement, the French insisted that Scotland become involved and invade England. In the spring of 1436, Margaret left for France, and in August that year, James led a large army to lay siege to the English-held Roxburgh Castle. But the siege had to be abandoned after two months – another blow to his already bruised reputation.

James called another general council in October 1436 to raise taxes to advance the war against the English. But this time, he was met with a severe rebuff and an unprecedented attempt by Sir Robert Graham, a servant to the king's uncle, Walter Stewart, Earl of Atholl, to arrest him. The knight was imprisoned and finally banished from Scotland. But the king failed to see the bigger picture. He interpreted Graham's action as a random, one-off event by a disgruntled loose cannon. Not for one moment did James realise that a plot was being hatched within his own royal household to depose him.

To kill a king

In part, James's difficulties can be traced back to his grandfather Robert II's siring of so many illegitimate children by his mistress, Elizabeth Mure, of which his father Robert III was one. Although the couple married in 1348 in an attempt to legitimise their offspring, a section of the Scottish nobility never came to terms with this and saw the children of Robert II's second marriage to Euphemia as the rightful heirs to the throne.

In part, the problems can also be put down to James's reign of terror and intimidation of rivals. James didn't set out to tame his lawless nobles; he set out to annihilate them. There were 15 earldoms when James assumed power in 1424; by the end of his reign, there were 8, and of these only 4 were in the hands of the same families. In elite circles, complaints about tyranny began to be made more loudly. Clearly, James's days as king were numbered – he had made too many enemies and not enough friends.

On 24 February 1437, James was murdered in his bedroom in the Dominican friary at Perth. The king's cousin Sir Robert Stewart was chamberlain of the royal household and part of the conspiracy cooked up by his father and the king's uncle, Walter, Earl of Atholl. Walter was also the son of Euphemia. Sir Robert used his privileged position to allow a small band of assassins, led by Sir Robert Graham, to enter the building. James's servants alerted him to the danger, and he tried to escape via a sewer, but it was blocked. Trapped, with nowhere to go, the king was brutally murdered.

Even so, the conspirators failed to achieve their ends. A wounded Queen Joan was able to send a message to Edinburgh to shield the young Prince James from any attempts to embroil him in the conspiracy. A period of civil war ensued, but a coalition fighting in the name of the queen and her young son defeated Atholl and his co-conspirators.

Atholl, Sir Robert Stewart and Sir Robert Graham were tortured for three days before being executed. Graham felt justified and said:

> Yet I do not doubt but that you shall see the day and time that you shall pray for my soul, for the great good that I have done to you, and to all in this realm of Scotland, that I have thus slain and delivered you of so cruel a tyrant.

History has delivered a different verdict than Graham's. Today James I is seen as a moderniser, a king who tried to raise the stature of the monarchy against the powerful members of the Scottish nobility. The attempt cost him his life, but his policy of reducing the power of the great magnates was to be continued by his son, James II.

The Reign of James II

On 25 March 1437, James II, nicknamed 'Fiery Face' because of a red birthmark on his face, was 6 years old when he was crowned king at Holyrood Abbey (rather than the traditional site of coronation, Scone). Another break from tradition was anointment by the bishop of Dunblane rather than St Andrews.

James II's minority brought the usual contest for power waged by the major players among the Scottish nobility. However, there was a twist: due to a combination of war, forfeiture and youth, only two adult earls were left in

Scotland at the end of 1437. The main power brokers were Joan, Queen Dowager, and Archibald, 5th Earl of Douglas. The latter headed up the government as lieutenant general, but his death in 1439 saw power divided between William Crichton, 1st Lord Crichton, Lord Chancellor of Scotland (sometimes in co-operation with the earl of Avondale), and Sir Alexander Livingston of Callendar, who had possession of the young king as the warden of Stirling Castle. A struggle ensued between the major players – one that would end in the defeat and exile of the powerful Black Douglas earls and a further enlargement of royal resources and prestige.

The minority of James II

With the powerful Douglas family temporarily weakened by Archibald's death, Livingston took the lead by placing Queen Joan and her new husband, Sir John Stewart, under 'house arrest' at Stirling Castle on 3 August 1439. They were released a month later, but only after

✔ Agreeing to put James in the custody of the Livingston family

✔ Giving up Joan's dowry for the young king's maintenance

✔ Confessing that Livingston had acted only with thought for the king's safety

Crichton was jealous of the house of Douglas. He organised a dinner in the name of the king on 24 November 1440, to which an invitation was sent to the 16-year-old William, 6th Earl of Douglas, and his brother, 11-year-old David. A black bull's head, the symbol of death, was placed before them. After a mock trial, Crichton had the Douglas brothers murdered in front of the 10-year-old king. Ever since, the event has been known as the 'Black Dinner'. No wonder.

The Black Douglases

On 3 July 1449, James II, having reached adulthood, married 15-year-old Mary of Guelders, great-niece of Philip the Good, Duke of Burgundy, at Holyrood. This marriage removed James II from the clutches of the Livingston family, whom he had not forgiven for the brief arrest of his mother and her husband.

By the autumn of 1449, Sir Alexander and two of his family had been arrested. By mid-January of 1450, the Scottish Parliament had found them guilty of treason and they were executed on Edinburgh's Castle Hill. The only powerful family left in Scotland was the Black Douglases, who at the time controlled three earldoms and was claiming a fourth. Their rule stretched over Galloway, Douglasdale, Annandale, Clydesdale, Lothian, Stirlingshire and Moray.

The king became obsessed with curbing the power of the Black Douglases. Because of this, relations between James and William, 8th Earl of Douglas, deteriorated to a fatal degree. Things came to a climax over the case of Patrick Maclellan of Bombie, Sheriff of Galloway, a staunch royalist, who had refused an invitation to join Douglas and the earls of Ross, Crawford and Ormond in an alliance against James.

Against the express orders of the monarch, Maclellan was imprisoned and executed by the 8th Earl of Douglas. Maclellan's execution led to the fatal confrontation between James and Douglas in Stirling Castle on 22 February 1452. James, 23 years old at the time, personally led a murderous and vicious attack on Douglas by stabbing him in the neck. Douglas's body was further mutilated by the king's men and thrown from a window into the garden below. Douglas had no fewer than 26 stab wounds.

Horrific as it was, the 8th earl's murder did not mark the end of the Douglas family. Instead, it caused a civil war of sorts between the Douglas family and the crown from 1452 to 1455.

James's military campaigns against his Douglas rivals during this period tended to end indecisively, and he faced the possibility at times of being overthrown and forced to flee Scotland. But while James was in England, he was introduced to the black arts of kingship – in particular, the use of bribery and corruption. Thanks to his predecessors and his own systematic annihilation of the nobility in Scotland, James had at his disposal a massive amount of patronage over lands, titles and offices of state. He was prepared to use them to bribe the allies of the Douglases to change sides; the most important of the defections was that of the earl of Crawford after his defeat by a royalist army at the Battle of Brechin in May 1452.

Three years later, James struck a decisive blow against the Douglases at the Battle of Arkinholm, near Langholm, Dumfries-shire. The head of the family, James Douglas, 9th Earl of Douglas, had gone to England to rally support, but his three younger brothers were present at the battle. Of the brothers, Archibald Douglas, Earl of Moray, was killed and his head presented to the king; Hugh Douglas, Earl of Ormond, was captured and executed shortly afterward; and John Douglas, Lord of Balvenie, escaped to England. With the fall of the last Douglases' stronghold, Threave Castle, Kirkcudrightshire, after a two-month siege, the main rivals to the king had all been eliminated.

In the months that followed, the Scottish Parliament declared the Douglas lands and possessions forfeit and permanently annexed them to the crown. The forfeited estates brought in an extra £2,000 a year to the crown in rents. Other lands were given to the Gordons, Campbells and Huntlys in exchange for loyalty. The Red Douglas, Earl of Angus, was given the lordship of Douglas.

With the head of the Douglas family in permanent exile in England, James finally had the freedom to govern as he wished – a freedom he bequeathed to his successors. The destruction of the Black Douglases, along with the forfeiture of the Albany Stewarts in the reign of his father, cemented the consolidation of royal power in Scotland. Future Stewart kings of Scotland never had to face such a powerful challenge from a rival family to their authority again.

Accidents will happen

James's style of centralised government was more like the English and French styles than the governments of his ancestors, which had relied on alliances with powerful noble families to keep the peace. He surrounded himself with bureaucrats and clerics rather than nobles. He carried on as his father had done to place Scotland and its monarchy in a European context. Isabella, his second sister, was married off to the duke of Brittany in 1442, and two other sisters had foreign matches made for them in 1444. He also tried to increase the standing of Scotland in Europe through military expeditions against the English, which proved lethal.

Ending the English occupation of Roxburgh Castle had become a bit of a *cause célèbre* for James and the Scottish nobility. In 1460, James laid siege to the castle, taking with him a large number of a new type of cannon he had had imported from Flanders.

On 3 August, James was attempting to fire one of them, known as 'The Lion', when it accidentally exploded, killing him outright. A contemporary described his death:

> as the King stood near a piece of artillery, his thigh bone was dug in two with a piece of misframed gun that brake [broke] in shooting, by which he was stricken to the ground and died hastily.

Led by George (the Red) Douglas, 4th Earl of Angus, the Scots carried on with the siege, and Roxburgh Castle fell a few days later. But for James, it was a little late. At the age of 29, he was laid to rest at Holyrood, and his widow became regent of Scotland (see Chapter 9).

Economic and Social Life in Medieval Scotland

Medieval Scotland was a hierarchical society. Most people lived on the land, rather than in towns, and they owed allegiance to their social superiors in some form or other.

Hierarchy signified massive inequalities in the distribution of wealth and power. At the very top of the pile was a tiny group made up of the monarch and the greater nobility; at the bottom were the peasants and other labourers. The earl of Mar, for example, between the years 1412 and 1422, received £4,238 from the crown in the form of pensions and annuities for no specific purpose. At that time, a skilled worker would have earned perhaps £10 a year.

But because the nobility included lesser nobles and *lairds* (small landowners), it was far from being a uniform category. The same applies to the peasantry.

The unwashed

Peasants made up about 98 per cent of Scottish society in the Middle Ages. They were generally looked down upon by those above them. Abbot Walter Bower, in his noted chronicle of the period, the *Scotichronicon,* compared them to dogs. But the term *peasantry* was a catch-all for a really diverse group of people.

During the first half of the 13th century, there were free and unfree peasants. The *unfree,* or serfs, were tied to the landlord and forced to perform labour services; like slaves, they could be bought and sold. But this form of exploitation was dying out toward the end of the 13th century. Landlords wanted rents not services, although peasants were still forced to grind their corn in the masters' mills and, of course, were subject to the masters' justice.

Above the unfree were the *husbandmen* – the wealthiest peasants who hired labour from among the landless. But even their livelihood was precarious because all tenants and sub-tenants were on short leases that could be withdrawn at a moment's notice.

Strangely enough, in spite of the massive inequalities in landed society, the Scottish peasants never revolted as they did in England in 1381. A number of reasons have been put forward to explain the relative calm in Scotland:

- ✔ Wars increased the sense of national identity, and that blunted social antagonisms. We were all in it together!

- ✔ Landowners were more sensitive to their tenants' problems.

- ✔ Scotland was more of a kin-based society, where members of the kindred look after each other.

Although toil was unremitting and work backbreaking, there was also ample room to enjoy some recreation. The harvest celebration was an annual event and included a march with music and the making of 'corn dollies'. Holy or saints' days were also times of rest. The seasonal rhythms of work (where work was lighter in the winter and heavier during the summer) provided time for people to enjoy themselves away from work. So, it wasn't all doom and gloom – people could have some fun.

Wrestling and other sports, like golf and football, were popular but banned in churches and churchyards. In 1424, killjoy James I legislated against football, and in 1458, his son James II prohibited golf in favour of archery – the peasants were the archers. Archaeological digs have shown that people at this time also played dice and chess and even ice-skated in the winter!

There was theatre of sorts with travelling bands of players performing plays – surprisingly, plays featuring Robin Hood were among the most popular north of the border. Perhaps the peasants were sending an indirect message to their superiors – after all, Robin took from the rich and gave to the poor!

There were only two things the peasantry shared with their noble superiors: bawdy ballads and prostitution. Ballads were part of a long-established oral tradition, and while they originally reflected aristocratic values, as time wore on they increasingly focused on the lower orders. It is difficult to know how widespread prostitution was and who participated in it, but later James IV paid for the services of 'Janet bair ars' and the Edinburgh town council in 1556 issued an edict preventing prostitutes from dressing as 'honest men's wives'. We can only assume that such practices existed in the 14th and 15th centuries.

The urban elite

The ruling urban elite was formed of the burgesses, drawn mainly from the ranks of merchants and, to a lesser extent, craftsmen. Of Dunfermline's 1,000 inhabitants in the early 16th century, only about 140 were burgesses. They were organised in clubs or *guilds*; admission to these guilds involved the payment of 40 shillings plus a donation of wine and spices. The guild members elected the town's officers. But there was conflict when craftsmen agitated successfully for greater representation on town councils and the right to establish their own guilds.

The wealthiest townsmen were socially ambitious and coveted a place in rural aristocratic circles. Not all doors were closed to them and some did succeed in breaching the barriers of blood and kin. For example, in the late 14th century, Sir John Forrester of Corstorphine was a burgess of Edinburgh, a *bailie* (magistrate) and a rural landowner.

The Highlands and the clans

Before the 14th century, no one in Scotland drew a distinction between Highland and Lowland Scotland. But from there, it was common to describe the Highlands as lawless, feud-ridden and barbaric.

Distinctions were now being made regarding culture, dress and language, as a contemporary source makes clear:

> The manners and customs of the Scots vary with the diversity of their speech. For two languages are spoken amongst them, the Scottish [Gaelic] and the Teutonic [English]: the latter of which is the language of those who occupy the seaboard and the plains, while the race of the Scottish speech inhabits the Highlands and the outlying Islands. The people of the coast are of a domestic and civilised habits. . . . The Highlanders and the people of the Islands . . . are a savage and untamed race, rude and independent.

The source of this anarchy was put down to clan rivalry. However, there are a great many misconceptions regarding clan society. The word *clan* is derived from the Gaelic word *clann* meaning 'children' and was used by chroniclers in the late 14th century. But not all clan members were related through blood or by common ancestry. The most common membership of a clan was through bonds of *manrent*. In return for the protection of a chief, the entrant would offer his allegiance as a 'native man'.

The idea that clan members were direct descendants of a common ancestor is farfetched. One example will suffice to explode that myth: Clan Donald encompassed vassal kindreds such as the MacLeods and MacLeans bound together through marriage as much by genealogy. Indeed, the MacLeods were of Norse descent; the MacDougalls and MacDonalds were a mix of Gaelic and Scandinavian; while the Frasers and Sinclairs and some branches of the Stewarts were of Anglo-Norman stock. So, there was no such thing as the typical clan, nor was there a clan 'system'.

Saints and sinners

The clergy in medieval Scotland were highly distinctive: they were *tonsured* (shaved head) and clean shaven. There were about 4,000 of them – some were lay or secular clergy, and others were monks, friars and canons-regular. There were 15 nunneries, compared with 100 monasteries for men.

Some of the clerics were highly educated; by the late 14th century, around 20 per cent had attended university. The higher the position, the more educated the cleric was. Between 1350 and 1425, it was estimated that 80 per cent of bishops were university graduates. They didn't study solely in Scotland – they were cosmopolitan. Scottish students could be found attending Oxbridge until the 13th century, in addition to studying in Paris, Orleans and Bologna. In later years, Cologne and Leuven were the favoured destinations; this trend continued despite the existence of the universities of St Andrews and Glasgow.

Those at the top of the Church mainly came from privileged and landed families and tended to share the nobility's lax attitude to morality. In 1426, the abbot of Iona complained that his predecessor had kept noble women as concubines, fathering offspring and using the monastery's wealth to provide dowries for his bastard children.

Clerics were also good businessmen with an eye for a profit. The monasteries and abbeys controlled the wool trade in Scotland. Melrose Abbey had a flock of sheep in the 1370s that numbered close to 15,000; the Cistercian monasteries had a combined flock of 40,000 sheep. Clerics also had extensive properties in seaports to export the raw wool, although they ran into difficulties in the 15th century (see the next section).

Trading networks

Trade was highly important in the medieval economy. Scotland exported basic stuffs such as fish, wool, leather and animal skins, and imported sophisticated luxury imports such as wine, wheat, clothing, furniture, artistic goods and timber – mainly for the nobility. Its main trading partner at this time was not England but Flanders – the most densely urbanised region of northern Europe. Bruges was the main port for Europe and the destination for Scottish exports. However, trade links were forged with other parts of Britain; wheat was sought in England and Ireland.

But as the 15th century wore on, internal difficulties and a recasting of the Flanders economy saw links weaken and wool exports from Scotland fall dramatically, later to be followed by a decline in hides and skins. Wool exports in the 1480s were only a quarter of what they had been in the 1320s. As a result, demand for imports fell, which was compounded by a decline in the money supply and the manipulation of the currency by the crown that led to a fall in the value of the Scottish pound by a third compared to the Flemish pound. Put another way, in 1400, the Scottish pound had less than three-tenths of the silver it had in 1296; by 1470, less than three-twentieths.

Some towns in Scotland suffered as a result of the disruption of trade. Urban decline was evident: Roxburgh was a thriving town in the 13th century, but by the 15th century it was largely abandoned.

Chapter 9

Renaissance Scotland (1460–1542)

In This Chapter

▶ Focusing on the Renaissance

▶ Considering the reigns of James III, James IV and James V

▶ Looking at everyday life in Renaissance Scotland

The eight decades between 1460 and 1542 represented a flourishing of art and culture in Scotland, referred to by historians as the Renaissance. The term *renaissance* means 'rebirth', and the Renaissance was all about a rediscovery of the classical world of ancient Greece and Rome (in contrast to what was thought of as the barbaric Gothic world of the so-called 'Dark Ages').

The Renaissance began in 14th-century Florence and spread to the rest of Europe over the course of the next few centuries. The artists and intellectuals who were at the forefront of the Renaissance thought of themselves as *humanists* – they focused on what it meant to be human. Because of this, artists like Leonardo da Vinci moved away from concentrating only on religious themes and depicted the beauty of nature and even ordinary people, rather than devils, saints and God. Scholars also tried to provide more rational approaches to understanding the world. Machiavelli, in his famous work *The Prince,* tried to describe political life as it really was.

No one at the time called this period the Renaissance. That term came later, in the 19th century.

The Renaissance

The Renaissance was important, not only because it bequeathed to us some wonderful art, architecture, literature and music, but also because it marked the transition of the ruling elite in Scotland from a warrior caste to a more civilised and refined one. The influence was not simply restricted to a tiny few. The adoption of humanistic values provided a basis for future achievements in education and laid the foundations for what would later be known as the Scottish Enlightenment (see Chapter 13).

Although the Renaissance suggests a more cultured world with respect for human life, progress and knowledge, the old black arts of backstabbing, murder and war continued unabated in Scotland in the late Middle Ages.

Monarchy

From James III onward, the nature of kingship in Scotland began to change. The Stewart kings began to think of themselves as supreme rulers. This idea had its roots in Roman law: *Rex in regnosuo imperator est* (The king is emperor in his own kingdom). By declaring themselves 'emperors', kings were claiming that they alone were in a position to dispense justice.

In 1469, the Scottish Parliament passed a law declaring that James III possessed 'full jurisdiction and empire within his realm'. To let everyone know that James was supreme ruler, a massive publicity campaign was carried out. Silver coins (called *groats*) were minted; on these coins was the image of the king wearing a closed, arched, imperial crown in place of the open circlet of earlier kings. This coin was the first to be minted with the monarch's portrait on it outside of Italy. Soon, the image of the king began to find its way into heraldry, royal seals, manuscripts and sculptures.

These images of the king were important for a number of reasons:

- They promoted a cult of the monarch.
- They furthered royal authority over the powerful feuding landed families of Scotland.
- They fended off English claims to feudal superiority over Scotland.
- They created a sense of national sovereignty and, with it, territorial consolidation.

Art

The Stewart kings from James III through to James V all imported commissioned work of a particularly high quality from French and Flemish artists.

The St Salvator's mace of the University of St Andrews was made for Bishop Kennedy by a Parisian goldsmith, Jean Magelle. Another important work of art is the altarpiece in Trinity College Church in Edinburgh by Hugo van der Goes. The most important artistic work of the period is the illuminated manuscript *The Hours of James IV and Margaret Tudor,* which dates from 1503, produced by Simon Bening, and given by James to his wife to commemorate their marriage.

Unfortunately, there are no signed paintings by Scottish artists from before the reign of James VI. Also, much of the artwork in churches was destroyed by Protestant zealots during the Reformation, so we can only guess at the richness of Scotland's religious artistic heritage.

Architecture

The advent of artillery had made castles irrelevant in warfare, but that didn't stop monarchs building and rebuilding them. Monarchs have a thing for palaces, not only because palaces advertise their wealth and status but also because palaces are pretty nice places to live.

Palace building began in earnest with James III, accelerated under James IV and reached a peak in the reign of James V. The two most enduring and important examples of Renaissance palaces are Stirling Castle and Falkland Palace in Fife. Between 1501 and 1541, James IV and James V of Scotland transformed the old castle of Falkland into a beautiful royal palace, but the most impressive architectural work was at Stirling (see Figure 9-1) and includes the King's Old Building, the Great Hall and the Forework.

Figure 9-1:
Stirling
Castle.

© iStock.com/Martin McCarthy

James IV also renovated the Chapel Royal, one of two churches within Stirling Castle at this time. In 1501, he received approval from the pope for the creation of a college of priests. His successor continued and expanded his building programme, creating the centrepiece of the castle, the Royal Palace, built under the direction of Sir James Hamilton of Finnart, assisted by stonemasons brought in from France.

There was also rebuilding at Holyrood and the Castle in Edinburgh. The north wing was added to Linlithgow Palace in 1518. Church building accelerated too in the period of the late 15th and earlier 16th centuries with the establishment of around 40 new collegiate churches.

All these new buildings were built in the Romanesque fashion with pillars and columns prominent (the entrance to the Chapel Royal at Stirling is a good example). But Scottish architects didn't always slavishly follow the patterns and styles from abroad; instead, they mixed local styles and materials with the more obvious Continental influences.

Education

The Renaissance put tremendous stress on the importance of education to build a rounded, honourable person who was equally comfortable with wielding a sword and reading a philosophical text. The subjects that made up a Renaissance education were poetry, grammar, history, moral philosophy and rhetoric.

James IV was the ideal Renaissance king. The Spanish envoy Pedro de Ayala, in a report to Ferdinand and Isabella of Spain, said of him:

> His knowledge of languages is wonderful. He is well read in the Bible and in some other devout books. He is a good historian. He has read many Latin and French histories and profited by them.

Of course, the monarch, like other important people, was privately tutored by eminent scholars, but what about the rest of the population? Grammar and song schools had initially been attached to cathedrals or collegiate churches, but as the years rolled by, they were found in the royal burghs and some small towns. Although primarily concerned with the education of boys, 'sewing' schools for girls existed in Edinburgh by the end of the 15th century.

What boosted literacy – at least among the well-to-do – was the passing of an act by the Scottish Parliament in 1496 that required all the sons of barons and freeholders to attend grammar schools to learn Latin. By this measure, it was reckoned that 60 per cent of the Scottish nobility were literate by 1500. However, the common people were left mostly illiterate until the Reformation stressed the necessity to read the Bible (see Chapter 10).

The universities were really training colleges for the clergy. But ambitious laymen began to enter universities to receive an education that would allow them to challenge the monopoly that clerics had established in posts in government and the law.

Scotland already had two universities by the time James III assumed the throne: St Andrews (1412) and Glasgow (1451). During the Renaissance period, Aberdeen University was founded in 1495 as King's College (another college, Marischal, was added in 1593). St Leonard's College was added to St Andrews in 1512 and the original St John's College of the university was re-founded by Cardinal James Beaton under the name St Mary's College in 1538 to counteract the 'heresies' resulting from the emerging Scottish Reformation and emphasise traditional Catholic teachings.

The universities of Scotland were part of a European culture, and many graduates went abroad to complete a second degree. Indeed, many of the lecturers and tutors had been trained in humanist studies in important centres of learning such as Paris and Cologne. Some of the greatest European scholars of that period were Scottish – for example, Hector Boece, the first principal of the University of Aberdeen, and John Major or Mair, who wrote in Latin a *History of Greater Britain.* It was through the universities that new ideas of humanism – and later Protestantism – entered Scotland.

Literature

Literature was perhaps Scotland's greatest contribution to the Renaissance. James IV's decision to grant permission for a printing press to operate in Edinburgh in 1507 allowed for a wider distribution of Scottish literary works. The titans of literature in this period were

- ✔ Robert Henryson, a school teacher from Dumfries

- ✔ William Dunbar, poet at the royal court of James IV

- ✔ Gavin Douglas, Bishop of Dunkeld

- ✔ Sir David Lindsay, Lord Lyon, King of Arms

Gavin Douglas's most important work was a Scots translation of Virgil's epic Latin poem *The Aeneid,* which was the first version of any of the great classical works to be written in a language native to the British Isles. The others wrote in a lyrical and satirical style. Henryson's major work was *Morall Fabillis,* which is a series of 13 interconnected fables. In the 'The Lion and the Mouse', in veiled prose, Henryson advised James III that the common people should be considered part of the political equation. In *The Thissil and the Rois,* Dunbar advised newly married James IV against philandering, not that it did much good – the Stewarts, between them, sired scores of illegitimate children! But the most biting satire was Lindsay's *Ane Satyre of the Thrie Estatis,* which poked fun at corrupt state officials and clergymen, and is considered by many to be the greatest Scottish play ever written.

Music

Not very much is left of pre-Reformation music, but most historians would agree that Robert Carver, a canon of Scone Abbey, was the outstanding composer of the Renaissance period. *The Carver Choirbook* contains music for five masses and two shorter pieces, as well as some English and Burgundian music. It is reckoned that it took a highly trained choir to sing Carver's *polyphonic* (many voices) compositions, such as the one employed by the Chapel Royal at Stirling Castle.

Two other composers of note in the reign of James V were David Peebles and Robert Johnson, but only fragments of their work remains. Much of this can be put down to the Reformation, particularly during its Calvinist period (see Chapter 10), as steps were taken to destroy any traces of the Catholic musical tradition. Song schools were closed, manuscripts were destroyed, choirs were disbanded and organs were removed from churches.

However, prior to this development, monarchs had prided themselves on being Renaissance princes in their musical ability. The lute was the favoured instrument. Both James IV and James V were skilled lute players, and James IV also played the clavichord. Other instruments such as the harp, viol and fiddle were also popular at court. No secular chamber music from this time really survives to this day, far less the kind of music that ordinary people listened to and sang.

The Reign of James III

Like the other Stewart kings, James was a minor when he came to the Scottish throne. His father, James II, had died in an accident in 1451 when James was only 9 years old, and he was crowned a week later at Kelso Abbey in Roxburghshire. His mother, Mary of Guelders, was appointed guardian by the Scottish Parliament, until he assumed power. However, Mary died three years after her appointment, and her place was taken by Bishop James Kennedy of St Andrews. His death in 1465 signalled the beginning of a power struggle for control of the young king.

While hunting in 1466, James III was seized by the Boyds of Kilmarnock and held captive until his assumption of power in 1469. From 1466 to 1469, Lord Robert Boyd, aided by his brother, Alexander, assumed the position of regent.

He made quite a number of enemies simply by doing what they all did in power: promoting his family. Boyd's son, Thomas, was made earl of Arran and married off to James's sister, Mary.

But it wasn't all bad. In 1469, Lord Boyd arranged the marriage of James to Margaret, the 12-year-old daughter of Christian I, king of Denmark and Norway. As part of the dowry, Scotland received Orkney and Shetland. Scotland assumed the territorial boundaries with which we associate it today. Margaret bore James three sons, one of them, James IV, the future king of Scotland.

The Boyds got little thanks for their trouble. James was annoyed at the presumption of Lord Boyd in marrying off his sister to his son, Thomas. When the Boyds left the country on the diplomatic business of arranging the marriage, their regency was overthrown and they were indicted as traitors. The elder Boyd escaped to England, but little is known of the future whereabouts of his son, Thomas. The family of Sir Alexander Boyd was executed in 1469, and the marriage of Mary was declared void in 1473.

Threat over? Don't believe it!

A little family bother

James was the only Stewart king to contend with a legitimate adult brother – in fact, two: Alexander, Duke of Albany, and John, Earl of Mar. He disposed of John in 1480, during his period of imprisonment in Edinburgh for treason. James's other brother, Alexander, had fled to France the year before, likewise accused of treason. Initially welcomed by the French king, Alexander soon fell out with him for refusing to back his plans to invade Scotland.

The immediate source of the disagreement between the Stewart siblings was the relationship with England. James wanted to build stronger ties with the English king, Edward IV, and what better way to do this than by arranging in 1474 for his son, the future James IV, to marry the latter's daughter, Princess Cecily? The Scottish nobility were not too happy with this arrangement because it went against the grain of longstanding hatred of the English born of the Wars of Independence (see Chapter 7). What annoyed them even more was the imposition of taxes to pay for the alliance and the marriage. Maybe that's why it never went ahead!

By 1479, the alliance was beginning to crack and war was in the air. In 1482, the English king sent an invasion force of 20,000 men north, commanded by the duke of Gloucester, the future Richard III and Albany, now calling himself Alexander IV, a claimant to the Scottish throne and a client of Edward IV. James rallied his troops to meet at Lauder Bridge to repel the invasion, but instead of doing their patriotic duty, the nobles promptly arrested the king and took him to Edinburgh Castle, where he was held prisoner by two of his earls, Atholl and Buchan, and the bishop of Moray.

But the English invasion soon ran out of money, and Gloucester seemed content with the capture of Berwick (the last time it would change hands between England and Scotland) and left Scotland. The 'Lauder Lords', as they were known, tried to form a workable government with Albany, who was styled the 'lieutenant general' of the new regime. But the regime was doomed from the start because it owed its existence to England. Three years followed in which James, through promises of land and power, managed to persuade important figures (such as John Stewart; Lord Darnley, keeper of Edinburgh Castle; and the bishop of Dunkeld) of his right to reclaim the throne. The Renaissance concept of principle and honour didn't seem to register with the Scottish elite. They were up for sale!

What sealed Albany's fate was the death of his patron Edward IV in April 1483, forcing him to leave Scotland for England. In July 1484, there was one more attempt to seize the throne. This much smaller force invading Scotland was defeated at the Battle of Lochmaben, where his ally, one of the exiled Douglas family, was captured, while he fled south again. The invasion had no support from Richard III and failed to find any Scottish support even in the former estates of Albany and Douglas.

In 1485, Albany fled for the last time, again to France, and shortly afterward he was killed in a joust in Paris, allegedly by a splinter entering his eye.

Our friends in the north

James didn't face difficulties only with his brother; he also had to deal with the rebellious lord of the Isles. The territory of the lord of the Isles was vast and included the Hebrides (Skye and Ross from 1438), Knoydart, Ardnamurchan and the Kintyre peninsula. Although nominally part of Scotland, successive lords of the Isles fiercely asserted their independence from the crown. In 1462, the last lord, John MacDonald, made a treaty with Edward IV to invade Scotland, but the invasion never took place – the War of the Roses got in the way. In 1475, the English produced documents to prove the treasonous behaviour of MacDonald.

James III stripped MacDonald of much of his land, giving his second son the earldom of Ross and parcelling out Kintyre and Knapdale to the earl of Argyll. MacDonald was allowed to retain his title, but it was no longer hereditary: the holder had to be approved by the crown. This proved to be a huge loss of prestige, and MacDonald was overthrown as chief of Clan Donald by his illegitimate son, Angus Og, in 1480. In the same year, Og razed the king's castle at Inverness to the ground and inflicted a defeat on James's army – one of only two defeats of a royal force by rebels in the medieval period.

The existence of a serious rival to Stewart power in the Highlands and Islands remained a barrier to the centralising strategy of the king to make himself supreme ruler. It was never solved in James's reign and was bequeathed to his son and heir to deal with.

Business as usual

James III assumed the throne of Scotland once again, and it seemed as if nothing had happened. On 5 March 1486, Pope Innocent VIII blessed a golden rose and sent it to James. But that was the calm before the storm.

The king was never popular with a large section of the Scottish noble elite, and his policies only increased their opposition to his rule. He continued to seek an alliance with England, which was a bit mad given all that had happened. He also refused to travel to administer justice, a key function of medieval monarchy, preferring to hole up in Edinburgh. There was also the issue of favouritism. A group of favoured lesser nobles – 'the familiars' – were advanced as full lords of the Scottish Parliament in 1488, which antagonised the more powerful magnates. Among 'the familiars' was his second son, whom he favoured above his first. His wife, Margaret of Denmark, had been banished to Stirling. Trouble was brewing!

The opposition in Parliament, led by the earls of Angus and Argyll, were in open revolt. With the king's eldest son, who was only 15, as their figurehead, they engaged in battle with James's army at Sauchieburn, near Stirling, on 11 June 1488. It was highly exceptional that a sovereign had to yield to an army in the field – rebellions tended to fail. But the battle was a disaster for the monarch, and he died in mysterious circumstances after it. Some said he was assassinated, others said he fell off his horse and died of the injuries, and others claimed he was killed in battle. We'll never know the true cause of death. But hey, the king is dead. Long live the king!

The Reign of James IV

Another Stewart minor was on the throne of Scotland, and that immediately produced challenges to royal authority. Within two years of being crowned king, James IV faced two major risings. As a result, he quickly realised that these risings were the product of pretentious nobles being excluded from a share of power due to favouritism.

After 1495, James tried to find a more balanced form of membership of the king's council. This allowed him to bypass Parliament, the theatre where disaffected nobles could moan and generally sow the seeds of discontent. After 1496, the Scottish Parliament met only three times in 17 years, whereas between 1488 and 1494 it had met nine times.

But James also realised the full value of a monarchy based on shock and awe, particularly when it came to impressing the nobility. The Scots have always held an affection for the 'hard man'. So, to fulfil the Renaissance ideal of the monarch as emperor within his own realm, James set about extending royal authority to those parts of the Highlands and islands that thought of themselves as beyond the monarch's jurisdiction. In this, he was well placed: he spoke Gaelic and visited the Highlands six times in the first seven years of his reign.

The lordship of the Isles

After the murder of Angus Og by his Irish harpist in 1490, MacDonald tried to reassert his claim to the lordship by approving his nephew Alexander of Lochalsh's plan to recover the earldom of Ross. After ravaging the Black Isle, belonging to Urquhart, King James's sheriff of Cromarty, Lochalsh, was defeated by the Mackenzies at the Battle of Blar na Pairc in Strathconon, Inverness-shire. James sailed to Dunstaffnage Castle, near Oban, to receive the surrender of MacDonald and the homage of the clan chiefs of the Western Isles. MacDonald was subsequently charged with and found guilty of treason. By an act of Parliament, all his lands and titles were forfeited to the crown. As a favour, he was allowed to retire to the Abbey of Paisley, and according to the treasurer's accounts, he died at Dundee in around 1502 or 1503.

The Highlands and Islands were now under royal control. Or were they?

Real difficulties in maintaining royal rule in these remote areas remained, mainly because the Isles men would not accept it. When Torquil Macleod of Lewis refused a royal command in 1501 to hand over the heir to the lordship of the Isles, Donald Dubh, who had escaped from custody, the king was obliged to use massive military force to punish his insubordination. This sparked a rebellion by the Isles men, and they attacked Badenoch, territory held by the king's lieutenant, Alexander Gordon, Earl of Huntly, and then went on to burn Inverness.

The entire military force of the kingdom was called out to deal with the rising, including a naval squadron under Sir Andrew Wood and Robert Barton, which was sent to reduce the castles of the Island chiefs. Dubh and Macleod continued to play cat-and-mouse with James until they were captured after the siege of Stornoway Castle, Lewis, in September 1507. The rebel Dubh was left to rot in prison for 38 years; he was released in 1545, while Macleod died in exile in 1511.

This was not the end of northern insubordination. A much bigger (but unsuccessful) rising took place in 1545, the year of Dubh's death. The policy of pacification might not have always been successful, but it shows the determination of the monarch to ensure that his rule was supreme.

The Renaissance prince

James IV was a much more hands-on monarch than his father had been. He was especially interested in looking after the money side of things and created a more efficient system for collecting taxes. He used his wealth to build one of the finest Renaissance courts in Europe filled with *makar* (makers or creators), poets and musicians.

But in true Renaissance fashion, he also saw himself as a warrior king – a man of the sword. As part of the cult of honour, James frequently held jousts or tournaments. At one such joust in Edinburgh, lasting three days in 1508, he overcame opponents from Denmark, England and France. He could leap on a horse without the aid of stirrups and ride, it was claimed, for 160.9 kilometres (100 miles) in a day.

James's macho image was also strengthened by the building of an impressive fleet of 38 royal Scottish navy ships. Two dockyards were constructed for the purpose. One of the ships, *The Michael,* was the largest in Europe and cost £100,000 to build. It was equipped with 27 cannons, weighed 1,000 tons, was 73 metres (79.8 yards) long and had a crew of 300 men.

Our friends in the south

Plans to marry off James to Princess Cecily (see 'A little family bother', earlier in this chapter) didn't quite work out, but there was still interest in strengthening the ties between Scotland and England through marriage. After signing the Treaty of Perpetual Peace in 1502 with Henry VII, James further cemented ties between the two nations by marrying the English king's daughter, Margaret Tudor, in Holyrood Abbey in August 1503. He went on to sire four sons, only one of whom – his heir and successor, James V – reached adulthood. But he had plenty of heirs in reserve, with eight illegitimate children by four different mistresses!

The peace didn't last very long – James became embroiled in European power politics. The Italian Wars, as they were known, comprised a complicated series of affairs in which allies became enemies and enemies became allies. Basically, a league of European powers – the League of Cambrai – was initially set up at the behest of the pope in 1508 to curb the ambitions of the Venetians. But during the campaign, the pope became more afraid of France and left the League to join with Venice. An anti-French alliance – the Holy League – was established that included England, Spain, the Holy Roman Empire and the papacy. When Henry VIII attacked France in 1513, James sided with the French, proving that the 'Auld Alliance' was still able to inspire Scottish loyalties. He agreed to a loan of his fleet, which was fine, but he also agreed to send an army south to distract the English from France. Not so fine.

The Battle of Flodden Field

While Henry was absent from England at the siege of Thérouanne in France, James thought he could take advantage of this and amassed probably the largest Scottish army ever to invade England, with himself at its head. Both sides met at Flodden Field in Northumbria on 9 September 1513 (the battle is also known as the Battle of Branxton Hill). The English were led by Thomas Howard, the 70-year-old earl of Surrey. The outcome was a disaster for the Scots. Although outnumbering the English, they were slaughtered – 10,000 men were killed in two hours. (The Scots never do well when they're favourites, as our national football team has shown on more occasions than it would be polite to mention!)

The massacre was due to superior English tactics. The terrain seemed to favour the Scots – they commanded the top of the hill above Flodden Field, and the English had the bottom. But when James ordered the main charge, the Scots got bogged down in marshy ground at the bottom of the hill. In the hand-to-hand fighting that took place, the English billhook proved more effective than the 6.1-metre (20-foot) Swiss pike used by the Scots.

Outmanoeuvred and outfought, the cream of the Scottish nobility lay dead on the field of Flodden. Included in that number was the king, the last monarch from Britain to be killed in battle. Also among the dead were 9 earls, 2 archbishops, 2 abbots and 14 greater lords.

Some mystery surrounds the whereabouts of James's body. Hacked to pieces, it was supposed to be taken to London for burial in St Paul's Cathedral, but it lay unburied at Sheen Priory in Surrey, from where it disappeared after the Reformation. So, his final resting place remains unknown.

Flodden had shown that Scotland was part of an international system of politics and a sought-after ally by major powers, especially France. James had wanted to be seen as a European prince, and in this he had succeeded, but at what a cost! For centuries, Flodden remained a deep and hurtful memory to the Scots. Even today, some Scots make the pilgrimage and lay wreaths at the Flodden memorial at the foot of Branxton Hill. In the Border town of Selkirk each year, 80 horsemen take part in the Common Riding, the same number from the town who fought at Flodden. Only one returned carrying a captured English banner, a replica of which is proudly paraded by the horsemen.

The Reign of James V

The reign of James V was notable in a number of ways. It saw the further extension of the power of the monarchy, as well as the continued commitment of the Stewarts to the principles of the Renaissance and the positioning of Scotland within Europe's elite nations through marriage. But these developments pale into insignificance with the emergence of radical – or, if you like, 'heretical'– religious challenges to the Catholic Church and the authority of the papacy: the Reformation. The conflicts created by religious dissent would last for more than a hundred years.

The politics of regency

Another Stewart king bites the dust, and another minor takes his place. James V was only 17 months old when his father was killed in battle. So, a regent had to be appointed to rule until James reached his majority. Cue backstabbing and treachery!

James IV's widow, Margaret Tudor, was appointed regent, but that came to an end with her marriage to Archibald Douglas, 6th Earl of Angus, ten months after her husband's death. Douglas, like his new bride, was an Anglophile, hardly a popular position with the Scottish nobility, given that they had suffered such catastrophic losses at Flodden. Disgruntled nobles wrote to the cousin of James IV, John, Duke of Albany, to invite him to assume the regency. This was the man whose father, Alexander, Duke of Albany, had plotted with the duke of Gloucester to overthrow James III, so perhaps he was not the wisest choice!

The toing and froing only highlighted the fact that there were two factions within the nobility: the pro-English minority and the pro-French majority.

Albany was really a Frenchman – state papers had to be translated into French for him, and he was committed body and soul to Francis I of France. In 1521, Albany returned to France to renegotiate the Auld Alliance as the Treaty of Rouen; as a result, there was talk of a joint Franco–Scottish invasion of England in 1523, but it was all hot air. French troops did arrive in Scotland, but they left within six weeks, waved a hearty *au revoir* by their Scottish hosts who had had to feed them. The Scottish nobility had no stomach for another war with England so soon after Flodden. By 1524, Albany had departed the scene and retired to France, which opened up a power vacuum.

The Red Douglas

Douglas was determined to fill the void. He had got on the wrong side of the queen mother by fathering an illegitimate child, and ever since she had been secretly trying for a divorce. In alliance with Albany, Margaret managed to have Douglas charged with treason. Hell hath no fury like a woman scorned!

Douglas was exiled as a prisoner to France in 1522, but he managed to escape to London two years later. In November 1524, he returned to Scotland with the support of the English king and tried to force his way into Edinburgh, but he was repelled by Margaret and her supporters. Repulsed, he retired to his ancestral pile, Tantallon Castle, to lick his wounds.

Douglas also took the time to plot, and he returned to Edinburgh three months later with a larger force. This time, he successfully entered the city and called a parliament. Douglas immediately secured a power base for himself by appointing his family and allies to key positions in the Church and government; he became chancellor.

In July 1525, the ruling estates in Scotland decided that the young king, for his own safety and education, should be placed in what they called 'company'. The company was made up of his stepfather, Douglas, and Gavin Dunbar, Archbishop of Glasgow. It was to be on a rotational basis – Douglas was to have the guardianship of the young king for a fixed period of four months, from July to November 1526. But at the end of the term, he refused to hand over the king, who was held prisoner in Edinburgh Castle for almost three years. When his mother, Margaret, objected, Douglas put her and her supporters to flight.

Douglas was now in charge, and it wasn't all bad. As lord warden of the marches, he sorted out the anarchy and disorder in the Scottish Borders. He also concluded a peace treaty with England in August 1526. Attempts to free the king from his clutches were also repelled. With a much smaller force, Douglas defeated John Stewart, 3rd Earl of Lennox, at the Battle of Linlithgow Bridge in early September of that year. Lennox, who had the support of Queen Margaret and Cardinal Beaton, was wounded, and on surrendering to his opponents, he was murdered and his base in Stirling was occupied by Douglas's men.

However, in 1528, James escaped the clutches of Douglas and fled Edinburgh for Stirling. A small army of loyal supporters and enemies of Douglas gathered around the king. Fearing the worst, Douglas bolted for England in May 1529, where he took an oath of allegiance to Henry VII and was given a pension by the English for his troubles.

His relatives did not fare as well. James took revenge on those Douglases still in Scotland. Not only were their lands confiscated by the crown in July 1537, but Douglas's third youngest sister, Lady Glamis, was found guilty of conspiring against the king's life and was burnt at the stake on Castle Hill, Edinburgh.

The Renaissance prince

Like his father, James V thought of himself as a Renaissance prince. His spending on the royal palaces exceeded £50,000 – more than the total sum spent by the previous four Stewart kings combined. This was possible because he was able to generate greater income than the others. He had the Scottish Parliament pass a law allowing him to *feu* (rent) out crown lands; he made sure his taxes were collected and paid; he even had a flock of 10,000 sheep grazing on the royal estate at Ettrick, near Selkirk. Through these and other schemes, James was able to increase royal household income by around 40 per cent, or from just over £9,000 per year in 1509 to £15,000 per year by the time of his death in 1542.

However, the best way he had of raising royal income was through marriage because it brought with it a dowry. In Europe, James was considered a highly eligible marriage prospect, with Holy Roman Emperor Charles V and Francis I of France interested in finding him a suitable bride. But by invoking the Treaty of Rouen, which provided for the Scottish king a daughter of France, James was able to secure the hand of Francis's 16-year-old daughter, Madeleine, in marriage on 1 January 1537 in Paris's Notre Dame Cathedral.

James returned to Scotland with his bride in May 1537, but Madeleine died two months later of consumption. Another bride was provided by the French king – the daughter of the duke of Guise, Mary. She was a widow of 22, already with two sons, but she came with a dowry of 150,000 French livres, which allowed James and his new wife a lavish lifestyle. They married on 12 June 1538, and Mary bore him two sons. Both sons died in infancy, but a daughter born in 1542 at Linlithgow Palace survived; she later became Mary, Queen of Scots.

James's early experiences of noble duplicity and treachery created an enmity within him against the elite in Scottish life. He tried to connect with the common people by wandering the country in disguise, listening to his people talk. His nickname was 'Gudeman of Ballengeich' – *Gudeman* means 'landlord' or 'farmer', and Ballengeich was a road next to Stirling Castle.

This distrust was also evident in the way James promoted lesser men above the more traditional ruling elites. In the Scottish Borders, he bestowed on them the warden of the marches; in the Highlands, he refused to grant the 4th earl of Argyll lord lieutenancy of the Isles and gave it instead to his sworn enemy MacDonald of Islay. The lords of the north and west of Scotland were also warned regarding their pocketing of the king's tax revenues. By these means, James was able to create a group of nobles who owed their elevation to him and, hence, their loyalty.

James V and the Reformation

After Martin Luther, a German priest, nailed his *Ninety-Five Theses* to the door of his local church in Wittenberg, Germany, in 1517, complaining about corruption within the Catholic Church, particularly the selling of indulgences, the papacy was faced with a doctrinal revolt.

In Scotland, the late medieval Catholic Church was in a state of disarray even before the attacks of Protestant critics like Luther. The problem was that the Church at a local level was ceasing to exist as churches fell into disrepair through neglect and war. The priesthood had similarly declined and was generally made up of illiterate and debauched men. In contrast, the closed abbeys and monasteries enriched themselves at the expense of the wider interests of the Church. Only 23 monks lived in the vast Melrose Abbey; the monks at Incholm kept women in their monastery; and the Church hierarchy ignored the laws of celibacy, with Cardinal Beaton of St Andrews fathering eight illegitimate children. By the 16th century, it was estimated that 40 per cent of all legitimations of bastards were for the offspring of the clergy.

James V also appointed many of his own illegitimate children to lucrative ecclesiastical positions, such as Robert Stewart, 1st Earl of Orkney, son of Euphame Elphinstone, who became commendator of Holyrood Abbey. So, many of the monasteries were run by men with little interest or training in religious affairs. You can see that the critics had a point.

Critical Protestant literature was being smuggled in from England and the Low Countries. Such was the extent of the smuggling of banned texts that the Scottish Parliament passed a law in 1525 prohibiting the import of Lutheran books and tracts. But banning them only made people more interested in these subversive texts. Banning this kind of literature was one thing, but preventing its circulation was another. From 1525, William Tyndale's translation of the New Testament was smuggled in and avidly read by literate Scots.

James was a staunch Catholic and opposed the spread of heretical ideas in Scotland. He actively pursued Protestant reformers, the most famous of whom was Patrick Hamilton, a great-grandson of James II. Hamilton had studied under Luther in Wittenberg and Erasmus at Louvain. When he returned to Scotland in 1527, he set about preaching the reformed religion. He concentrated less on the abuses of the Catholic Church, and instead emphasised a doctrine that was much more dangerous: 'Faith unites Man to God.' In this faith, every man was his own priest, so there was no need for bishops or cardinals or the entire hierarchy of the Catholic Church.

Archbishop Beaton of St Andrews had Hamilton arrested. In 1528, when Hamilton refused to recant, he was burned at the stake for heresy, becoming Scotland's first Protestant martyr.

The execution itself was horrific. It was a damp, wet February day in St Andrews and the fire was difficult to stoke. Hamilton endured six hours of torture. But his death was a propaganda coup for the reformers, as an adviser to Beaton pointed out:

> My lord if ye burn any more . . . ye will utterly destroy yourselves. If ye burn them, let them be burned in deep cellars, for the reek of Master Hamilton has infected as many as it blew upon.

Hamilton was the first of 21 martyrs executed between 1528 and 1558. James himself oversaw the burning of two heretics outside the walls of Edinburgh Castle in 1534. But with each execution, the dissent in the country grew, reaching epic proportions in the late 1550s (see Chapter 10).

James's defence of traditional religious beliefs also brought him into conflict with England. Henry VIII's desire to marry Anne Boleyn and divorce Catherine of Aragon ran into trouble when the pope refused to grant his wishes. In 1533, the English king reacted to the pope's refusal by renouncing the authority of the papacy and placing himself at the head of the Church in England.

To reconcile the Scottish king to his religious policy, Henry arranged to meet him at York in 1536, but James refused the invitation. For his defence of the established Church against the heresies coming from south of the border, a grateful Pope Paul III sent James a blessing symbolised in the gift of a cap and a sword. But to the English, it was a clear sign that James had thrown in his lot with the Catholic Church and France. There was a telltale clue: he had married two French women, one the king of France's daughter!

Two English plots to murder the king were discovered, and James also foiled an attempt by Henry to have him kidnapped. Although in 1540 the English king made another attempt to win the support – or at least the neutrality – of James for his religious policy, the relations between the two countries had become very hostile. Another meeting was arranged in 1541 at York, but the Scottish nobility refused to let their king leave the country in case he might be held prisoner by the English. There was, after all, some precedent for this!

The breakdown in communications led to a number of border clashes. In August 1542, the Scots, led by the earl of Huntly, inflicted a heavy defeat on the English army at Haddon Rig. In October of that year, furious, Henry sent north an English force of 20,000 men, under the duke of Norfolk; it burnt Kelso and Roxburgh as it progressed.

James ordered his nobles to meet him at Fala Muir, just outside Edinburgh, but the response was lukewarm to say the least. The memory of Flodden, and the fact that the Scots saw themselves as pawns in the larger power struggles between France and England, influenced the decision not to answer the call, or the refusal to march on the English border. At the town of Lauder, the Scottish army disbanded. It didn't matter. The English army had decided to leave Scotland – they had run out of beer!

The Battle of Solway Moss

Ever the optimist, James issued another call to arms and, with around 15,000 men under the command of Sir Oliver Sinclair, marched into England. There, they were confronted by an English army only 3,000 strong at Solway Moss on 24 November 1542. The battle can scarcely be called a battle – it was more like a farce that ended in humiliation for the Scots.

For a start, the morale of the Scottish army was low and there was no recognised command structure. Although Sinclair, James's favourite among the Scottish nobility, was the appointed commander, most of the generals refused to accept this. So, disunity among the leaders precipitated the break-up of the army almost as soon as the battle began. Outflanked and outmanoeuvred, the Scots surrendered. As it turned out, only 7 English soldiers and 20 Scots were killed in combat, but many more drowned in the River Esk, and 1,200 Scottish prisoners were taken. They included Sinclair and the other main commanders, the earls of Cassillis, Glencairn and Maxwell.

The shameful nature of the defeat saw the death, less than a month later, of James V, who was only 30 years old. Some say he died of a broken heart; others claim he died of a fever. We'll never know. He was buried at Holyrood Abbey along with his first wife and his two infant sons. The tomb was destroyed during the English occupation of Edinburgh in 1544.

With the defeat, the international status of Scotland changed from player to pawn. Prior to the disasters of Flodden and Solway Moss, Scotland appeared a valuable ally to those powers, especially France, engaged in fighting European wars. But everything rested on the military threat posed by the Scots, and after 1542, the potency of that threat was considerably diminished.

Everyday Life in Renaissance Scotland

How did all this affect ordinary Scots as they went about their daily lives? How did people survive in an age of private wars, foreign invasion and political uncertainty; of economic hardship and insecurity; of dislocation in religious and cultural life? How did they cope from day to day – lairds and tenants, merchants and craftsmen, rural labourers, urban dwellers in service jobs, wives, widows and unmarried women? In this section, I shed some light.

The economy

Life in Renaissance Scotland may have been short, nasty and brutish for the majority of the population, but there were degrees of deprivation. Indeed, compared to the hundred years after 1550, things were, economically speaking, much better for the ordinary Scot. That can be put down to a number of reasons:

- **Population:** The population had fallen to around 700,000 in 1500, which meant there was less pressure on resources.
- **Famines:** Famines were rare compared to the second half of the 16th century.
- **Living standards:** The living standards were higher.

The economy was one of subsistence – people generally laboured to supply their own needs, some of which was used to pay rent to landowners. Indeed, the land conferred status and influence on the holder, but the nobility had no way of marketing and profiting from the sale of the produce of the land. The way to increase one's cash balance was to find a post within the government or procure a pension, preferably from England or France. Thus, the market had little place in providing greater income for the nobility, far less the necessities for the bulk of the population. What trade there was in luxury goods was for the aristocracy, all of which was irrelevant to the peasantry.

The diet of the common people consisted of oatmeal, meat (mutton and beef), dairy products and a little fish. As the 16th century wore on, the poorer Scots in rural areas were forced, because of rising prices, on to an oatmeal diet, while in the towns it was bread and ale. However, they weren't on the brink of starvation. There was periodic feasting associated with harvests, weddings and funerals.

Social life

The social structure in late medieval Scotland was hierarchical. Everyone knew their place and, more importantly, how to keep it. Here's what the hierarchy looked like, from top to bottom:

- ✔ **King or monarch:** He was at the top of the pyramid.

- ✔ **Dukes and earls:** Immediately below the king or monarch was a small number of dukes (usually descended from very close relatives of the king) and earls. They formed the senior nobility.

- ✔ **Barons and lords of Parliament:** Below the senior nobility came the barons, and, from the 1440s, fulfilling the same role, the lords of Parliament, the lowest level of the nobility (but given the right to attend the meeting of the *Estates* (all the ranks listed above who comprised the Scottish Parliament). They amounted to about 50 or 60.

- ✔ **Lairds:** Below the nobility were the lairds, roughly equivalent to English gentlemen. Most were in some sense in the service of the senior nobility, either in terms of land or military obligations. Although serfdom had died out in Scotland in the 14th century, through a system of justice these lesser nobles still exercised a great deal of control over their tenants through their right to try them in what were called *barony courts*.

- ✔ **Peasants:** At the bottom of landed society came the peasantry, who made up about 80 per cent of Scottish society. They had no rights and could be evicted at short notice. They also, unlike in England, had no access to common land or free pasture.

In the towns, the wealthier merchants were the ones who held local office as burgesses, bailies or members of the town council. But don't run away with the idea that they were the Richard Bransons of their day. Most merchants lived with their families in one room, usually above their shops or business premises. They owned few material possessions – perhaps a towel, a table-cloth, a basin, at least one cup, a bed for sleeping in and a bench to sit on. The very wealthiest – the burgesses – might have a feather bed with sheets. They were hardly wealthy in the way we recognise the urban elite today, but they were represented in the Scottish Parliament as the Third Estate. Below them were the craftsmen and workers who made up the majority of the urban population.

Scotland was barely urbanised in this period. In 1550, only 2.5 per cent of Scots lived in towns of more than 2,500, one of the lowest rates in Europe. The towns or burghs themselves were small, usually consisting of one street, the High Street, with lanes or *wynds* off it. Glasgow had a population of between 2,500 and 3,000 in 1500, compared to Edinburgh's 10,000. The royal burghs had the right to monopolise foreign trade and to send a representative to the Scottish Parliament. However, like the smaller burghs, of which there were many, their main function was to act as markets for locals and those from farther afield to sell their produce. As early as 1500, the town council of Edinburgh complained of the 'greitt confluence of simpill peipill'(great gather-ing of common people), who thronged daily through the burgh's 14 markets from as far away as Perth or Dumfries.

The city, through its port in Leith, also was the main centre of the export trade in Scotland, which mainly consisted of primary products such as coarse wool, animal skins and hides, and fish. In fact, a staggering number of animals entered along Edinburgh's Cowgate to be slaughtered and their skins exported. In 1499,the burgh exported 44,325 sheepskins, 28,740 skins of other animals and 24,347 hides. It may have brought in some much needed foreign cash, but did that compensate for the stench? No wonder that when installed as regent Mary of Guise vacated the Cowgate for other less smelly parts of the city, as did Cardinal Beaton!

Although women played a subservient role to their fathers, husbands and sons, in the burghs they enjoyed certain rights and privileges. The wives and widows of burgesses controlled the brewing trade and 288 female brewers were recorded as active in 1530. Moreover, one in five households was made up of single women. Domestic service was the main occupation for women with three out of four working in this part of the economy. Nearly all worked only for board and lodgings but then so did most men.

For those women who survived childbirth (and at least one-third did not), they could generally expect to live longer than men. Because of this, a woman having three or four husbands in her lifetime was not exceptional. Plus, females were allowed to marry from the age of 12; for boys, the minimum marriage age was 14, but in the 16th century this increased to their 20s. On marriage, women kept their own surnames, but there were barriers to marrying a member of one's kin group. For noble families, a papal dispensation was required for a marriage to take place. Divorce was unheard of, but in cases of adultery there existed the practice of 'separation from bed and board'.

In late medieval Scotland, life was short, and when death occurred, all the windows and doors were opened immediately, to let the spirit escape. The clock was stopped and not started again until the burial was over. Unlike today, everything was draped in white (black in the great houses) and a wake was held, known as the Lykewake, lasting for two or three nights. During that time, respect was paid to the dead, but it was also an occasion for eating and drinking and even dancing. It was important to have a good send-off, but funeral expenses could impoverish a family. Thus, for the poor, there were coffins, known as *biers,* which had a hinge that allowed the body to be dropped into a grave, allowing the coffins to be reused.

Part IV
The Unmaking of a Nation (1540–1750)

© iStock.com

Go in depth on the Treaty of Union of 1707 in a free article at www.dummies.com/extras/scottishhistory.

In this part . . .

- Look at the Union of the Crowns in 1603 and the subsequent attempts by James VI and I and his son Charles I to unite England and Scotland through religious reforms and the civil wars they provoked.

- Examine the reasons behind the Treaty of Union of 1707, the failure of the Darien Scheme and the famine of the 1690s.

- Consider the economic and political consequences of union for Scotland and how the Scots got drawn into the slave trade.

- See how Scotland was governed after voluntarily giving up its own parliament.

- Understand the Jacobite rebellions in the 18th century and how defeat in 1745 forever changed Scotland in general and the Highlands in particular.

Chapter 10

From Reformation to the Union of the Crowns (1540–1625)

In This Chapter

▶ Looking at the regency of Mary of Guise

▶ Understanding the Scottish Reformation

▶ Focusing on the reign of Mary, Queen of Scots

▶ Studying the reign of James VI

▶ Understanding the Union of the Crowns

*T*he period from 1540 to 1625 was a momentous one – it changed Scotland from a Catholic country to a Protestant one. But it was a long, drawn-out process and not without bloodshed – monarchs were toppled and beheaded, as in the case of Mary, Queen of Scots – but out of this period came not only the Protestant ascendancy but also the Union of the Crowns of England and Scotland in 1603. A Scottish king, James VI, held the crown of both nations as James I. He saw the need to build a more binding union than that of the crowns and began to lay plans to first unite the Churches of Scotland and England as a prelude to the creation of new state, Great Britain. Did he succeed? Read on.

Regency and Reformation

The defeat of the Scottish army at the Battle of Solway Moss in November 1542 hastened the death of the already fever-ridden James V the following month. His death meant that the Scottish throne fell to his daughter, Mary. The problem: Mary was only six days old when her father died! So, a regent had to be appointed to run the country until Mary was able. The job first fell to James Hamilton, the second earl of Arran, great-grandson of James II and a Protestant, who held office for 12 years.

Arran's first task was to sign the Treaty of Greenwich of 1543, in which peace was agreed between England and Scotland on the basis of a marriage between Henry VIII's son, Edward, who was 5 years old at the time, and Mary, who was 1. The marriage would become binding when Mary reached her tenth birthday. But that didn't please everyone – in particular, the Scottish chancellor, Cardinal David Beaton; Mary's mother, Mary of Guise; and assorted nobles, who were Catholic and pro-French.

The English king adopted the age-old strategy of bribery and corruption in order to get his way. Arran's son was promised the hand of Princess Elizabeth; Scottish prisoners taken at Solway Moss were released on the basis that they would push forward the marriage of Edward and Mary. Just when Henry thought he had an agreement, a week later Arran reneged, reconverted to Catholicism and went over to the pro-French side.

Claiming that England had delayed too long in ratifying the agreement, the Scots signed an alternative agreement with France. Arran did all right: the French duchy of Châtelherault was later given to him. The infant Mary was crowned queen of the Scots on 9 September 1543, the 30th anniversary of the Battle of Flodden.

Rough wooing

Henry was understandably furious and the earl of Hertford (later duke of Somerset) was instructed to draw up an invasion plan. The purpose was not to gain territory but to punish the Scots for their treachery.

The objective was made clear in an Edict of the English Privy Council:

> Put all to fyre and swoorde . . . burn Edinborough towne, so rased and defaced when ye have sacked and gotten what ye can of it as there may remayne forever a perpetuel memory of the vengeance of God.

This was the beginning of what Sir Walter Scott would later call the 'Rough Wooing'; a period from 1543 to 1550. The English burned and looted from Edinburgh to the Scottish Borders. The Palace of Holyrood and the Abbey Church were plundered as part of the slash-and-burn policy, but the English failed to take Edinburgh Castle. The effect of this brutality was to unite the warring factions in Scottish society against 'our auld inymeis of Ingland'.

The Scots defeated a larger English force consisting of mainly mercenaries at Ancrum Moor, near Jedburgh, in early 1545, which only made Henry even angrier. Henry decided on the military option as the only possible solution for getting the Scots to agree to the marriage proposal.

As part of his strategy, Henry used reforming preachers to destabilise the Scottish government. One such tool in this policy was the itinerant preacher and political activist George Wishart who had entered Scotland in 1543. Two years later, Cardinal Beaton had him arrested and burnt as a heretic in St Andrews in front of the castle, while he looked on.

Five months later, on 29 May 1546, Beaton was assassinated by a band of local Fife lairds, acting with the approval of Henry VIII. They occupied the castle and awaited help from England, which predictably never came. The earl of Arran laid siege to the castle, but the Castilians, as they were known, held out and were joined by John Knox in April 1547.

The arrival, on 29 June 1547, of a French fleet off St Andrews brought the siege to an end. The 150 occupants of the castle surrendered a month later and most, like Knox, were sent to France as *galley slaves* (men chained to benches and made to row for long periods while an overseer watched over them with a whip in hand in case of slacking).

The other part of the plan was to send an invasion force of 16,000 to conquer Scotland. An English army defeated a larger Scottish force at Pinkie, near Musselburgh, on 10 September 1547, a day referred to as 'Black Friday'. Thousands were killed and 1,500 were taken prisoner. The Scottish army was chased to Edinburgh, but again, the castle successfully resisted the English onslaught.

The English headquarters were based at Haddington. From there, they maintained their control of southeastern Scotland, building a series of more than 20 forts between Berwick and Dundee – but at a huge expense (around £1 million). It was all to no avail – in July 1548, Mary was moved to France, and the Scots signed a treaty approving her marriage to the French dauphin, Francis, in return for a guarantee of Scottish sovereignty.

With the help of the French the English invasion force at Haddington was placed under a siege in 1548. The next year, their headquarters were abandoned, due to a variety of reasons:

✔ The death of Henry VIII in January 1547

✔ Rebellions in Cornwall and East Anglia

✔ The fall of the duke of Somerset in a palace coup

✔ French attacks on the English garrison at Boulogne

In 1550, Mary de Guise, accompanied by nobles and clerics sympathetic to England, went to France. Like Arran, now referred to as Châtelherault, the French king 'bought them completely'. This was the finest group of Scotsmen that money could buy!

The regency of Mary of Guise

With Arran bought off, the way was clear for Mary of Guise to assume the position of regent, which she did in 1554. Although initially she did her best to keep everyone happy – from Catholics to Protestants (see the next section) – in the end, her policies alienated the Scottish nobility.

It wasn't so much religion, but patriotism and greed that brought her down. The two main grievances were taxation and French influence.

Taxation

Taxation rose considerably under Mary's regency, to support French soldiers' pay and to maintain the royal residences in France and Scotland. The wedding of Mary, Queen of Scots, to Francis alone cost the Scottish taxpayers £60,000. Scottish nobles were used to a low tax regime, and the new demands stirred up a great deal of discontent among them.

French influence

The Scottish people also resented the growing French influence, particularly the promotion of favourites to positions of power and the use of foreign troops to deal with public disorder. The marriage of Mary to Francis in 1558 also held out the possibility of Scotland becoming a province of France, because the treaty gave him the right to rule Scotland if she died before he did. This became more than a possibility when the dauphin succeeded to the French throne in 1559 as Francis II and Mary as queen consort of France.

The lords of the congregation

In December 1557, Protestant nobles – including the earl of Morton, the earl of Argyll and the earl of Glencairn – joined together as the lords of the congregation to oppose the marriage of Mary to Francis. They rightly saw that the French were trying to woo Scotland into a war with England in which Scottish sovereignty would eventually be lost.

The tempo of opposition increased with the issuing of the 'Beggars' Summons' on the first day of 1559, warning friars to leave their houses in favour of the poor and infirm by what they called 'flitting Friday' (12 May). The other event was the arrival after 19 months as a galley slave of John Knox in Scotland. He stirred the passions of the mob, and riots took place in Perth the day before 'flitting Friday' in which the houses of the Black and Grey friars and the Carthusian monks were destroyed, as well as the tomb of James I.

Following religious riots in Perth, the lords gained support and were able to see off a joint French/Scottish force led by Châtelherault and D'Oysel, the French king's lieutenant. Next to fall was Stirling, quickly followed by Edinburgh and

Perth. John Knox was made minister of Edinburgh. Seeing which way the wind was blowing, Châtelherault and his son, the earl of Arran, changed sides and faith in September and became leaders of the lords of the congregation. Châtelherault was Protestant once more!

However, the regent wasn't finished yet: a French force of 3,000 men was sent to Scotland, and they drove the Reformers back to Stirling. The Protestant cause was hanging by a thread until an English fleet arrived in the Firth of Forth in January 1560, an event that caused the French to retreat to Leith. The Scots and the English agreed a treaty to expel the French from Scotland, but that proved unnecessary because the regent died on 11 June 1560. Her death opened the way for both the English and the French to leave Scotland under the terms of the Treaty of Edinburgh concluded on 6 July 1560. It also put the Scottish Parliament in the hands of the Protestant lords.

Reformation

The Reformation was rather late in coming to Scotland, so to understand this development, you have to go back a few decades. Ever since Martin Luther nailed his *Ninety-Five Theses* to the door of his local church in Wittenberg, Germany, in 1517, complaining against corruption within the Catholic Church (particularly the selling of indulgences), the papacy had been facing a doctrinal revolt. This revolt would end with a national system of religion replacing what had been an international one.

Luther's disenchantment with the Church and its doctrines was shared by large numbers of people, both high and low, in Scotland. The Church had long been a target of criticism for its worship of money rather than religion. While the monasteries and religious orders grew in wealth, local churches decayed and the clergy were poor and uneducated. Many of the commendators who ran the abbeys were not even clerics. Also, many of them were put there by royal favour. Six of James V's illegitimate sons held abbeys as commendators.

Lax morals were also a concern. Cardinal Beaton had eight illegitimate children and Bishop Hepburn of Moray had nine! In his *Ane Satyre of the Thrie Estatis,* first performed at Cupar, Fife, in front of James V in 1540, David Lindsay expressed a savage critique of the Church, which reputedly made the king laugh out loud.

However, not all aspects of the Church were corrupt. Here are some of the positive contributions the Church made:

- The Church founded three universities in the 1400s and added the College of St Mary's in St Andrews in 1548.
- Many friars were highly regarded theologians and preachers.

- Some of the monasteries adopted high moral standards, such as the Carthusians at Perth and the Observant Franciscans.

- In 1548, the Church tried to introduce reforms aimed at improving the morals of the clergy by banning *concubinage* (living as man and wife without being married) and preventing non-qualified persons from holding offices.

But it was all too little too late. Attendances at Mass had already fallen away dramatically.

But it wasn't all about low standards and greed: the Protestant faith was preaching something more revolutionary. Protestants rejected the following:

- Papal authority – they referred to the pope as merely the 'bishop of Rome'.

- Praying to the Virgin Mary and the saints.

- The ceremonials and rituals of the Roman Catholic Church – they regarded them as idolatrous and blasphemous.

- The use of Latin in services – they favoured the vernacular.

- The Church hierarchy of bishops and cardinals – instead, they put the forth the revolutionary concept of everyman being his own priest.

When the Reformed Scottish Parliament met in 1560, acting in the name of the people, with an unprecedented attendance of 100 lairds drawn from all over the country, it passed a set of policies that amounted to a revolution in faith by

- Banning the Catholic Mass

- Rejecting the authority of the pope

- Accepting a Protestant Confession of Faith

Ideas about how the new Church was to be organised were set out in the *First Book of Discipline* (1560). This was a blueprint for the future of Scotland in which the Church and national life were to be brought into harmony with Scripture. The *Book* endorsed the following:

- The establishment of reformed ministries throughout the country.

- A national system of education and relief for the poor.

- Administration of an examination to all candidates for the ministry, to ascertain their suitability for the position.

- Oversight by 12 regional 'superintendents', who were better paid than ministers and played the part formerly performed by bishops.

✔ Involvement by laymen in religious matters. Each parish was to appoint a *Kirk session* (a committee made up of church elders and the minister to enforce godly obedience and discipline). A General Assembly was to be held once a year for the whole church, with laymen in attendance, to decide on ecclesiastical policy.

✔ Importance placed on the church sermon as the focal point of worship, with ministers being instructed to speak loudly in Scots.

✔ Communion at long tables, replicating the Last Supper.

✔ No kneeling before altars.

✔ No Christmas. The Reformers didn't like special days of worship – devotion was meant to be taking place with the same amount of fervour every day.

✔ No distractions, like statues or paintings – St Giles's walls were whitewashed and its side chapels dismantled, and the same thing happened in St Andrews.

However, there was one potential but unpredicted obstacle to establishing the Godly Commonwealth: the return of Mary, Queen of Scots (see Figure 10-1).

Figure 10-1: Mary, Queen of Scots.

© iStock.com

The Reign of Mary, Queen of Scots

Mary's first husband, Francis II, died of a septic ear a year after coming to the throne of France. Mary, who was only 17 at the time, was forced to leave France for Scotland. But as a devout Catholic, her entry into Scottish society in August 1561 could not have been more intimidating.

The Edinburgh mob tried to break into Mary's private chapel at Holyrood to stop a Catholic Mass from being held. Eight days later, Mary's official entry into the capital was turned into a showpiece for the Protestant faith. The queen was presented with the keys of the city by a boy who appeared to be descending from the clouds and who also gave her an English Protestant Bible and psalm book.

Conversing with John Knox

A few days after Mary arrived back in the capital, her 'conversations' with John Knox (see Figure 10-2) began. Many historians see the Reformation played out as a drama between the two of them, but don't make too much of these conversations. Mary and Knox met only four times, and only in the first two and a half years after her return. There was a lot more going on than just theological disputes between Catholics and Protestants.

Figure 10-2:
John Knox.

© iStock.com

John Knox was already in print against what he called, in his famous work of 1558, 'The first blast of the trumpet against the monstruous regiment of women'. What he meant by 'monstruous regiment' was that rule by women was unnatural – an affront to nature and God. It was specifically aimed at Catholic female rulers; that is, Queen Mary I of England and Mary of Guise. Knox wrote:

> how abominable before God is the Empire or Rule of a wicked woman, yea, of a traiteresse and bastard.

So, it was pretty predictable how his meetings with the young queen would go – badly! Knox felt that, given his age, knowledge and preaching skills, he could browbeat the young queen into submission. He said of her:

> If there be not in her a proud mind, a crafty wit and an indurate Heart against God and His Truth my judgment faileth me.

But Knox miscalculated. Mary was an attractive, tall (nearly 183 centimetres [6 feet]!) and cultured woman who was also politically astute. She was certainly no pushover. She recognised that the different faiths had to be tolerated; as much as she would have liked, there could be no undoing of the Reformation. As such, she appointed Protestants to the Privy Council and her closest advisors – her half-brother, James Stewart, Earl of Moray, and William Maitland, her secretary – were of the Protestant faith. Mary also agreed to practise her Catholicism in private while seeming in public to endorse the victory of Protestantism.

She avoided introducing unpopular taxes that had played a part in bringing down her mother. With a yearly income as dowager queen of France of £30,000, she didn't have to. In fact, the only national tax she introduced was one to pay for the baptism of her son and heir in 1566.

None of this stopped Knox's attacks on Mary – they were fairly constant. But Knox himself became the subject of scandal when, in his 50s, he married the 17-year-old daughter of one of his friends!

Finding a husband

Scotland was not Mary's first choice as a monarch. France was first. While reigning with her husband, Francis II, she had designs on the throne of England, because her grandmother was a sister of Henry VIII. Some Catholics in England felt she had a more legitimate right to the throne than Elizabeth, the daughter of Anne Boleyn, whom they considered to be a bastard (because they didn't recognise Henry VIII's divorce), and who was, of course, a childless virgin!

Mary considered a few potential suitors. One of them was Don Carlos, son of the king of Spain, but unfortunately, he turned out to be insane. In any case, Elizabeth did not approve of Don Carlos, and she made it clear to Mary that if she wanted to inherit the throne of England, Elizabeth would have the final say regarding who was a suitable candidate for marriage. Elizabeth even suggested her lover, the earl of Leicester, Robert Dudley, as a husband for Mary. There was a bit of humiliation involved!

However, a more credible candidate was Mary's first cousin Henry Stewart, Lord Darnley (the 'long lad' as Queen Elizabeth called him; he was more than 183 centimetres [6 feet] tall), a grandson of Margaret Tudor and next in line to the throne should Mary die prematurely. Let's keep it in the family! The couple married at Holyrood Chapel according to the rites of the Catholic Church on 29 July 1565 – something that met with the disapproval of the Virgin Queen, who imprisoned Darnley's mother in the Tower of London as an act of revenge. Elizabeth felt the marriage should not have taken place without her permission, because Darnley was both her cousin and an English subject. Any child resulting from the union of Mary and Darnley would have an even stronger claim to the throne of England than their parents did.

The marriage and the prospect of a Catholic dynasty brought an immediate armed response led by Mary's half-brother, the earl of Moray. This was easily put down by Mary who pledged her own jewels to pay her soldiers. Not a shot was fired in anger in what became known as the Chaseabout Raid. Moray was forced to flee across the border to England.

Mary needed friends, but she made the wrong ones. She called to Catholic Spain for assistance. At home, she spent more and more time with foreigners who were not of noble birth. She gave some of them – such as David Riccio, Franceso de Busso and Sebastien Danelourt – positions of importance. All this alienated moderate Protestants, who had been previously loyal to her.

The murder of David Riccio

Riccio (also spelt Rizzio) arrived in Scotland in 1561 with the ambassador of Savoy. His musical ability immediately won the queen's favour. Mary liked masque balls, cards and dancing, as well as archery, hunting and golf, and she had a fondness for literature and poetry – she was every inch the Renaissance monarch (see Chapter 9 on the Renaissance). So, there was an immediate rapport between Mary and Riccio, although others at court found him arrogant and conceited.

Darnley, who was only 19, and who was now considered by Mary to be useless on all levels, began to suspect that the relationship between Mary and Riccio was more than sovereign and subject. She was pregnant, and Darnley thought Riccio was the father. Jealousy led Darnley to hatch a plot with several other Scottish nobles to murder Riccio in such a way as to terrorise the queen. On the evening of 9 March 1566, they broke into the supper room of Holyrood Palace where Mary was dining with Riccio and her half-sister, Janet, and in front of Mary, stabbed Riccio 56 times.

It wasn't just a cuckold's revenge – Darnley also hoped that the attack would cause Mary to miscarry. She never forgave Darnley for the incident and said to Lord Ruthven that 'it is within my belly that one day will avenge these cruelties and affronts'.

On 19 June 1566, the future James VI was born in Edinburgh Castle. With witnesses present, Mary made it clear that the father of the child was Darnley. She said:

> My Lord God has given you and me a son, begotten by none but you. This is the son who will unite the two kingdoms of Scotland and England.

But there was a problem for Mary: the birth of her son weakened her position – Scotland now had a male heir, and Mary was dispensable. As politically astute as ever, Mary sidefooted her opponents by pardoning the rebels involved in the Chaseabout Raid. In December that year, Mary pardoned the murderers of Riccio. This meant inviting the traitorous Moray back to Scotland.

Darnley has to go

The rift between Mary and Darnley had become a chasm too wide to bridge. But as Mary grew cold toward Darnley, she grew fonder of James Hepburn, Earl of Bothwell. It was Bothwell who organised the baptism of Mary's son according to the rites of the Catholic Church, while Darnley was ill with syphilis. It didn't go unnoticed that Bothwell's father had sought a divorce to marry Mary's mother in 1543.

However, the problem for the queen was that she couldn't risk divorcing Darnley, because it might lead to James being declared illegitimate. A better idea was to remove Darnley altogether. At the end of January 1567, Darnley, an ill man, was brought to Edinburgh and housed in a house at Kirk o'Field. On the night of 9 February, while Mary attended a masked wedding ball at Holyrood, the house was blown up. But this is where the mystery begins.

Although the property was blown to pieces, Darnley and his servant, dressed in their nightshirts, were found some way from the house, showing no marks of having been touched by the explosion. Darnley had been smothered. Who did it? Unfortunately, we don't know for certain. There is a mass of speculation but little hard evidence. The finger could have been pointed at a number of characters, not the least of whom was Bothwell. He was the popular villain of the piece, along with Mary. When she entered Edinburgh, the women didn't shout, 'Burn the papist!' – they shouted, 'Burn the whore!'

Bothwell was made to stand trial for Darnley's murder in Edinburgh on 12 April. He clearly had supplied the gunpowder, but it never came out because the trial never took place! On the day of the trial, Bothwell packed Edinburgh with his men and prevented the prosecutor from entering the city. No one came forward in support of the charge, so the jury acquitted him.

With that little problem out of the way, a marriage was arranged with Mary, who was pregnant at the time by Bothwell. A divorce authorised by Mary was rushed through between Bothwell and his wife, Lady Jane Gordon, and they were married in May 1567. The marriage was according to the rites of the Reformed Church, which is proof that Mary was not a devout Catholic, but it did little to appease the opposition. They saw the marriage as scandalous and proof, if ever it was needed, that Mary was untrustworthy and immoral. That was the spark to set off another rebellion by the lords of the congregation.

The opposition and those loyal to Mary and Bothwell met at Carberry Hill, near Musselburgh, on 15 June. There was no battle, and no one was killed. In return for allowing Bothwell to escape, the queen was imprisoned on the island in Loch Leven, Fife, branded the 'Scottish whore' by Knox. Bothwell ended up in Demark where he died ten years later a madman in a Danish jail. His departure from Scotland was timely – five days later, the so-called Casket Letters were discovered in Edinburgh Castle, which implicated Bothwell and the queen in Darnley's murder. Whether the letters were forgeries is open to question. The only copies that survive are English ones, so your guess is as good as anyone else's.

However, the impact was hugely adverse for Mary. She was forced to abdicate in favour of her son on 24 July. James VI, who was only 1 year old, was crowned the first Protestant king of Scotland at Stirling on 29 July in what was the least attended coronation in Scottish history. By December, the Protestant Confession of Faith was made a test for anyone who wanted to hold crown office.

A revolution had taken place in which a monarch was deposed by the people – even if 'the people' in this instance were the noble elite. So, there was a major difference between the Reformation in England (which was pushed through by the monarch, Henry VIII) and the Reformation in Scotland (where it took place in spite of and against the monarch). As Archbishop of Canterbury Matthew Parker said, 'the people are the orderers of things'.

The queen fights back

Mary wasn't completely devoid of support. On 2 May 1568, 18-year-old William 'Willie' Douglas rescued her from Loch Leven and she joined up with those lords sympathetic to her, such as Argyll and Hamilton. A force of 5,000 to 6,000 men was raised quickly. At Langside, near Glasgow, on 13 May they faced a much smaller army of around 4,500 led by Moray. But it ended badly for Mary and her supporters – 300 of her men were killed, and Mary was forced to flee to England, never to return to Scotland and never to see her son again.

Elizabeth I of England was faced with quite a dilemma. Mary was her cousin and heir presumptive to the English throne, so Elizabeth couldn't deny her shelter. Elizabeth also didn't like rebellions, and if she recognised the government of Moray, it would appear to be condoning the overthrow of the monarchy.

The solution was to hold an inquiry at York in October 1568 in which Moray was allowed to state the case for rebellion. The Casket Letters were used to blacken Mary's character, but she was able to point out that her marriage to Bothwell had the support of most of the Scottish nobility, whereas Moray had only managed to attract one-tenth of the same nobles to the coronation of James VI. Plus, Bothwell had been acquitted of the charge of murder by a Scottish court.

The inquiry moved from York to Westminster – a clear sign that Mary was winning the argument. By January 1569, Elizabeth had to concede that there little evidence to 'conceive of an evil opinion of her good sister'. But that didn't mean she wasn't under suspicion. After all, Mary never renounced her claim to the throne of England. She had to be under constant surveillance, and the next 16 years of her life were spent in the custody of the earl of Shrewsbury as she was moved from castle to castle.

Although she was effectively under house arrest, Mary nevertheless proved a nuisance to Elizabeth, mainly because unhappy Catholics in England saw Mary as kind of rallying figure. Now divorced from Bothwell, Mary fell in love with the Catholic Thomas Howard, 4th Duke of Norfolk, and secretly arranged to marry him – until Elizabeth got wind of it and threw him in the Tower.

Mary became involved in all sorts of plots to overthrow Elizabeth and have herself declared queen of Scotland and England. She supported a rising against Elizabeth in the north of England in November 1569 and conspired with Norfolk and the duke of Alva in the early 1570s to overthrow her. The plot was discovered, and Norfolk was executed for high treason in January 1572.

Mary has to go

For her part in the Norfolk plot, Mary was deprived of any claim to the English throne and was warned that she would be made to stand trial if she was involved in any more plotting. But Mary couldn't resist it. So, a trap was laid for her.

A young nobleman, Anthony Babington, was the chosen vehicle for the conspiracy to assassinate Elizabeth, with the help of the Spanish, and put Mary on the throne. The long-term goal was an invasion by the European Catholic powers to re-establish the old faith. It became known as the 'Babington plot'.

Babington wrote to Mary on 7 July 1586, outlining his plans, which included a rescue scenario. Mary rather stupidly replied to him in her own handwriting, agreeing to be rescued but stressing that Elizabeth was not to be harmed. Little did Mary know that her letters were being intercepted and read by Elizabeth's chief spymaster, Walsingham, who added a few forgeries. Elizabeth's spy network accumulated enough material to arrest the conspirators, among whom was Mary herself.

Babington and his fellow conspirators were tried and executed in September 1586, and Mary was arrested and taken to Fotheringhay Castle, Northamptonshire. The 'trial' was a foregone conclusion. Mary was found guilty of plotting to harm the queen of England. But the court had no power to pass the death sentence – that was the monarch's decision. Elizabeth, who strangely enough had never met Mary, hesitated but signed the death warrant on 1 February 1587. It was said that she had the warrant placed among a batch of state papers requiring her signature so that it could be claimed she had signed it by accident.

Mary died at the age of 44, a Catholic, wearing under her gown a deep red shirt, the colour of martyrdom. The axe had to be used twice to behead her. The last words she spoke were in Latin: 'Into thy hands, O Lord, I commend my spirit.'

On Elizabeth's instruction, Mary's clothes were burned and her body and severed head were encased in a casket of lead and taken to Peterborough Cathedral. Mary had left instructions for her body to be buried at Rheims, France, with her Guise relatives. When her son, James VI, assumed the throne of England, he had Fotheringhay Castle pulled down and built a magnificent monument to Mary in Westminster Abbey.

What can we make of perhaps the most famous woman in Scottish history? Was her fall and ultimate death of her own doing? People remain divided on the question.

For the best part of 200 years or so after her death, Protestants saw her as an immoral tyrant rightly overthrown by Scottish defenders of liberties. Catholics saw it differently. To them, Mary was more sinned against than sinning, a martyr to the faith. More recently, the decline of religion in Scottish society has shifted historical perceptions of Mary. Nowadays, she is seen more as a feminist icon than a religious martyr – a woman who struggled against the odds in a male-dominated world, and lost. Whatever you think of her you can be sure that she will continue to divide public opinion for many years to come.

The Reign of James VI

James may have been only a year old when he was crowned king, but in spite of all the upheaval and unrest, the kingdom held together. James proved to be an astute politician who was able to play one faction off against another and, by doing so, reign for longer than any other Scottish monarch. In 1603, he became the first king of England and Scotland. As a committed centraliser, he tried to unify the countries under his rule, first through a policy to unite the Churches of England and Scotland, and later through the parliaments. But the key aspect of his unifying policy was that it was pragmatic that there was never any intention to force the Scots or the English into a marriage they didn't care for.

Civil war and revolution

James VI was only a year old when he came to the throne, and his minority involved the establishment of regency, which along with Mary's forced abdication plunged Scotland into a civil war. Mary's forces had been defeated at Langside in 1568, but her defeat and flight into England didn't exactly bring peace to Scotland – far from it. The civil war lasted for nearly 20 years, until Mary's execution. During that time, Scotland had four regents, three of whom were murdered and one of whom was executed. James VI was the subject of nine attempted kidnappings!

The first regent was the earl of Moray who was assassinated by James Hamilton at Linlithgow on 23 January 1570. The house where the shot was fired from belonged to the archbishop of St Andrews, John Hamilton, who was hanged without a trial for his part in the assassination plot at Stirling.

Moray was succeeded by Darnley's father, the earl of Lennox. By this time, Scotland was divided into two camps with two separate parliaments. The supporters of Mary (Marians), including Maitland of Lethington, who held Edinburgh Castle for her, had one parliament; Regent Lennox had another parliament, at Stirling. However, Lennox went the same way as Moray when he was shot in the back on 4 September 1571. This is getting worse than *The Godfather*!

Lennox was succeeded by John Erskine, Earl of Mar, in October 1571. But Mar was poisoned and died, funnily enough on his way home from a banquet hosted by his successor, James Douglas, 4th Earl of Morton! Douglas lasted for six years, and his achievements outweigh the other three put together. With the help of English troops, he successfully ended the Marian occupation of Edinburgh Castle in 1573. He also addressed the problem of placing the Reformed Church on a sounder basis. The Concordat of Leith of 1572 put the Church under the control of bishops nominated by the crown, but this was a big mistake! It only encouraged further conflict.

Under the leadership of Knox, the Reformed Church in Scotland had accepted Calvinism, which was opposed to religious hierarchy. According to Knox's teachings, there was no scriptural basis for bishops because there was no mention of them in the Bible.

Knox died in November 1572, and his place was taken by an equally radical Protestant scholar and theologian, Andrew Melville, who had returned to Scotland in 1574 as principal of Glasgow University. Along with 29 other ministers, Melville drew up the *Second Book of Discipline* in 1578. It repudiated royal control of the Church and instead laid plans for the establishment of a *theocracy* (rule by the godly).

As Melville put it to the king:

> Sirrah, ye are God's silly vassal; there are two kings and two kingdoms in Scotland: there is king James, the head of the commonwealth; and there is Christ Jesus, the king of the Church, whose subject James the Sixth is, and of whose kingdom he is not a king, not a lord, not a head, but a member.

Few people in the political elite were prepared to endorse the setting up of a theocracy, but many were suspicious of creeping Catholicism and signs of immoral behaviour on the part of the young king.

The king and his lover

Concerns came to a head with the arrival in Scotland of the king's father's cousin, the 37-year-old Esmé Stewart, from France in 1579. Although James was only 13, he began a scandalously open affair with Esmé. According to an English observer, 'oftentimes he will clasp him about the neck with his arms and kiss him'.

James bestowed on his lover the earldom of Lennox; then a year later, in 1581, James made Lennox Scotland's only duke and a privy councillor. To counter his influence, the nobility forced the king to sign the Negative Confession of Faith in 1581, which repudiated all forms of papistry. But there was a price to pay. At the behest of Lennox, Captain James Stewart accused Regent Morton of being an accomplice to the murder of Darnley. He was executed on 2 June 1581 by 'The Maiden', a guillotine he had invented!

Morton's execution led the nobility into open revolt at the influence of Lennox over the king. In August 1582, in what became known as the Ruthven Raid, the Protestant earls of Gowrie and Angus lured James into Ruthven Castle and imprisoned him, an action endorsed by the General Assembly. They refused to let him go until he signed a proclamation declaring himself to be a free king and ordered Lennox to leave Scotland. Lennox duly did so, returning to France where he died soon after bequeathing his embalmed heart to his former lover.

The king did not escape from Ruthven until June 1583. When he did, he had Gowrie, whose father was one of the nobles who murdered David Riccio, executed. The following year, he set about imposing himself on his kingdom.

It's witchcraft

James became fascinated by witches after his return from Denmark in 1590. He attended the North Berwick witchcraft trials, which was the first major persecution of witches under the Witchcraft Act of 1563. Seventy people were accused of trying to bring about his death and that of his new bride (details on her in the next section) by conjuring up the storms that delayed the monarch's return to Scotland.

The most celebrated trial was that of Agnes Sampson who was personally examined by James at Holyrood Palace. She was fastened to the wall of her cell by what was called the *witch's bridle* (a four-pronged instrument forced into the mouth in such a way that two of the prongs pressed on her tongue, and the other two against her cheeks). The poor woman was also deprived of sleep. Given all she had gone through, it wasn't really surprising that Sampson was prepared to confess to the 53 indictments brought against her. She was strangled and burned as a witch.

James was convinced that witches were a threat to his reign and wrote a tract condemning the practice, called *Daemonologie* (1597). Due to his influence, 400 people (mainly women) were accused of witchcraft in 1597; of this total, around 200 were executed. However, after 1599, James's views became more sceptical, especially over the ways to extract evidence (that is, sleep deprivation and pin-pricking to find the 'Devil's mark' on the body).

Restoring royal authority

There were three issues for James to sort out:

- ✔ The militants in the Church
- ✔ The lawless nobles
- ✔ The royal finances

Initially, the third issue was more easily solved than the first two. In 1586, a year before his mother was executed, James signed a pact with Elizabeth I to keep the peace. In return, he was given a pension of £4,000 a year, but it wasn't enough to cover royal expenses. The solution was to get a wife, particularly a rich one! In 1589, James did just that when he married 14-year-old Anne of Denmark. Her large dowry put the royal finances on a firmer footing. She was crowned queen consort of Scotland on 17 May 1590 in the Abbey Church at Holyrood and went on to bear James seven children (in spite of James's preference for his own sex), although only three survived beyond infancy.

The crown's improved economic position allowed James to confront those nobles who continued to challenge his authority. In the early 1590s, the Catholic earls of Huntly, Angus and Errol, along with the king of Spain, hatched a plan to land troops in Scotland and from there mount an invasion of England. On 3 October 1594, the earl of Huntly defeated a government force under the command of James and the earl of Argyll at Glenlivet. But it proved to be a pointless victory – with Mary dead, there was no figure that the rebels could rally round, so there was no backing for further action. Glenlivet proved to be the last protest by the landed elite against James.

Dealing with the Church proved to be a ding-dong affair. The pendulum seemed to swing one way and then another – at times in favour of the king, at other times in favour of the Church. However, in the end, the crown was the winner.

As a boy, James had been tutored by George Buchanan, one of Europe's greatest Latin scholars. Buchanan tried to instil in him the concept of contractual kingship. This meant that the monarch ruled with the consent of the 'people' (not Joe Bloggs, but the landed elite). If the monarch failed to perform his duty to the people, they had the right to remove him.

As he got older, James had no time for this and burned Buchanan's writings at the first opportunity. James believed in the divine right of kings to rule. He was put there by God, and only God could remove him from the throne. James outlined his views in two publications – *Trew Law of the Free Monarchies* and *Basilikon Doron* (Royal Gift) – both written in 1598. In the latter book, written for his son Henry, he explained to him:

First of all things learn to know and love that God, whom ye have a double obligation; first, that He made you a man; and, next, for that He made you a little God to sit on his throne, and rule over other men.

It was only to be expected that holding such views would bring the monarch into conflict with the radical clergy in the Reformed Church. In May 1584, James passed the 'Black Acts', which reaffirmed royal control over the Church and upheld the authority of bishops. As a result, Andrew Melville and some of his followers were forced to flee Scotland for England.

The 'Golden Act' of 1592 restored the privileges of the Kirk (the Church), but with one important proviso: the General Assembly was only allowed to meet with the permission of the monarch and Parliament, and by 1606, bishops were restored to membership of the Scottish Parliament. By this time, James's severest religious critic, Andrew Melville, was in the Tower of London; after four years' imprisonment, he was allowed to leave England for France, where he died a forgotten man in 1622. Ain't no stopping him now!

The Union of the Crowns

Elizabeth I died in Richmond Palace on 23 March 1603, and as next in line to the throne James was crowned I and VI king of England, Scotland, Ireland and France. He couldn't wait to get out of Scotland and bade farewell to his subjects in St Giles's Cathedral in early April. He headed south, promising he would return every three years. In fact, in the next 22 years, he returned only once, in 1617, and that was to prove highly controversial.

James soon changed the title of his kingdom to Great Britain, Ireland and France, and went out of his way to promote new symbols of Britishness: histories were written, flags were designed and coins were minted. He also tried to integrate the hundreds of Scottish carpetbaggers who followed him south into the institutions of court and government. Eight Scottish nobles and 12 English were installed as Knights of the Garter; one in five members of the English Privy Council was Scottish.

In a speech to the English Parliament, James spoke of the natural evolution of the two countries into one state:

> I desire a perfect Union of Lawes and persons, and such a Naturalizing as may make one body of both Kingdoms under mee your King . . . for no more possible is it for one King to governe two Countreys Contiguous, the one great, the other less, a richer and a poorer . . . than for one head to governe two bodies. . . .

Of course, James also promoted his favourites who received lavish gifts of land and titles. The most notorious was Robert Carr of Ferniehurst who was made a knight in 1607 and later earl of Somerset. It was said that the king kissed Carr and another favourite, Francis Osborne, 'after so lascivious a mode in public'.

However, James's attempts to engineer a complete union between England and Scotland were rejected out of hand in 1607 by the English Parliament. The Scots were also wary of Stewart plans – they felt that they might be turned into 'a conquered and slavish province to be governed by a Viceroy or Deputy'. The example of Ireland was clearly in their minds. So, early plans by the monarchy for a more complete union were scuppered because there was no enthusiasm for it north or south of the border. But it did not dent James's commitment to the idea of union.

Not surprisingly, James was more concerned with English matters of state than Scottish. As an absentee monarch, he developed a system of what was known a 'government by the pen'. As he put it in a speech to the English Parliament in 1607,

> Here I sit and govern it [Scotland] with my pen, I write and it is done, and by the Clerk of the Council I govern Scotland now, what others could not do by the sword.

But while English affairs took up most of his time, James did not completely ignore his native land. Indeed, James set himself a number of objectives as absentee monarch, all of which were designed to increase his power north of the border:

✔ Bring about an end to the lawlessness in the Border and Highland regions of Scotland and quell rebellion in Ireland.

✔ Find a way of settling differences with the Kirk.

✔ Make Great Britain a reality.

The third objective proved trickier than the other two.

Law and order

James had a pretty low opinion of the Scots, particularly of the Highlanders, as he makes clear in *Basilikon Doron:*

> [Those] dwelleth in our mainland, that are barbarous for the most part, and yet mixed with some show of civility; the other, dwelleth in the Isles, and are utterly barbarous, without any show of civility.

Indeed, although his tutor George Buchanan was a native Gaelic speaker, it was the fashion at his court in Scotland to ridicule Gaelic culture and the Irish legends of the kings of Scotland.

He used his newfound wealth and power to crush the lawless spirits in the Scottish Highlands. Feuding, cattle stealing and extortion were all part and parcel of everyday life in the north. In fact, the word *blackmail* derives from the protection rackets used by the Highland clans to coerce Lowland farmers into providing black meal in return for a guarantee not to steal animals from them.

To extend his authority in the region, James made an example of the MacGregor clan, who held lands from Argyll to Perthshire and were well-known thieves. In 1602, they stole 300 heads of cattle, 100 horses and 400 sheep from the Colquhoun clan. The following year, they slaughtered 200 of the Colquhouns in a battle. James had the MacGregors hunted down like dogs.

But James realised that he could not achieve a stable society in the Highlands and Islands through force alone. So, in 1609, he ordered Andrew Knox, Bishop of the Isles, to hold a meeting with some of the main clan chiefs. The outcome of the deliberations was known as the Statutes of Iona. Under the terms of the agreement, Highland chiefs were to dispense with 'Irish manners, dress and custom', as well as have their eldest sons or daughters educated on mainland Scotland and learn to speak, read and write in English and persuaded to renounce Catholicism in favour of the Reformed Church. He also used other loyal clans, such as the Campbells, to pacify the area and stamp out any signs of disobedience.

This policy was extended to Ireland. James believed that colonising Ulster would quell the rebellion that had been engulfing the province for nine years and win over the 'rude and barbarous Irish' to 'civility' and Protestantism. Catholic landowners found their lands confiscated and Protestant settlers from England, Scotland and Wales replaced them. This was the beginning of the plantation system, which, over time, created a Protestant north and a Catholic south in Ireland. It also destroyed the Gaelic aristocracy of Ireland and their links with the west coast of Scotland.

The Scottish Borders, or the 'middle shires' as the king preferred, notorious for *reiving* (robbing), were also to be pacified. In 1605, a commission comprising five Englishmen and five Scotsmen was set up to police the Border areas. On the Scottish side, Sir William Cranston had a force of 25 mounted police, who were remarkably successful in bringing law and order to the region. More than 140 Border reivers were hanged in the first year of operations.

Kirk and king and nation

James considered himself a Protestant but he had no time for the militants within the Scottish Church. (He once remarked to a delegation of Presbyterians, 'I give not a turd for your preaching'!) What he wanted was a more manageable Church like that in England of which he was the head. So, his plan was to Anglicise the Scottish Church. This was a double whammy – not only would he have a less Bolshie set of clerics to deal with, but by uniting the Churches of the two nations, James would lay the platform for further integration, eventually leading to a united Great Britain: one king, one kingdom.

By 1610, James had increased the number of bishops in Scotland to 11 and set up what was known as the Courts of High Commission to enforce ecclesiastical law on the English model. The arrangement worked rather well – the Church in Scotland could be at one and the same time Presbyterian and Episcopalian (bishops).

Most Scots were happy with the situation, but James went a bit too far for their tastes when, on his only visit to the country in 1617, he announced further innovations. He tried to bring the Kirk more into line with the practices of the English Church by what were known as the Five Articles of Perth:

- ✔ Communion to be received kneeling

- ✔ Observance of Holy Days like Christmas and Easter

- ✔ Confirmations to be carried out by bishops and not ministers

- ✔ Communion to be allowed in private for the sick and infirm

- ✔ Baptism to be allowed in private

The first article smacked of popery to many Scots because the practice had been to receive communion sitting around a table in imitation of the Last Supper. The General Assembly that met in Perth in 1618 at first rejected them, but they were bullied by the king into accepting them (although many ministers refused to implement them). This got the king very angry, and the General Assembly didn't meet again for another 20 years. The Scottish Parliament was also reluctant to ratify the Articles; it took three years of persuasion before the Parliament did so, in 1621.

James may have seen a united Church as a major step on the road to complete union between Scotland and England, but he was not prepared to send an army north (unlike his successor, Charles I) to enforce the Articles. At the end of the day, James was a pragmatic ruler who realised that persuasion was more effective than force in bringing about changes. But he didn't live long enough to achieve his goal. He died on 27 March 1625 during a violent attack of dysentery. He had been a reigning monarch for around 50 years, but what kind of monarch?

Unusually for a monarch then or since, James was an intellectual who spoke several languages and was responsible for the development of the idea of the divine right of kings to rule. He was also a consensual ruler who tried to integrate all shades of opinion. Of course, he had his favourites, like George Villiers (later Earl of Somerset) and Robert Carr (later Duke of Buckingham), but he made sure they never dominated decision-making. Indeed, when faced with opposition, James worked to find a compromise rather than resort to brute force.

But even though he preferred peace to war, that did not stop James from using the sword when dealing with those he considered responsible for lawlessness in the Borders and the Highlands. The fading out of blood feuds in Scotland can also be put down largely to the actions of the king. Like most monarchs, he was vain and his manners were coarse for the taste of the English court, but at the end of the day his longevity as monarch shows James to have been a highly competent and politically astute ruler.

Chapter 11

King, Commonwealth and Revolution (1625–1690)

In This Chapter

▶ Looking at the reign of Charles I

▶ Considering the reign of Charles II

▶ Studying the reign of James II and VII

▶ Understanding the Glorious Revolution

▶ Focusing on the first Jacobite Rebellion

▶ Looking at everyday life in 17th-century Scotland

*T*he years between 1625 and 1690 were nothing short of momentous. During this period, the course of modern Scottish and British history was set in motion. In the name of Christ, all manner of atrocities were committed and thousands died. Why were Christians killing Christians, you might ask? The reason is simpler than you may think.

The Presbyterian Church in Scotland didn't want bishops running its affairs, because that smacked of popery, but the king did. That led to a clash of wills that eventually spilled over into open defiance and then into war. The Bishops' Wars, as they were known, soon engulfed Ireland and England, and civil war broke out, which ended with the execution of Charles I and Scotland occupied by English forces led by Oliver Cromwell. The Restoration of the monarchy in 1660 put an end to occupation and republicanism, but it turned out rather badly for the Stewarts. James II and VII was overthrown in 1689, and the rule of an unashamedly Protestant king and queen, William and Mary, began. The Catholic threat had been finally scotched and a constitutional monarchy was established, committed to the Protestant faith. No more popery, no more the divine right of kings to rule! Was it worth it? Find out here.

The Reign of Charles I

Charles I came to the throne in 1625 following the death of his father James VI and I. Like his father he believed that he was an instrument of God and therefore had a divine right to rule – he wasn't answerable to his court, to his parliament or to his people, only to God. Sounds delusional, but this is what Charles and others who supported him at the time believed.

However, unlike his father, Charles lacked the wisdom and the political skills to sustain his reign for more than 24 years. Too arrogant, too stupid and too aloof, Charles succeeded in alienating his people north and south of the border.

Although he was crowned king of England, Ireland and Scotland in 1625, Charles waited for eight years to have his coronation in Scotland – and what a provocation it caused! The queen, Henrietta-Maria, was a Catholic and held a Mass in Edinburgh. Ornately dressed bishops were in attendance at the coronation ceremony, and there was a lot of kneeling before the altar. Presbyterians were almost apoplectic at the open display of popish sympathies. It all seemed like a massive snub to Calvinist Scotland – something that people didn't expect, because Charles had been born in Dunfermline Palace in 1600 and had been baptised at Holyrood by a Presbyterian minister. Still, he had left Scotland before his fourth birthday and returned only once, in 1633, for his coronation. So, maybe Scotland's hopes were misplaced.

The Book of Common Prayer and more trouble for Charles

The furore over the coronation was nothing compared to Charles's attempts to impose the English *Book of Common Prayer* on the Scottish Church without any consultation. Although it was drafted by Scottish bishops, the new prayer book was clearly the work of Charles's chief adviser, Archbishop William Laud.

The first reading of the book took place on 23 July 1637 in St Giles's Cathedral in Edinburgh, and it led to a riot. One of the serving women, warming the pew for her mistress, Jenny Geddes, reputedly threw a stool at the dean of the Cathedral, John Hanna, saying the immortal words: 'daur ye say Mass in my lug (dare you say Mass in my ear)?'

The ferment in Edinburgh spread like a plague to other parts of the country. The earl of Montrose summed up the general mood when he claimed that the book had emerged 'from the bowels of the whore of Babylon'!

This was the final straw for the Scottish nobility. Charles had succeeded in alienating the very people who should've been his natural supporters. But it wasn't just the coronation and the prayer book that left them feeling hacked off; there were other issues as well:

- ✔ **The Act of Revocation of 1625:** The act threatened to repossess all the lands gained by the nobility during the Reformation.

- ✔ **Promotion of bishops to the most important offices of state:** Archbishop John Spottiswoode was appointed chancellor, the highest political office in Scotland. This policy was hugely resented by the politically ambitious nobles, like John Stewart, Earl of Traquair and Lord Treasurer.

The Privy Council, the ruling executive in Scotland, suspended the reading of what now was known as 'Laud's Liturgy' and pleaded with the king to take a step back. But Charles was not for turning. He chose to make a stand on his authority, turning a crisis into a full-scale rebellion against kingly powers.

In December, an alternative government was formed in the shape of what was known as the 'Five Tables', a body made up of nobles, ministers, barons and burgesses, as well as an executive committee. Charles treated the Tables with contempt. He issued a new proclamation demanding obedience, pointing out that he and he alone was responsible for the new prayer book. The response was not what the king expected!

The National Covenant

The Tables meeting in Greyfriars Church in Edinburgh in February 1638 greeted the royal proclamation with derision. Rather than submit to royal authority, they presented the king with a challenge of their own making – the National Covenant. The following extract from the document contains the core of the argument against unrestrained royal authority:

> we declare before God and men, That we have no intention nor desire to attempt anything that may turn to the dishonour of God, or to the diminution of the King's greatness and authority; but, on the contrary, we promise and swear, That we shall, to the uttermost of our power, with our means and lives, stand to the defence of our dread sovereign the King's Majesty, his person and authority, in the defence and preservation of the foresaid true religion, liberties and laws of the kingdom; as also to the mutual defence and assistance every one of us of another, in the same cause of maintaining the true religion, and his Majesty's authority, with our best counsel, our bodies, means and whole power, against all sorts of persons whatsoever; so that whatsoever shall be done to the least of us for that cause, shall be taken as done to us all in general, and to every one of us in particular.

On the surface, it seems a fairly inoffensive statement of loyalty to the king. The architects of the document – Archibald Johnston (a lawyer) and Alexander Henderson (a minister) – had no desire to appear radical. But the National Covenant had buried within it something truly revolutionary: in a nutshell, it said that as long as the king was prepared to uphold the 'one true religion' – that is Presbyterianism – he would enjoy the full devotion and support of his people. But should he fail in this, then the people had the right to remove him.

So, there was no acceptance or recognition of the divine right of kings to rule – it was rule by the consent of Parliament and the General Assembly.

The National Covenant was signed by the political elite present but then distributed throughout the country for wider subscription. This gave the Covenant the status of expressing the settled will of the Scottish people. Those signing the document were known as the Covenanters.

Royal reaction

The marquis of Hamilton convinced Charles that he ought to reconvene the General Assembly of the Church of Scotland to meet in Glasgow in November 1638, for the first time in 20 years. The goal of reconvening the General Assembly wasn't clear, but the outcome was:

✔ They swept away everything that the Stewarts had worked for in trying to build a British Church (see Chapter 10):

  • Laud's Liturgy

  • The Five Articles of Perth

  • The Court of High Commission

  • The bishops (who had been banned from attending the General Assembly)

✔ The one true religion was declared the government of Scotland.

The General Assembly presented Charles with a dilemma of major proportions: how could he rule by divine right in England but only by the consent of Parliament and the General Assembly in Scotland? An impasse had been reached.

The royal solution was to send an army north, but that was risky because it meant recalling the English Parliament (which had not sat for 11 years) to vote funds for war. Charles wanted to avoid that, so a woefully ill-equipped army was sent north. The first of the Bishops' Wars began.

The Scots blocked the royalist advance at Berwick, and a treaty was drawn up between the king and the Covenanters. The Covenanters agreed to set aside the decisions of the 'illegal' Glasgow assembly. In return, Charles agreed to reconvene another assembly in Edinburgh and to a new sitting of Parliament. The treaty provided a breathing space but not a permanent peace – anyone with an ounce of sense knew that Edinburgh would simply confirm the decisions arrived at in Glasgow. But the Edinburgh Assembly went one stage further by separating Church and state – churchmen were banned from holding political office, and bishops were declared contrary to God's law.

While Charles was drawing up his plans for another war to enforce his authority north of the border, the Scots caught him off-guard. A Covenanting army under the command of Alexander Leslie, veteran of Continental wars, marched into the north of England. In August 1640, they defeated royal forces at the Battle of Newburn in the second Bishops' War.

Newcastle became the Scots' headquarters. They were now in a position to cut off coal supplies to London. Charles had no choice but to sue for peace. While in Edinburgh, between August and November 1641, he reluctantly recognised a Presbyterian Kirk and the right of Parliament to sit every three years. Worse still, he had to agree to write a blank cheque to cover the Scottish army's daily expenses in the north of England until peace was reached.

Charles was broke and there was no way he could afford to make good his promise to the Scots. He had no choice but to recall the English Parliament, which was anything but friendly to him! This began a chain of events that used to be called the English Civil War but is now known as the Wars of the Three Kingdoms.

The Wars of the Three Kingdoms

While Charles was in Edinburgh, things kicked off in Ireland. Catholics there had decided to massacre their Protestant brethren. An agreement with the English Parliament saw a Covenanting force of more than 11,000 men sent to Ulster to pacify the Irish rebels. While this was happening, England was sliding into civil war. The recalled Parliament made demands of Charles that would've stripped him of his royal authority. Rejecting these demands, Charles raised his standard at Newark in August 1642 and battle commenced. Such was the reputation of 'invincibility' of the Covenanting army that both the king and the parliamentarians sought military assistance from the Scots.

The Scots entered the civil war in England on the side of the parliamentarians. But there was to be a price for this assistance: the Solemn League and Covenant, in September 1643. By the terms of the Covenant, Presbyterianism, the one true religion, would also become the faith of the English. In reality, the wording was a bit vague, and it would have to be agreed to by the

English Parliament before it could be implemented once the war was over. There wasn't really much chance of this happening, but it sounded promising enough for the Scots to ally themselves with the English parliamentarians against Charles.

In January 1644, an army of more than 18,000 troops, 3,000 horses and 600 dragoons marched into England; another 8,000 troops followed in June. This tipped the scales in favour of Oliver Cromwell and Parliament, and the Royalists were well beaten at Marston Moor, near York, on 2 July 1644 and again at Naseby on 12 June 1645. God's army was invincible – or was it?

That invincible reputation came under close scrutiny in Scotland's own civil war. Between 1644 and 1645, a former leading Covenanter, James Graham, 1st Marquis of Montrose, in alliance with Irish rebels, inflicted a series of defeats on the Covenanters, at places such as Tippermuir, Inverlochy and Kilsyth. For his services, Montrose was made lord lieutenant and captain general of Scotland by a grateful Charles. The war was effectively ended when Montrose's army was defeated on a misty morning at Philiphaugh, near Selkirk, on 13 September 1645. But another blow was struck at the invincibility of the Covenanting army when Irish rebel forces under the command of Owen Roe O'Neill defeated the Scots at Benburb on 5 June 1646. Maybe God wasn't on their side after all?

We've got to talk about Charles

Charles surrendered to the Scottish army at Newark in May 1646. But what were they to do with the defeated king? What was he worth to them? God's own people decided to sell him to the English in 1647 in return for part payment of arrears of pay for the army amounting to £4.8 million in Scottish money. As one historian put it, they had entered England as part of religious crusade and left as mercenaries!

Handing the king over to Cromwell didn't go down well in some quarters north of the border. The 2nd earl of Lauderdale visited Charles in Carisbrooke Castle on the Isle of Wight. He promised him military support if he would agree to impose Presbyterianism on England for a trial period of three years. With his fingers crossed behind his back, Charles agreed and a treaty called the Engagement was signed in December 1647.

The treaty split the Covenanters in two. Most of the nobility favoured the treaty and were known as the Engagers, but the clergy and some of the more militant among the nobility refused to believe Charles's sudden conversion to the one true religion. So, when the duke of Hamilton led the Scottish army south, it was understrength, although still around 20,000 strong. The army was met at Preston by Cromwell's New Model Army of only 8,000 and cut to pieces in a battle lasting three days in August 1648. Charles himself was executed on 30 January 1649.

The Reign of Charles II

When news reached Scotland of the defeat of the Engagers at Preston, Presbyterian communities in the southwest of Scotland staged what proved to be a *coup d'état*. Known as the Whiggamores (the 'sour milk men' – *Whigg* is a Scots word for 'sour milk' or 'whey', the main diet of the poor), they marched on Edinburgh with the support of Cromwell. A radical Presbyterian government was formed led by lairds, merchants and parish ministers.

The first thing the government of the saints did was to pass the Act of Classes, which disqualified the leading Engagers from holding office; it also abolished all the legislation passed by previous Scottish parliaments. But the Whigs, as they came to be known, for all their radicalism, opposed the execution of the king.

In reaction to the execution, the Scottish government immediately offered the crown of not only Scotland but also England, Ireland and France to Charles's son, who at that point was in exile in The Hague, Holland. A bit presumptuous!

Charles II was proclaimed king by the Scots, but only on the basis that he was to be a covenanted king and that Presbyterianism was to be imposed on England and Ireland. No trial periods this time round. Charles II was willing to sign up to the Presbyterian agenda, but he wouldn't agree to unilateral imposition of it in other parts of Britain.

In early 1650, he sent the exiled Montrose to Scotland to renew war against the Covenanters, but his ragbag army was defeated at Carbisdale in April that year. Montrose was hanged and quartered at the Mercat Cross in Edinburgh. All the officers captured were put to the axe. 'Jesus and no quarter' was the rally cry of the Covenanters – now you know what that meant!

With no cards left to play, Charles II signed the Treaty of Breda with the Scots, accepting the conditions of the Scottish commissioners regarding the Covenant, and arrived in Scotland in June 1650.

Charles II may have been playing at being a Presbyterian, but how he was made to play! As one observer put it, 'He was made to observe the Sabbath with more rigour than the Jews.' This was a bit of a shock to the system – Charles had pretty much lived the life of a libertine in Holland. While at Falkland Palace, Fife, card playing, dancing and of course fornication was frowned upon. The young prince was preached at, prayed at and forced to listen to endless sermons. However, soon he was put out of his misery.

The Cromwellian occupation

On hearing the news of Charles II's arrival, the English Commonwealth declared war on Scotland. The former allies had fallen out badly with each other. But the strategy in forming a Covenanting army was weird to say the least. Instead of recruiting as many men as possible, the Scottish Parliament decided to purge the army of anyone suspected of low morals or of being king's men rather than Kirk men. Within three days, 80 officers and 3,000 men were sent home. God's army was no match for the New Model Army, and at Dunbar, near Edinburgh, they were routed. The English were in control of Edinburgh and most of the south of Scotland.

The Scottish army was pushed north. In a desperate attempt to increase the pool of soldier material a resolution was put to the General Assembly to annul the Act of Classes, a decision that split the Kirk. The majority of ministers who accepted the resolution were known as the Resolutioners, and the minority who opposed were known as the Remonstrators.

After formally signing the Solemn League and Covenant, Charles II was crowned king at Scone, near Perth, on 1 January 1651. Although there was bad blood between him and the Covenanters, he persuaded the Scots to have one last throw of the dice. An army was raised and an invasion of England began in the hope that English Presbyterians and Royalists would flock to join it. But as usual, the English failed to turn up! Cromwell's army met the Scots at Worcester on 3 September 1651 and destroyed them. After hiding up an oak tree, Charles escaped to France. Scottish resistance was over.

Some Scots will boast that although we've lost battles, we have never been conquered. Well, that view was shot to pieces –not only were the Scots conquered, but they were also incorporated via the 'Tender of Union' into the English Commonwealth! Scotland had 30 representatives (half of them English officers) in the Westminster Parliament. General George Monck was put in charge of Scotland.

Was it so bad? Well, being occupied by a foreign army of never fewer than 10,000 men would never be an enjoyable experience, and there were a few Royalist pockets of resistance until 1655. Passes were needed to move from one part of the country to another, and the total amount the Scots had to pay in taxes to pay for their subjugation was £90,000 year!

But, on the plus side, 'honest George' without any consultation with the Scots went about improving the justice and tax systems in more efficient and fairer ways. By 1655 it was said, 'a man may ride all over Scotland with £100 in his pocket, which he could not have done these five hundred years'.

The Restoration of the monarchy

The tight grip of the English occupiers began to loosen, although this had nothing to do with the Scots and more to do with the political chaos in England caused by the death of Oliver Cromwell in 1658. 'Honest' George Monck and his Scottish ally, Cameron of Lochiel, formerly sworn enemies of royalty, marched south in 1660 to restore parliament and the monarchy. Those who marched with him became the king's prestigious Second Foot Guards (later, the Coldstream Guards).

Charles II received his English coronation on 1 May. The 'Merry Monarch', as he was known, proved to be far from jovial when it came to Scotland – which he never visited again during the rest of his reign.

What did the Restoration mean politically for Scotland? In a nutshell, it restored five things:

- ✔ The monarchy
- ✔ The Privy Council
- ✔ The Scottish Parliament
- ✔ The Scottish judiciary
- ✔ The bishops

This didn't happen overnight – in fact, it took more than two years to introduce all these changes – but by the end of 1662 it was pretty much in place. An Act of Rescissory, passed on 1 January 1661, declared null and void all legislation passed by the Covenanting and Cromwellian regimes. It seemed like the last 30 or so years had all been a dream – no, a nightmare!

Purge, purge and purge some more

However, these changes came at a price for those who had run Scotland prior to restoration. The marquis of Argyll who had collaborated with the Cromwellian regime was executed, and his severed head was placed on a spike outside the Tolbooth in Edinburgh, replacing the severed head of the royalist Montrose. Montrose's remains were dug up and given a state funeral and interred in St Giles's Cathedral, Edinburgh, coincidentally facing Argyll.

The Scottish authorities resolved to make a public example of a minister, so the Rev Dr James Guthrie was singled out as one of the leading opponents of Charles I's religious policies. He was hanged and dismembered at the Mercat Cross, Edinburgh, on 1 June 1661. His snow-white head was cut off and was fixed on a spike in the Netherbow, where it remained for 27 years. Archibald Johnston, one of the drafters of the National Covenant of 1638, after being captured in France was hanged in 1663 and his severed head was placed on a spike, also in the Netherbow in the capital.

There was a determined drive to remove any vestiges of Covenanting rule. Both the National and Solemn League Covenants were declared treasonable. Those still subscribing to them were subject to execution for treason. An Oath of Allegiance to the crown was passed by the Scottish Parliament in February 1661. Those in the Kirk and the universities with Covenanting sympathies were driven from their posts. One-third of the Scottish clergy were ejected from their posts (in England, it was only one-tenth). In the southwest of Scotland alone, around 200 ministers were removed – a kind of religious equivalent of the later Highland Clearances!

The death rattle of the Covenanters

Some of the ministers didn't wait to be ejected – they voted with their feet rather than accept the authority of bishops and the monarch's control of the Kirk. After all, to the Covenanters, Charles II had signed the Solemn League in 1650 and his renunciation of it was tantamount to blasphemy. So, denied churches to preach in, they took to the fields. These field assemblies – or *Conventicles* – became the basis of resistance to the Stewart monarchy.

The Scottish government under the earl of Lauderdale tried to suppress the Conventicles through military force. This led to an armed revolt in 1666, known as the Pentland Rising. Around 1,000 men from southwest Scotland attempted to re-enact the Whiggamore Raid (covered earlier in this chapter) and march on Edinburgh. They were poorly equipped and driven back just outside Edinburgh, then crushed at Rullion Green on the slopes of the Pentland Hills by government forces under the command of 'Bloody' Tam Dalyell of the Binns. Fifty were killed; of those captured, 21 were executed and the others were banished to Barbados.

Still, the rising did encourage the Lauderdale government to take a softer line with the protestors, and a limited amount of toleration was granted. Two Indulgences were passed in 1666 and 1672, which restored a total of 132 dissident Presbyterian ministers to their parishes. Feeling that this would sidefoot the more militant Covenanters, Parliament passed the Act of Supremacy of 1669–70, making Charles II head of the Scottish Church and attending illegal Conventicles punishable by death.

These policies offset the positive impact of limited toleration and only served to increase the popularity of the Conventicles – some were attracting more than 10,000 worshippers. The Conventicles were guarded by armed men, so they began to look more like armies at prayer rather than worshippers.

To intimidate the dissidents, the government introduced, in 1678, the 'Highland Host', a force of 8,000 men from the eastern and southern Highlands. The Host soon gained a reputation for plundering the southwest of Scotland of shoes, money and horses. Although they weren't from the Gaelic heartland, they came to be seen by the Presbyterians not only as thieves but also as agents of Catholic or Episcopalian oppression. Something had to be done! The first response was assassination; the second, armed rebellion.

One of Charles's right-hand men in Scotland, the much-hated Archbishop James Sharp of St Andrews, was hacked to death in front of his daughter, Isabella (they were a bit more relaxed about celibacy then!), on Magus Muir, 3.2 kilometres (2 miles) from St Andrews on 3 May 1679. That action sparked an armed rebellion of 5,000 men in the west of Scotland. The rebels defeated a government force under James Graham of Claverhouse at Drumclog, on the border of Ayrshire and Lanarkshire.

The victory was short-lived – later that year, at the Battle of Bothwell Bridge, the duke of Monmouth, Charles's illegitimate son, mowed down the Covenanting army. Twelve hundred prisoners were taken and herded into Greyfriars Churchyard in Edinburgh – still known as the Covenanters' prison. Of that number, 340 had agreed within a fortnight not to take up arms against the king. More than 200 who refused to sign were put on a ship to the West Indies, but the vessel went down off Orkney and they all drowned.

The Cameronians are coming, the Cameronians are coming!

There was one last throw of the Covenanting dice. Richard Cameron, ordained as a minister in the Scots Church in Rotterdam, was a fundamentalist and a republican who had no time for monarchy or bishops. Indeed, he was so radical that he even scared the radicals within the Covenanting movement!

Cameron and his followers (known as the Cameronians) were Scotland's 17th-century version of the Taliban. Cameron said that Charles was 'the enemy of God and one of the most vile adulterers that ever lived'. He publicly declared war on the king in what was known as the Sanquhar Declaration of June 1680:

> We for ourselves do by thir presents disown Charles Stewart, that has been reigning (or rather tyrannising . . .) on the throne of Britain . . . we being under the standard of our Lord Jesus Christ . . . do declare war with such a tyrant and usurper and the men of his practices, as enemies to our Lord Jesus Christ, and his cause and covenants.

The government immediately offered a reward of 5,000 merks for his capture, and Cameron was hunted down and killed in a skirmish at Airds Moss in the River Ayr valley on 22 July 1680. The Cameronians continued the struggle after their leader's death, but it was David against Goliath without the sling! One of Cameron's disciples, James Renwick, was the last Covenanting martyr, executed in 1688.

The Killing Times

In the 1680s in Scotland (a period that became known as the 'Killing Times'), the Scottish government under the control of James, Duke of Albany and York, and later king, began to crack down severely on dissident Protestants.

The most important piece of legislation was the Test Oath of 1681, which forced those wishing to hold office to swear allegiance to the crown. Some high-profile refuseniks were the 8th earl of Argyll and James Dalrymple of Stair, Lord President of the Court of Session, both of whom were found guilty of treason and driven into exile.

Government troops under the command of Claverhouse forced people to take an oath acknowledging the king as supreme in matters of religion. If they refused, punishment was execution on the spot. It was king first and Jesus Christ second. In 1685, a hundred individuals – nearly all belonging to the Cameronians – were executed under the legislation and many other Covenanters were imprisoned.

At Wigton, Dumfries-shire, Margaret MacLachlan, age 65, and Margaret Wilson, age 18, were tied to stakes and drowned by the incoming tide of the Solway Firth for refusing to repudiate the Sanquhar Declaration. By October 1684, 160 men, women and children were imprisoned in Glasgow in what were said to be appalling conditions.

The Killing Times have to be put in perspective. More witches were burnt than Covenanters executed; more Quakers were imprisoned in England than Covenanters jailed in Scotland. But the important thing to grasp was not the extent of the killing but the damaging impression it made on the minds of Presbyterian Scotland.

The Reign of James II and VII

In February 1685, Charles II died of a stroke at the age of 54. Without a legitimate heir, his death brought to the throne his brother James II and VII, a self-confessed Catholic. James had none of the diplomacy and tact of his grandfather, James I and VI, but all the arrogance and stupidity of his father, Charles I. His reign lasted only a stormy three years.

Given his open Catholicism, his accession to the throne was surprisingly met with little opposition even in Presbyterian Scotland. James was master of the country, having thoroughly destroyed the Covenanting movement – the source of any likely opposition.

The proof of his mastery came early in his brief reign when he survived a plot hatched by Protestant exiles in Holland to overthrow him. The plotters were his nephew, the duke of Monmouth, and Archibald Campbell, Earl of Argyll. Argyll left Holland in June 1685 with three ships and 300 men, mainly from his own clan, the Campbells. He raised his standard at Kintyre, an act that coincided with Monmouth's landing in southwest England.

The trouble was that no one was really interested in supporting this rebellion. Argyll found it difficult even to raise the bulk of his own kinsmen. Both men suffered the same fate. Monmouth was defeated at the bloody Battle of Sedgemoor on 6 July 1685; Argyll didn't even get the chance to fight! He was captured at Inchinnan, near Renfrew, and taken as a prisoner to Edinburgh. There was no need for a trial – Argyll had already been tried and sentenced to death (see 'The Killing Times', earlier in this chapter). The king confirmed the earlier death sentence and ordered that it be carried out within three days of his captors receiving the confirmation. Seventeen of Argyll's followers were also executed, and another 150 were transported to the West Indies. His co-conspirator, Monmouth, was beheaded along with 250 of his men.

James's victory over the ragbag armies of Argyll and Monmouth convinced him that he had the support of the Scottish people and, in particular, the Highland clans. Moreover, the economy was growing and he was in a very strong financial position. So, he felt that he had a personal mandate to bring about changes in the religious life of the country.

Perhaps James was delusional, but at the opening of the Scottish Parliament in 1685, he sent a letter requesting new penal laws against disobedient Presbyterians. Under royal pressure, Parliament passed an Act that stated the following:

> whoever should preach in a conventicle under a roof, or should attend, either as preacher or as a hearer, a conventicle in the open air, should be punished with death and confiscation of property.

In March 1686, James followed up with another letter – this time to the Scottish Privy Council, advocating toleration for Catholics. This paved the way for the Declaration of Indulgence of 1687, also known as the Declaration for Liberty of Conscience, in which all subjects were free to practise their own particular faith free from persecution.

It sounded good, but there was a subtext: James saw Protestantism as a 'false' religion and promoted Catholicism and Catholics as much as he could. But this was in a country where only 2 per cent of the population was Catholic, and they were mainly found in the Western Isles. So, from the outset his policy of religious toleration was viewed in Scotland and in England with suspicion. Catholic converts, such as the earl of Melfort, were placed in high office at the expense of Protestants. James further outraged Presbyterians by setting up in Holyrood Palace of all places a Jesuit college, a printing press and a Roman Catholic chapel. No wonder the Edinburgh mob tore up the place! Toleration seemed to be of benefit only to Catholics.

James didn't only annoy and upset the Scots; he was also doing an excellent job of provoking the English. One of his most contentious actions was to fill the Irish army with Catholic officers and promote Catholics to heads of university colleges. He also dispensed with Parliament. The game changer was the birth of a son, James Edward Stewart, by his second wife, Mary of Modena, in 1688. The thought that the boy would be brought up a Catholic and continue his father's policies well into the future was too much for the English. He had to go!

The Glorious Revolution of 1688

Fearing that James II and VII would join with the French and attack the northern Protestant states, and without consulting the Scots, the English opposition invited the Dutch ruler, Prince William of Orange, and his wife, Mary, James's daughter by a first marriage, to accede to the throne. William landed in Devon with an army of 14,000 men on 5 November 1688, but there was no one to fight. James and his family had run off to France. It seemed that James had abdicated, so there was no constitutional problem in offering the throne jointly to William and Mary.

The Glorious Revolution was quick and virtually bloodless, although for the Scots and the Irish there was nothing peaceful or speedy about it.

The new monarchs' first act was to convene Parliament and issue a Bill of Rights for the English, which established a constitutional monarchy and declared that no Catholic could be king or queen or hold any official post.

But the Scots couldn't claim that James had abdicated because he hadn't been present in Scotland when the crisis broke. Thus, the Scots put forward a different constitutional argument: by running away, James had forfeited his crown. That failed to satisfy opinion in Scotland, and a crisis loomed.

The solution was to call, at the request of William of Orange, a Convention of the Scottish Estates on 16 March 1689 to consider the rival claims of the two candidates for the crown of Scotland. The claim of James VII was set out in a letter hastily written on board a ship at Brest, as was William's, but it was considered so extreme and stupid, with no guarantees for the Protestant faith, that it proved a major factor in making up the Convention's mind to offer the crown to William II. Only five of those present voted in favour of James.

Depriving James of the crown was followed on 11 and 13 April by two momentous documents – the Claim of Right and the Articles of Grievance. The content of them can be summarised in five key points:

- ✔ No Catholic could be monarch or bear office.
- ✔ No Royal Prerogative could override the law.
- ✔ Parliament was to meet frequently and be free to debate.

✔ The consent of Parliament was necessary to raise *supply* (funds for war).

✔ There would be no bishops.

This was the basis on which William accepted the throne of Scotland on 11 May 1689. These actions provoked the first Jacobite rebellion.

The Jacobite Rebellion of 1689

The rebellion of 1689 was the first of a number of attempts to put the Stewarts back on the throne (see Chapter 12). Claverhouse, now Viscount Dundee (or 'Bonnie Dundee', as Sir Walter Scott referred to him in a poem written in 1830), raised the standard of the deposed king on Dundee Law in early April. Then, with 50 followers, he headed north to raise an army.

On 27 July, he defeated a formidable government force under the command of General George MacKay at the Pass of Killiecrankie, Perthshire. The battle was short, as a contemporary account makes clear:

> It was past seven o'clock, Dundee gave the word. The Highlanders dropped their plaids. It was long remembered in Lochaber that Lochiel took off what was possibly was the only pair of shoes in his clan, and charged barefoot at the head of his men. . . . In two minutes the battle was won and lost.

The Highland charge proved successful at Killiecrankie, as it had on many previous occasions. Mackay was less complimentary about his men, calling them 'the vilest cowards in nature'. But although short, Killiecrankie was an extremely bloody battle. More than 30 per cent of Dundee's 2,500 men were killed, as were around 60 per cent of Mackay's force of 4,000. The way was open to set the Highlands alight with the spirit of rebellion, but there was a problem: the charismatic Viscount Dundee was killed in battle by a stray bullet. Nevertheless the Jacobites continued the fight, and the army grew to somewhere between 3,000 and 5,000 men.

Another problem arose: the Cameronians. The Jacobites were fierce, but the Cameronians were fierce and 'madd' as one government officer put it. These religious fanatics who had been hunted down by Claverhouse had a chance to even up the score. Eight hundred Cameronians, led by 20-year-old William Cleland, met a far superior Jacobite force at Dunkeld, Perthshire, on 21 August 1689 and held out in a four-hour siege of the town.

The siege led the Highland army to withdraw, both sides claiming an inconclusive victory. After Dunkeld, the rising lost impetus and was finally defeated at Cromdale, near Grantown-on-Spey, on 1 May 1690. With the Jacobite threat neutralised, at least for the time being, William turned his attention to Ireland. James's Irish army was crushed by William at the Battle of the Boyne on 12 July 1690.

On the back of the defeat of the Jacobites, the Presbyterian Church was re-established in June 1690 and the abolition of patronage and the Act of Supremacy followed in July. Over the next few years, some 182 ministers were ejected from their charges for refusing to say prayers in public for William and Mary; in the period 1689 to 1702, the total reached 664. However, the purges signified that after all the blood that had been spilled and the thousands who had died, once and for all, Scotland was to be a Presbyterian state.

Everyday Life in 17th-Century Scotland

Seventeenth-century Scotland has long been thought of as a country of abject poverty, religious fanaticism, lawlessness and violent disorder. While all this is true, to some extent, it's also something of an unfair characterisation.

Scotland was not uniquely poor – plenty of places around the world saw poverty. Scotland can only be judged to have been economically backward when compared to the most advanced economies of the time.

As to violence, the continuation of clan warfare into the 17th century and the existence of blood feuds did make the country seem disorderly compared with much of western Europe, and royal power admittedly was relatively weak. But incidences of private violence were uncommon. Yes, rebellions took place, but they were few and far between.

In constructing such a picture of Scottish society, there seems to be an English bias. English rebellions against the arbitrary power of the monarch in the 17th century are depicted as a part of a respectable constitutional struggle to bring about representative government with a parliament limiting royal power. But when the Scots rebel, this is interpreted as a symptom of the almost innate tendency of the Scottish people to disorder and violence, fuelled by religious fanaticism. In this section, I try to correct the distortions of Anglo-centric history.

Living conditions

Life in the 17th century was frequently nasty, brutish and short for the majority of Scots. Housing conditions were pretty primitive, underlined by the fact that no examples of ordinary homes survive from this period (suggesting that the homes were of poor quality). Houses were usually of the one-room type, and humans shared them with farm animals in the winter – hygiene was not an issue!

The common people had a monotonous diet – generally oatmeal in various varieties, from porridge to cakes (giving Scotland the nickname 'land of the cakes'). Kale or cabbage dishes were also common. Bread was made from peas – only the rich could afford wheat. The diet was primarily vegetarian with occasional bits of fish and meat.

Famines were accepted as a way of life, manifestations of the will of God. But they could have a devastating effect on death rates (see Chapter 12 for the impact of the 1695 famine). Plagues, likewise, could kill thousands. In 1644, it was estimated that 9,000 people died of the plague in Edinburgh alone; three years later, plague wiped out about a quarter of Aberdeen's population of 9,000.

Worst off were those who, even in good years, lacked the means to survive, having neither land nor craft to support them. Wandering beggars were a major problem in Scotland, as they were in all European countries at this time. The naturalist John Ray visited Dumfries in 1662 and remarked that the countryside abounded 'with poor people and beggars'.

The attitude of the authorities was to punish rather than help those beggars they considered to be able-bodied (that is, able to work but for whatever reason not doing so), and to help those they considered deserving (that is, women, orphans, the old and the infirm). The able-bodied were subject to branding and whipping.

The number of beggars could swell by the thousands during harvest failures as men, women and children left home in search of food. The movements of people we see in the developing world in places like Ethiopia and Somalia during famines is similar to what it was like in the 17th century for the hungry.

Emigration: Let's get out of here!

Large numbers of Scots left for greener pastures in the 17th century. The total may have reached a quarter of a million by 1700. Around 50,000 settled in Ireland, but many went farther afield. Poland attracted a great many Scottish merchants, soldiers and pedlars with an estimated exile community of between 30,000 and 40,000. The loss of population to England is unknown, but it must also have been substantial.

These are only guesses, but one thing we do know for certain is that between 1625 and 1642 the Privy Council sanctioned the enlistment of more than 47,000 young men, about one in five of that age group, to fight as mercenaries for foreign powers. The Munro clan alone had 3 generals, 8 colonels, 5 lieutenant-colonels and 30 captains fighting in the Swedish army of Gustav Adolph.

The social structure

The social structure in rural Scotland differed from the social structure in urban Scotland. In this section, I explain the differences between the two.

Rural Scotland

Scotland, like other European states, was a hierarchical society where the authority of the big landlords could be all-pervasive. The landlords dispensed justice – they had the right to try all crimes except treason, until the establishment of the High Court of Justiciary in 1672. Obeying your landlord was wise, even if he ordered you to defy royal authority, because the king and his government were remote and seldom in a position to punish disobedience. Even if the king could, he punished the landlord and not his men.

So, the power wielded by the landlords was awesome. But did that mean that tenants had no rights? Yes and no. Most of the land leases were unwritten, so tenants were at the mercy of landlords and could be evicted at any time. But there were common-sense and traditional limits to the exercise of power. A landlord wanted – and needed – more than just rent money from his tenants. He needed their loyalty to serve him in battle; that in it put a brake on how much he could screw out of them in rent and to what extent he could use eviction as a means of intimidation.

Many tenants claimed that they had a hereditary or 'kindly' right to their land, and sensible landlords recognised this. The concept of kinship was strong in Scotland, and it created a social bond between the tenant and the landlord. As head of the kin group, the landlord expected the unquestioning loyalty of his kin group, but in return, he had certain obligations to his tenants to respect their rights and to look after them, particularly in time of trouble or distress. One example might be the McNeil chief on Barra, who took it upon himself to find wives and husbands for widowers and widows, replace cattle of tenants lost in bad weather and maintain old people in his own home.

Urban Scotland

In 17th-century Scotland, very few people – only about 3.5 per cent of the total population – lived in towns. By 1700, this figure had increased to a little more than 5 per cent, still well below England and Wales.

Edinburgh was far and away the largest town in Scotland. In 1640, it had around 30,000 inhabitants; the population rose to somewhere between 40,000 and 47,000 by 1690. Glasgow was the next largest town, with a population of around 10,000 in 1630; like the capital, it experienced a burst of growth in the second half of the 17th century. By the 1630s, there were only ten towns in Scotland with a population of more than 4,000; an old, established town like Dunfermline had only 220 houses in 1624.

What attracted people to the towns was the range of services and entertainment they provided. Craft workers like wigmakers, silk weavers and confectioners found a clientele for their goods. For the better off, particularly the nobility, a whole range of financial and legal specialists were on tap. The largest occupational group in the towns was domestic servants, followed by tailors.

The social impact of religion

By the time of the National Covenant in 1638 (see 'The National Covenant', earlier in this chapter), the Presbyterian Church had established a strong presence in every parish in Scotland, a development that transformed the lives of those in the countryside more than any other economic or social change.

The Protestant faith emphasised that man's primary loyalty was to God, and no matter what your position was in society, through prayer, you could get direct access to him. This idea was potentially subversive – it was literally saying that in cases of conflict, God's will overrode loyalty to landlord or monarch.

The necessity of communing directly with God led the Covenanters to stress literacy – you had to be able to *read* the Bible to find the word of God. By the mid-17th century, a good proportion of men could read in Scotland. The purpose was Calvinist indoctrination, but when people were literate, who knows what else they might read?

The Presbyterian Kirk might have had literacy standards, but its impact on the social life of the common people was negative, to say the least. Popular culture in the form of traditional festivals, rituals, customs and beliefs were suppressed as ungodly. How much of traditional peasant culture was destroyed by these zealots is difficult to say, but the destruction was extremely thorough.

The repression went beyond popular culture to virtually all aspects of life and behaviour. There was a particular emphasis on trying to bring the sex lives of the people into conformity with biblical teachings. The Kirk had strict views on incest, extending it to cover relations between a man and a woman with no blood relationship. So, a widow could not marry the kindred of her late husband, and a man couldn't marry any of his late wife's kindred.

As to sexual intercourse, it was a pleasure confined to marriage. Fornication and adultery were frowned upon, and the Kirk went to great lengths to root out what it called 'filthiness'. Those who transgressed against the sexual code were ritually humiliated on Sundays in front of the congregation, or publicly flogged, or banished from the community if they persisted. For those considered guilty of sexual crimes of a deviant nature, capital punishment was imposed.

In 1675, a man convicted of having carnal knowledge of a mare at Inveraray sheriff court was sentenced to death. He was first strangled and then burnt at the stake. The horse didn't get off lightly either – it was also put to death!

It's witchcraft

Women (and sometimes men) accused of being witches were put to the stake; around 4,000 people were burnt to death as witches between 1590 and 1662. The Restoration began with the largest witch hunt in Scottish history. Scotland was not alone in this – a general witch craze was afflicting most of western Europe in this period.

But how could you tell who was a witch and who was not? A common way of providing evidence to use against suspects was the Devil's Mark. When a man or a woman made a pact with the Devil, the Devil supposedly left his mark on them. Professional witch-prickers were employed to search them out. They would prick the suspect, and if the suspect didn't bleed, he or she was seen to be in league with Satan!

Eventually, witch-pricking came to be seen as fraudulent. After the 1670s, the whole idea of witchcraft was being discredited. Among the elite, there had been growing scepticism, even at the time, that many witch hunts had been about score settling among neighbours and that innocent people were being executed. The use of torture to exact convictions became increasingly regarded as unreliable. This growing scepticism about witchcraft may have reflected the spread of literacy and learning in Scotland, which was beginning to overtake superstition as a way of understanding the world.

Although in decline, witch hunts were not eradicated as late as 1697. A child made accusations of witchcraft against 20 individuals, 7 of whom were put to death.

Culture and education

The aim of the Presbyterian Church to establish a parish-based educational system available to all may not have been realised in the 17th century, but at least it was a worthy ambition. Schooling did spread – for example, Fife had only 3 schools before the Reformation, but by 1633 it had 43. Even remote counties in Scotland saw a rise in the number of schools. The growth of schools saw an increase in literacy.

'Literacy' might only mean that someone could sign his name on a marriage register. How far a person could read or write in sentences is anyone's guess.

On the basis of these crude literacy tests, Scotland was a fairly literate society, certainly more so than the north of England. Illiteracy was unknown among the male ranks of the nobility; around three-quarters of male craftsmen and tenant farmers could write their names. Illiteracy increased the further you went down the social scale; among women of the lower orders it was pretty much universal.

Scotland also had five universities compared to two in England. Most of the scholars had been trained on the Continent; indeed, more than 50 Scots had graduated from Leiden University in Holland by 1700. Although the main purpose was to train the Presbyterian clergy, the universities also provided an education for the sons of the nobility. The latter were schooled in Latin, history, philosophy and science, allowing them access to a common European culture.

Higher learning created a thirst for knowledge, which laid the foundation for the emergence of the book trade. Most of the published books and pamphlets dealt with religious themes, but after 1680 there was a focus on more earthly issues. Only between 25 and 50 items were published in any given year up to 1695, but in 1695 this number increased to 250. Some of the well-to-do had enormous libraries – Archbishop Robert Leighton of Glasgow owned 4,000 volumes.

Although much despised, James II and VII oversaw the creation of two new cultural establishments that shaped Edinburgh's development as a centre of the Enlightenment (see Chapter 12): the Advocate's Library (now the National Library of Scotland) and the Royal College of Surgeons. James also established royal appointments, such as the historiographer royal in 1681 and the geographer royal in 1682. Maybe he wasn't all bad?

The greatest cultural achievements were in the area of the law. The monumental work of Sir James Dalrymple of Stair, in his *The Institutions of the Law of Scotland Deduced from Its Originals* (1681), codified the civil law of Scotland. Sir George MacKenzie, in his *Institutions of the Law of Scotland* (1684), did the same for the criminal law.

The 17th century may have been a century of major religious and political upheavals, but it also saw a flowering of institutions and learning among the blood and gore, which would lay the foundations of the much more impressive cultural achievements of the 18th century. The country may have been poorer than the major international states such as England and Holland, but compared to countries of its own size, in many ways its experience was fairly similar.

In a European context, Scotland was not the exception to the rule – it was the rule!

Chapter 12

The Unmaking of a Nation (1690–1750)

During this period, Scotland's political leaders voluntarily gave away its sovereignty and became part of a new country called Great Britain. Historians continue to debate the reasons behind the decision of the Scottish Parliament to vote itself out of existence in 1707. But whether it was for the money or for something nobler, the fact is that the Scottish national identity, which had been built around opposition to English imperialism, had to recast itself – the Scots had to learn to become North Britons.

The Union was not popular with everyone. Many Scots, especially in the Highlands, still owed allegiance to the Stewart Dynasty, and in a number of revolts, they attempted to reverse the settlement arrived at in 1707. Through these struggles, Scotland was cemented into the Union politically, militarily and economically.

The 'Ill Years'

The 1690s proved to be a decade of disaster for Scotland. They began with the Glencoe Massacre. The middle years also witnessed famine on a massive scale, and the end of the decade brought with it the debacle of Darien. Not for nothing were the 1690s referred to as the 'Ill Years'.

The Glencoe Massacre

Following the defeat of the first Jacobite rising in 1689 (see Chapter 11), the Highland chiefs were called to swear allegiance to King William I's government. Due to technical issues connected with the timing, the clan MacDonald failed to register their allegiance by the closing date of 1 January 1692. The secretary of state for Scotland, John Dalrymple, was not too unhappy at the news, and a plot was hatched at the highest level of state to exterminate the MacDonald clan.

Dalrymple wrote to the king:

> Glencoe hath not taken the oath at which I rejoice. . . . It will be a proper vindication of the public justice to extirpate that sept of thieves. . . . It must be done quietly, otherwise they will make shift for both men and cattle. . . . Let it be secret and sudden.

King William I signed a document on 1 January 1692 ordering the massacre of the MacIains of Glencoe, an affiliated clan of the MacDonalds. The man chosen to lead the massacre was Robert Campbell of Glenlyon, a member of the sworn clan enemies of the MacDonalds, the Campbells, although most of his men were not. Campbell was acting not for his clan but for the king, and his orders came from the lord advocate, Dalrymple of Stair. Although the government ordered the attack by putting a Campbell in charge, the massacre was framed to look like a clan feud.

The orders were to:

> fall upon the rebels . . . and put to sword all under seventy. . . . You are to secure all the avenues, that no man escape. . . . This by the King's special command, for the good and safety of the country, that these miscreants be cut off root and branch.

Like the best-laid plans, this one didn't go very well. The armed reinforcement didn't arrive on time; the attack took place two hours before it should have. Only 40 of 150 MacDonald clan members were killed; the rest escaped. The chief of the MacDonald clan was shot in the back as he got out of bed; his wife was stripped naked and her rings were pried from her fingers by soldiers' teeth. In addition, their homes were burned and their cattle driven off.

The massacre caused a national outrage. It was no worse than the massacre on the Isle of Eigg two years earlier, carried out mainly against women and children, in which rape figured highly. But Glencoe was different because it was seen as a case of 'murder under trust', which was a heinous crime in Scotland, carrying the same penalty as treason. For almost two weeks the soldiers and clansmen had lived together – eating, drinking, gambling and playing shinty. Then the soldiers had attempted to slaughter the clansmen!

A parliamentary inquiry was set up, but the only one involved who took the high jump was Dalrymple, who was forced to resign in 1695. To sweeten the pill of dismissal, he was given an earldom in 1703.

The Glencoe Massacre backfired on the government because it increased support among the clans for the Stewart cause and strengthened the hand of the Scottish government against English interference.

Widespread famine

From 1695 to 1699, Scotland suffered a series of bad harvests that led to the deaths of thousands of Scots from starvation and disease. The Scottish population fell by around 15 per cent – in some parishes, that number was as high as 50 per cent!

Poverty was endemic, and the old system of poor relief could not cope with the numbers looking for help. The extent of the problem can be appreciated from two contemporary accounts. Patrick Walker, an itinerant pedlar, wrote that in the Highlands,

> Meal became so scarce . . . and many could not get it. . . . I have seen . . . women clapping their hands, and tearing the clothes off their heads, crying 'How shall we go home and see our children die in hunger?' . . . deaths and burials were so many and common, that the living were wearied in the burying of the dead.

A Lowlander wrote,

> Some die by the wayside, some drop down in the streets, the poor sucking babs are starving for want of milk, which the empty breasts of their mothers cannot furnish them, everyone may see death in the face of the poor that abound everywhere.

The attitude of the authorities was callous, to say the least. One university professor advised the hungry on which herbs were edible and suggested they eat cats. Ministers recommended fast days for the starving!

Those who could escape it got out. Fifty thousand Scots left for Ulster in the 1690s. Poland was also home to thousands of Scottish merchants, pedlars and soldiers. The loss to England has never been worked out, but during the 17th century something like a quarter of a million Scots left to look for a better future. This only made matters worse for the economy – the drain on population had a negative impact on growth.

The famine added to Scottish economic worries. When a solution to colonise was proposed as a way out, the Scots almost bit the hand of the proposer. But it ended in disaster.

The Darien Scheme

The *Darien Scheme* was an attempt to establish a Scottish trading colony on the Isthmus of Darien, now Panama. It's evidence of people's endless capacity for self-delusion, as long as the sales pitch is right.

The project was the brainchild of William Paterson, a financier from Dumfriesshire, based in London, who had spent some time in the West Indies and had been tinkering with the idea of establishing a colony since 1684. The establishment of the Company of Scotland Trading to Africa and the Indies in 1695 gave Paterson his chance to turn his dream into reality. The company's aim was to raise finance from both English and Scottish merchants, but opposition in the English Parliament quashed any hope of investment from that area. The Scots had to go it alone. They raised £400,000 in a couple of weeks (roughly equivalent to £42million today).

The proposal seemed, on the surface, to be absolutely brilliant. The new colony, New Caledonia, on the Isthmus of Darien, would link the Caribbean with the Pacific, which would cut out the hazardous journey around Cape Horn and establish itself as a great port linking the trade from the two oceans. Money made would enrich an impoverished Scotland.

The theory was good, but in practice the adventure was doomed to failure. Here's why:

- ✔ **The Scots were burrowing into Spain's Latin American Empire, so the Spanish weren't too pleased to see them.** In fact, a Spanish naval blockade of New Caledonia in 1700 finished off the Scottish colony. In the game of empires, sea power was everything; the Spanish had a large navy, whereas the Scots had only two frigates. So, Spain won.

- ✔ **The English weren't too helpful.** King William was cosying up to Spain in an attempt to stop Louis XIV inheriting the Spanish Empire on the death of Charles II. The Scots were getting in the way and had to be put in their place in spite of the fact that William was also the king of Scotland, a place he never visited. So, the English merchants were ordered not to provide the colony with supplies. The Scots weren't too happy with William!

- ✔ **The settlers were inexperienced and the climate was pretty tough; plus, disease was rife.** There were two expeditions. The first, in November 1698, left the port of Leith with 1,200 people; only 1 in 4 survived. Propaganda put out by the company suggested it was all going well and that encouraged a second expedition, in November 1699, of about another 1,000 people. But it was all a disaster and, in the end, only a few hundred of the 2,500 settlers survived the experience; most died from disease.

The Spanish forced a surrender of the settlers after only eight months.

The consequences of failure were profound:

✔ Economically, the scheme's failure was a massive blow to the country; something like a quarter of the liquid capital of Scotland was tied up in it. Investors included the great and the good, like the leading courtier the duke of Queensberry, down to merchants and financiers. Paterson himself lost a large sum of money.

✔ Constitutionally, there were questions raised regarding the Union of the Crowns (see Chapter 10). How could a monarch of both Scotland and England favour one over the other? Many people were furious over William's role in the collapse of Darien.

The English were held responsible. Anti-Englishness grew in the immediate aftermath. The *Annandale,* a ship hired by the Company of Scotland to trade with the Spice Islands, was seized by the East India Company because its mission contravened the company's monopoly in that part of the world. Fury broke out in Scotland, which led to the deaths of three innocent sailors in the port of Leith.

In July 1704, an English ship, the *Worcester,* was declared an East India Company-owned vessel. In revenge for the *Annandale,* its cargo was impounded and its crew farcically charged with piracy for having earlier sunk a Company of Scotland ship, the *Speedy Return.* The master of the *Worcester,* 21-year-old Thomas Green, and two crew members were hanged in Edinburgh on 11 April 1705 in spite of Queen Anne's instructions that they be pardoned. The hangings were an act of defiance, but in reality they only proved Scotland's political impotence. It was a spiteful response to wounded national pride. After all, Scotland was only a small country on the periphery of northern Europe.

Relations between the two countries could not have been bitterer at this point. Yet surprisingly, within two years of the hangings, Scotland and England would do something unique: form an incorporating union.

The Union Debate

Like any other great event in history, the union between Scotland and England is a complicated one. The result was the same for both countries, but the motivations for union were different. Indeed, the events leading up to union have all the hallmarks of the best political drama: backstabbing, threats, posturing, greed, bribery, corruption and occasional acts of principle.

Before I deal with some of these sordid issues, let me make two key points:

✔ There was nothing inevitable about parliamentary union, despite the Union of the Crowns in 1603 (see Chapter 10).

✔ The idea of parliamentary union was not a popular one in Scotland, and much of the pressure for it came from the English.

The Scots weren't too pleased with the English over the Darien Scheme (see the preceding section), but the English made matters worse by passing the Act of Settlement in 1701, which excluded the Stewarts and all Catholics from the English throne. Queen Mary wasn't producing any more heirs, and her younger sister Anne, despite 17 pregnancies, was unlikely to answer the call– her only surviving child, the duke of Gloucester, had died at the age of 11 in July 1700. So, the English decided to offer the throne on Anne's death to the Protestant Sophia, Electoress of Hanover, and granddaughter of James VI and I, but unfortunately she died two years before Anne. So, the electoress's son, George, Elector of Hanover, acceded to the throne of Great Britain in 1714.

The Scots may have agreed to this plan, but they were never consulted, so they were understandably angry. In retaliation for the Act of Settlement, the Scottish Parliament passed three pieces of legislation designed to assert Scottish independence:

- **The Act of Security (1704)** restated Scottish prerogatives in regard to the Scottish crown. After Anne, no future monarch of Scotland and England could take Scotland to war without the explicit consent of the Scottish Parliament.

- **The Act anent Peace and War (1704)** asserted the right of Scotland to pursue an independent foreign policy after Anne's death.

- **The Wine Act (1704)** allowed the import of wine from France into Scotland at a time when England was operating a blockade against French trade.

The English saw these acts as deliberate provocation. And to make matters even worse, the Scots had hinted that they could conceive of a future monarch who might be Catholic. After all, the Old Pretender, James Francis Edward Stewart, the son of the deposed James II and VII, was living it up in France at Louis XIV's expense and was ready, on the death of Anne, to restate the Stewart claim to the throne (see 'The Jacobite Revolts', later in this chapter).

The succession crisis, as it was known, had to be solved. The English knew that, and they scored a winning goal in the diplomatic tit-for-tat: the Alien Act of 1705. The Scots were given ten months to agree to the succession of Sophia and to make progress on the issue of union. Failure to do so would have dire economic consequences. All exports to England from Scotland would be banned.

As a contemporary put it, 'our country's fortunes depend on England: the only wealth we have comes from the cattle and horses we sell there'. He might have added linen as well. But the threat was real and that concentrated the minds of the Parliament in Scotland. It allowed Queen Anne to nominate 31 hand-picked commissioners from England and Scotland to discuss union.

Given the fractious relations between the two countries, it seems surprising that the deal was struck so quickly. In a poorly attended session, on 16 January 1707, the Scottish Parliament voted 110 to 67 for an incorporating union. The big question is why?

Bought and sold for English gold?

The question of why the Scottish Parliament voted for an incorporating union is something that divides historians as much as it does the Scottish public. Here are some possibilities:

- ✔ **Bribery and corruption:** People in this camp echo Robert Burns, who said that the Scots were 'bought and sold for English gold'.

- ✔ **Statesmanship:** According to the people who believe statesmanship was the reason, in difficult circumstances, the Scottish negotiators got the best possible deal for Scotland.

- ✔ **No alternative:** Another view can be best described as TINA (there is no alternative). People who see this as the reason for the union believe that Scotland was so impoverished that the country had no alternative but to negotiate for union, especially given the Alien Act, which had been passed by the English Parliament.

There is no doubt that some of the opposition in the Scottish Parliament were bought off.

The most celebrated case was the leader of the opposition Country Party, the duke of Hamilton. In return for getting the Scottish Parliament to agree to allow the queen to appoint the negotiation commissioners (ensuring minimal opposition), he was given an English dukedom in 1711.

On top of the promise of land and offices of state, there was the brown envelope! Earl of Glasgow David Boyle was given £20,000 to incentivise waverers to vote for union. The main Scottish negotiator, the 2nd duke of Queensberry, received more than £12,000 in 'back pay'. The leader of the *Squadrone Volante* (Flying Squadron), the 2nd marquis of Tweedale, who delivered the 25 or so votes of this independent grouping in the Scottish Parliament for union, received £1,750 in 'back pay'. The other leading Squad noble, Roxburgh, received a dukedom.

But the biggest sweetener of all was the 'Equivalent'. Article 15 of the Treaty of Union guaranteed to compensate those Scots who had lost money in the Darien Scheme. Just over £398,000 was set aside for compensation, which meant that the investors would not only get back what they put into the scheme but also receive 5 per cent interest. Because every well-to-do person had lost money in Darien, the Equivalent was a huge incentive to deliver the right result.

However, some of the sums used to bribe Scottish nobles were so small that it's difficult to make a case that it was simply votes for cash. Plus, many members of the opposition continued to speak out against union, particularly Lord Belhaven and Lockhart of Carnwath, who was one of the few commissioners opposed to union.

Also, you shouldn't view supporters of union as simply men on the make. There were many principled pro-Unionists, such as Sir William Seton of Pitmedden, who argued

> by this Union, we'll have Access to all the Advantages in Commerce, the English enjoy; we'll be capable, by a good Government, to improve our National Product, for the benefit of the whole Island; and we'll have our Liberty, Property and Religion, secured under the Protection of one Sovereign, and one Parliament of Great Britain.

Given the division of the world into major power blocs, for these men it was better to be a small fish in a large pond than a large fish in a small one. The Court Party and its ally, the *Squadrone Volante,* mustered enough votes to ratify the Treaty. Failure to ratify the treaty may have led to invasion from England because troops were massing on the border. So, union may have been a forced marriage of convenience, but what was in it for the Scots?

The Treaty of Union

The Treaty of Union passed by the Scottish Parliament on 1 May 1707 contained 25 articles or clauses that dealt with a variety of issues:

- **Economics:** Fifteen of the articles dealt with economic issues, like a single currency, taxation, weights and measures. The most outstanding was the right of Scots to have access to the largest free trade empire in the world, something for which the Scots had been clamouring for many decades. There was also guaranteed financial support to help develop Scottish industry, particularly linen and woollens, and of course there was the Equivalent (see the preceding section).

  The Equivalent and support for Scottish industry was good, but the weak Scottish economy was opened to competition from more advanced and efficient producers south of the border. Plus, Scotland may have been allowed to freely trade with the English colonies, but could its merchants take advantage of the new situation? Finally, Scotland would have to take on a proportion of English national debt and accept higher taxes. So, what you give with one hand you take away with the other.

  There may have been opportunities, but there were also threats.

- **Politics:** Scottish representation in the new Parliament was to be 45 members of Parliament and 16 peers of the realm sitting in the House of Lords.

  Scotland had the same level of representation as Cornwall did in the new Parliament of Great Britain. Scotland went from 227 members of Parliament in the Scottish Parliament to just 45 in the Westminster Parliament of 513 members, and only 16 seats in the House of Lords. How in a parliament that was overwhelmingly English were Scottish interests to be represented?

> ✔ **Religion:** By Article 2 of the treaty, this was to be a Protestant state as 'papists and persons marrying papists' were excluded from succession to the throne. The Protestant settlement of 1689 was ratified, and a further act guaranteeing the independence of the Presbyterian Church was added.

> ✔ **Law:** The independence of the Scottish legal system was also guaranteed.

Popular reactions to union

The majority of Scots had no say in the Union debates. As late as 1788, there were only 2,668 registered voters in Scotland. To say the Treaty of Union was unpopular in Scotland would be an understatement. One of the commissioners claimed that: 'The whole nation appears against the Union.' Even the very pro-Unionist Sir John Clerk of Penicuik stated that the Treaty of Union was 'contrary to the inclinations of at least three-fourths of the Kingdom'.

Public opinion was voiced against the Treaty as it passed through Parliament, with petitions from half of the shires and one-third of the burghs, as well as from presbyteries and parishes, totalling 80 in all. In November 1706, the presbytery of Lanark protested that union would render Scotland subject to 'strangers to our constitution . . . who may judge it for the interest of Britain to keep us low and entirely subject to them'.

The Convention of Royal Burghs also petitioned against the union; not one petition sent to the Scottish Parliament favoured an incorporating union. On the day the treaty was signed, the bellringer of St Giles's Cathedral, Edinburgh, rang the bells to the tune of 'Why Should I Be So Sad on My Wedding Day?'.

There were also riots. The anti-union mob in Edinburgh had kept up an almost daily harassment of known pro-Unionist members of Parliament during the parliamentary debates. In November and December 1706, there were riots in Edinburgh and Glasgow; in towns like Dumfries and Stirling, angry mobs burned the Treaty.

The English author and spy Daniel Defoe spoke of the Scottish protestors as a 'rabble' and the worst of its kind. To him the Scots were a 'hardened, refractory and terrible people'.

When the day of union arrived, the mob broke loose in Edinburgh and a riot ensued, spreading to Glasgow and several other Scottish burghs. Threats of widespread civil unrest resulted in Parliament imposing martial law.

The Union of Parliaments was pushed through against the popular will. Perhaps this was the greatest fraud against the Scottish people. But how would it be held together when so many were against it? The short answer is: by blood!

Economic consequences of union

One of the main selling points of union was the promise of greater future prosperity for Scotland. There were some grounds for long-term optimism:

- ✔ **Linen:** Gaining access to English domestic and colonial markets and enjoying the protection of British tariffs, output increased and laid the foundation for future industrialisation (see Chapter 13).

- ✔ **Tobacco:** The industry became hugely important and profits made in the trade were invested in building up the infrastructure of Clydeside and promoting industrial growth.

- ✔ **Agriculture:** Agriculture became more market orientated and a great wave of improvement began.

However, these benefits weren't apparent to contemporaries, as the number of riots taking place at the time clearly shows. One of the more serious riots was in 1725 in Glasgow as a direct result of the introduction of the Malt Tax, which raised the price of a barrel of beer by three pence – highly unpopular! Troops fired on protestors, leaving 8 dead and another 18 wounded. Order wasn't restored until two weeks later when General Wade arrived with foot soldiers and seven troops of dragoons.

There is very little evidence that there was much growth in the economy in the first half of the 18th century. Trade links with continental Europe and Scandinavia were disrupted. The woollen industry was undermined by English competition, as were paper-making and candle-making. Only black cattle exports seemed to grow (from 30,000 heads in 1707 to 80,000 in 1750), but the profits derived from the trade were of benefit only to a few Scots and there is no evidence that they were used to promote improvements in agriculture or the economy as a whole. In his *A Tour Thro' the Whole Island of Great Britain* (1726) Daniel Defoe admitted that the increase of trade and population, which he predicted would result from union, was 'not the case, but rather the contrary'.

The golden age of prosperity did not arrive, and economic disappointment provided the black cloth to attempts to destabilise the union.

The Jacobite Revolts

The Jacobites' goal of replacing the Hanoverians with the Stewarts has been the subject of a lot of myth-making over the years. So, let me set the record straight: the Jacobite cause was a dynastic one. It wasn't intended to restore the independence of Scotland (although some of its supporters may have harboured such hopes).

If you look at the Stewart past, it's almost wholly concerned with the unification of the two countries: one king, one church and one parliament (see Chapters 10 and 11). But the rebellions – and there were a number of them – became a peg on which the people could hang their dissatisfactions with the union. If you were denied high office (as many nobles were), if you were a Catholic or an Episcopalian and you resented the dominance of the Church of Scotland, if you were suffering as a manufacturer from English competition, you could vent your grievances by supporting the Stewart cause.

Although most of the armed support for the Stewart cause came from the Scottish Highlands, this was not a Lowlands versus Highlands confrontation, or a Scotland versus England one. Support for the Jacobite cause came from all over Britain. Even in the Highlands, not all the clans were for the Stewarts – major clans like the Argylls and the Campbells supported the Hanoverian government.

The 1715 rebellion

The exiled Jacobites in France were happy that the union wasn't popular in Scotland. In 1708, one exile, Simon Fraser of Lovat, convinced Louis XIV to launch an invasion using Scotland as a platform to attack England. The French didn't want to overthrow Queen Anne's regime; their goal was to force England to negotiate a peace and overturn the union settlement.

With the support of French troops, the Old Pretender, James Francis Stewart, (a man of 20 years!) was supposed to raise the standard in Fife or Lothian, but he contracted measles. The weather intervened and the French fleet was blown off course and eventually routed by Admiral Byng.

Still, the grievances began to stack up even higher:

- ✔ **The Equivalent** was three months late in arriving, and only a quarter of it was in coin; the rest was in English Exchequer Bills. It should have all been in coin.

- ✔ **The Toleration Act of 1712** allowed Scottish Episcopalian clergy to use the 'liturgy of England', and that really annoyed Presbyterians.

- ✔ **The Patronage Act of 1712** restored the rights of landowners to choose and appoint parish ministers.

- ✔ **The Scottish Privy Council** was abolished.

- ✔ **The Malt Tax** was applied by English members of Parliament to Scotland, provoking a boycott of Parliament by Scottish members of Parliament.

Every section of Scottish society was up in arms. The union was so unpopular with both the English and the Scots that when, in June 1713, Viscount Seafield, a man who in the past had laboured long and hard for union, moved in the House of Lords to have the union dissolved, the motion was defeated by only four votes!

Widespread discontent was the backdrop to what some historians have seen as the most important challenge to the union of 1707. Most sections of Scottish society were in some ways hacked off with the union. When Queen Anne died in 1714, there were disturbances all over England against the elector of Hanover, George I, assuming the throne. With England on the point of implosion, the time seemed ripe to re-establish the Stewart Dynasty.

The rebellion begins

In August 1715, under the pretext of a deer hunt, a plan for armed rebellion was hatched at the castle of the earl of Mar in Braemar in Aberdeenshire. On 6 September, the standard of James III and VIII was raised at Mar's castle. Let battle commence!

The plan was simple: march on Edinburgh, take the city and hook up with the Jacobites in the Borders and those in northern England, preparing the way for James to land in the southeast of England and head a victorious march to London to reclaim the crown. But as the national bard, Robert Burns, wrote: 'The best laid schemes o'mice an' men / Gang aft a-gley [go wrong]'.

The 1715 rebellion was a disaster from start to finish. The leader, the earl of Mar (popularly known as 'Bobbing John' because he shifted sides so often), was formerly an advocate of union and a Hanoverian, but he became a Jacobite when he lost office after the 1715 election. He was also an indecisive general. He sat in Perth, which he had captured in September 1715, waiting for further reinforcements, seemingly unaware that there were Jacobite risings in the Scottish Borders and in Northumberland. Failure to act decisively had dire consequences.

The death of the French king, Louis XIV, five days before the rebellion also meant that the Jacobites were denied the support of a major rival to Britain. Louis's successor, Philippe Duc d'Orleans, was more interested in negotiating a peace settlement with George I than encouraging a Jacobite rebellion.

The Battle of Sheriffmuir

The decisive battle of the rebellion took place at Sheriffmuir, near Dunblane, on 13 November 1715. The outcome was unclear in military terms, but politically it was a disaster for the Jacobites. With an advantage of four men to one, Mar's army was unable to defeat the government's troops. The momentum was lost, and Mar's opponent, the duke of Argyll, was left in control of the key road to the south.

Meanwhile, in the south, the Jacobites, under the leadership of Viscount Kenmure and William MacIntosh of Borlum, were defeated by government troops at Preston the day after Sheriffmuir. When James VIII eventually landed at Peterhead on 22 December of that year, the game was up and he returned to exile in France in February 1716, along with Mar, and never saw Scotland again. The French promptly requested that the Jacobite court leave, and Italy became the next haven for the Stewarts.

Retribution

The British state took revenge on the main participants in the rebellion. Viscount Kenmure was executed, and the peerages of Mar, Seaforth, Nithsdale, Panmure and Southesk were forfeited. Thomas Foster, who had raised the rebellion in the north of England, was executed too. No jury in Scotland would have convicted them, so other Scottish Jacobites were tried at Carlisle for treason and many were sentenced to death. An Act of Grace and Pardon was passed in 1717, which freed those Jacobites still in prison.

In the Highlands, a Disarming Act was passed in 1716, banning the carrying, but not the owning, of arms in public. This legislation applied only to clans considered disloyal to the house of Hanover.

The 1719 rebellion: They're at it again!

You may have thought that the debacle of 1715 would've put an end to Jacobite scheming and plotting, but not a bit. In 1719, another rebellion was instigated, this time with the help of Catholic Spain.

The plan was two-pronged. An invasion fleet of 29 ships carrying 5,000 Spanish troops, with arms for 30,000 more, left Cadiz in March 1719, intending to land in southwest England, where Jacobite sympathies were still strong. Another, much smaller invasion force carrying 307 Spanish infantrymen and George Keith, 10th Earl of Marischal, landed on the Isle of Lewis, where they joined up with 25 or so Jacobites under the marquis of Tullibardine. This was a diversion, though – the main event was to be in England.

However, the main Spanish fleet was decimated by a violent storm off Corunna where they were supposed to pick up the Old Pretender. The smaller force carried on, oblivious to what had happened. (If only the mobile phone had been invented earlier!) They made their base at the picturesque Eilean Donan Castle on the shores of Loch Alsh, until they were forced from it by the royal navy. By this time, augmented by a thousand clansmen, the 'plan' was to march on Inverness, but the two commanders could never agree on a strategy. The joint Spanish/Jacobite march was halted at Glen Shiel on 9 June 1719 by a combined force of English and Scottish troops from Inverness under General Wightman. It was the last battle involving foreign soldiers on British soil.

The main Jacobite leaders escaped. Keith fled to Prussia, where, in spite of a pardon, he lived the rest of his life and worked as the Prussian ambassador to France and later Spain. The 274 Spanish prisoners taken in battle were returned to Spain in October 1719.

Pacification of the Highlands

The British state had to ensure that these troublesome uprisings were extinguished for good. The first part of the strategy of pacification was to tame the martial spirit of the Highlanders. In 1725, a second Disarming Act was passed forbidding all Highlanders to carry arms and ordering them to hand in those arms that they owned to the authorities.

Another part of the policy was to increase the state's presence in that part of Scotland. In 1726, General George Wade, an Irishman with expertise in dealing with internal dissent, was appointed commander-in-chief in Scotland. Wade went about building forts and roads to connect them in the western and central Highlands. Using the labour of 600 men, in 11 years, 402.3 kilometres (250 miles) of road were built, including one from Perth to Inverness (the route of the current A9) and 28 bridges. These roads connected the four Highland garrisons. It was the British version of the Iron Curtain.

The strategy was a mixed success. Most of the blood feuds between the clans had run their course by the 1715 rising. The Highlands were more peaceable, but with an estimated 150,000 cattle going to markets in the south, rustling was still a problem.

Rob Roy MacGregor, a cattle thief and national hero, personified the problem of integrating the Highlands into north Britain. In 1711, wanting to expand his cattle herd, MacGregor borrowed the sum of £1,000 from James Graham, 1st Duke of Montrose, with whom he had been doing business for a decade. However, MacGregor's chief herder disappeared with the money, a fortune at the time even for a wealthy cattle and land owner. Declared bankrupt, a warrant was issued for MacGregor's arrest. He was branded an 'outlaw', and the good duke confiscated his lands and cattle, evicted his wife and children, and burned down his house.

For eleven or so years Rob Roy, with about 20 men, waged a personal war against Montrose, raiding his land and his cattle. He even found time to fight at Glen Shiel with the Jacobites. Although he was arrested a number of times, Rob Roy always managed to escape, making him a hero in the Scottish glens. He was finally caught by General Wade in 1725 and held in Newgate Prison in London. Daniel Defoe wrote a fictionalised account of his life in 1723 called *Highland Rogue,* making Rob Roy a legend in his own lifetime, and influencing George I to issue a pardon for his crimes just as he was about to be transported to the colonies in 1727. He died at the age of 63 in his house at Inverlochlarig Beg, Balquhidder, on 28 December 1734.

The Highland world Rob Roy was a part of was also coming to an end.

The 1745 rebellion

The '45 was the last and most celebrated of all the Jacobite risings. It's been romanticised and mythologised so much that it's difficult to separate fact from fiction. But from the start, it seemed mission impossible.

The French king, Louis XV, embroiled in a war over the Austrian succession with Britain, decided that it might be a good idea to invade his enemy (shades of 1715?). In March 1744, plans for a pre-emptive strike were drawn up, in which Scotland was to play a minor role. Three thousand troops were to land in Scotland, which was supposed to be a signal for a general rising of the Scottish clans; 12,000 troops were to land in England near London under the command of Charles Edward Stewart (Bonnie Prince Charlie, also known as the Young Pretender), shown in Figure 12-1. But the 'Protestant winds' blew fiercely, and the French fleet lost 12 ships off Dunkirk, 7 of them with all hands. The invasion plan was abandoned by the French, but it didn't deter the Young Pretender.

Figure 12-1:
Charles
Edward
Stewart.

© Hulton Archive/Getty Images

Charles pawned his mother's jewels to purchase cannons, guns and broadswords, as well as two frigates – the *Elisabeth* and the *Du Teillay.* The *Elisabeth,* with half the arsenal and 100 marines, was intercepted by an English man-of-war and forced to turn back. Charles, dressed as a divinity student, boarded the *Du Teillay* and set sail for the island of Eriskay, in the Western Isles. He landed on 23 July 1745 with only seven men, before moving on to the little village of Arisaig, near Fort William.

The reaction of the Scottish clans to the prospect of another rising was lukewarm – and you couldn't blame them. Strong supporters of the Jacobite cause, such as Cameron of Lochiel, told Charles to return to France, as did the chief of the MacDonald clan. The Catholic islands of Barra and South Uist took no part in the '45. When Charles raised his standard at Glenfinnan on 19 August 1745, only 1,200 men rallied, but when he took Perth on 4 September, more joined the cause. But he still had an army of only 2,000 men. Then Edinburgh fell on 17 September, and Charles had to fight his first battle four days later at Prestonpans, just outside Edinburgh, against an equal force of government troops led by Sir John Cope.

The Battle of Prestonpans must be one of the shortest battles ever fought – it lasted only ten minutes! Cope was court-martialled for incompetence but later acquitted. After this, the Jacobite army grew to 5,000 foot soldiers and 500 cavalry. The British government was in a panic and a new verse was added to 'God Save the King':

> God grant that Marshall Wade,
>
> May by thy mighty aid Victory bring,
>
> May he sedition hush,
>
> And like a torrent rush,
>
> Rebellious Scots to crush,
>
> God save the King.

Against the advice of his brilliant, but never trusted, commander, Lord George Murray, Charles decided to invade England. The progress was nothing short of phenomenal. By 4 December, only 27 days after crossing the border, the Jacobite army was at Derby, about 209.2 kilometres (130 miles) from London. At this point, things started to fall apart. Why?

> ✔ **They were outnumbered.** Only 200 Englishmen had joined the Jacobite army. The government troops under the duke of Cumberland and Marshall Wade numbered 30,000.

> ✔ **The Jacobite Council of War was divided.** Charles and his Irish favourites wanted to march on London; the Scottish generals wanted to retreat to Scotland.
>
> ✔ **The troops were tired, hungry and homesick.**

On 'Black Friday', 6 December 1745, the Jacobite army headed north. Was the decision a major miscalculation or a stroke of tactical genius? Who knows? But London was certainly in a panic – shops closed and the Bank of England feared a run on its deposits. However, north they went, inflicting a defeat on the government forces at Falkirk in January 1746.

Retreating further north, they took Fort Augustus, named after the duke of Cumberland, but failed to take Fort William. Cumberland was sent north to confront the Jacobite army. The decisive battle took place at Culloden just outside Inverness in April 1746. It was the last battle to be fought on British soil.

The Battle of Culloden

Against Murray's advice, Charles decided to stage a surprise night attack on Cumberland's army. Troops were marched 16 kilometres (10 miles) to Nairn, but 3.2 kilometres (2 miles) short of the town they realised that the British troops were far from asleep and they decided to head back. They had left at 8 p.m. and were back in camp by 6 a.m., exhausted and hungry.

The duke realised that the Jacobites were in no condition to fight, and he raised his troops at 5 a.m. and marched toward the Jacobite encampment. By 1 p.m. on 16 April 1746, both armies had taken up positions 457.2 meters (500 yards) apart. But the Jacobites were outnumbered nearly two to one. Large numbers of Lowland Presbyterians fought on the government side. Not fair.

Tactically, Cumberland had worked out how to deal with the famous Highland charge. With his men organised in two lines of fire, he expected the first to be broken but the second to hold with a row standing, a row leaning forward and a row kneeling. The firepower was continuous – as one row fired the other reloaded. The result: a massacre. By 2 p.m. it was all over. Between 1,500 and 2,000 Jacobites lay dead, compared to 50 government troops.

But the Jacobites still had an army of 4,000 men and Murray was convinced that they could regroup and carry on the fight. The battle was lost, but there was a war still to win. But Charles characteristically made the wrong decision and gave up the cause. He decided to return to the Continent and sent his followers a farewell message:

> I see with grief I can at present do little for you on this side of the water, whereas, by my going to France instantly, however dangerous it might be I will certainly engage the French court either to assist us effectually and powerfully, or at least procure you such terms as you would not obtain otherwise.

The summer's hunting

Charles was right: escape is a dangerous business, particularly when there's a reward of £30,000 on your head. For five months, government troops hunted him, but he continually evaded them by jumping from one island to the next.

With the help of loyal supporters, he took on various disguises. Dressed as a woman, 'Betty Burke', maid servant of Flora MacDonald, Charles crossed from South Uist to Skye in early June. By July, MacDonald was in jail, but the prince was still on the run. He successfully escaped to France in late September, never to return to Scotland. He died 42 years later, his body ravaged by drink and debauchery.

The Butcher of the Scots

The duke of Cumberland earned the title of 'Butcher' because of his savagery toward the defeated Highland soldiers. He issued an order of 'no quarter' to the wounded and allowed his troops to wage a campaign of rape, murder, theft and torture against the Highland population.

The leaders of the rebels suffered probably more than the common soldiers. Lords Balmerino and Kilmarnock were publicly beheaded. Lord Lovat, who had taken no part in the rebellion, was tried and executed in London; he was the last peer of the realm in Britain to suffer this fate. A grateful government increased Cumberland's Civil List allowance from £15,000 to £40,000 and Handel composed 'See the Conquering Hero Comes' in his honour. Who says butchery doesn't pay?

But the repression didn't end there. The British state took steps to destroy Highland culture and the power of the chiefs. The castles of Cameron of Lochiel, Glengarry, Lovat, MacPherson and Chisholm were burned to the ground. Forty chiefs lost their lands. Some of the more interesting suggestions in Parliament for dealing with the so-called savage Highlanders were the following:

- Sterilising all Jacobite women
- Destroying all seed corn so as to 'extirpate the inhabitants of the cursed country'
- Clearing the Highlands of people and re-colonising them with God-fearing folk in the south

However, the government ignored this advice and introduced legislation aimed at destroying the warrior society of the north:

- All Highlanders were to take an oath of loyalty to the king.
- The Disarming Acts were enforced with greater vigour.

✔ The wearing of Highland dress was forbidden through the Act of Proscription.

✔ The chiefs were stripped of their power to administer justice in their territories through the passing of the Heritable Jurisdictions Act of 1747.

National Identity: Turning Scots into North Britons?

Although the Jacobite rebellions were not primarily intended to restore Scotland's sovereignty, the problem of fashioning a British identity was one that needed addressing. How were the Scots to be turned into North Britons?

The Presbyterian elites of Lowland society had a massive stake in the union and feared a restoration of the Catholic Stewarts. Indeed, anti-Jacobite feeling was strongest in the most advanced areas of the economy. Glasgow celebrated the news of Cumberland's victory at Culloden Moor. The GLASGOW JOURNAL brought out a special large-print edition on 28 April 1746 to record 'the greatest rejoicings that have been at any time in the past'.

The Scottish literati also played its part in reconciling the Scots to their new identity. To them, the union was the key to liberation from Scotland's dark and fractious religious past and economic backwardness. They rewrote the Scottish past, rubbishing it as mythical and in many cases beyond belief. But by rewriting history to suit the Unionist agenda, Scotland, as later writers such as Sir Walter Scott pointed out, was in danger of losing connection with its past.

The solution was to allow them to be Scottish and at the same time British – a dual identity. Scottish identity was maintained by preserving the main institutions of Scottish society: the Presbyterian Church, the law, the education system and the right of Scottish banks to issue their own currency.

Political Management

What the English wanted more than anything from Scotland was security. After 1707, England expected peace and an acceptance of the Hanoverian regime from politicians in Scotland.

With the abolition of the Privy Council in 1708, it was up to a small number of law officers to administer Scotland. They reported to the English secretaries of state. Between 1713 and 1725, and again between 1742 and 1746, a secretary of state for Scotland existed, but generally it was the legal eagles who ran the show. If they couldn't deliver the goods, they were removed from office – as happened to Lord Advocate Robert Dundas after the Malt Tax riots of 1725 (see 'Economic consequences of union', earlier in this chapter). Scotland was being run from London via a few willing stooges.

But even if they were stooges for Westminster, how did they go about delivering the Scottish votes for the government? In a word, *management,* a euphemism for bribery and corruption. The system of political management was run during the classic period 1725 to 1741 by Archibald Campbell, 2nd Duke of Argyll, and his brother John, Earl of Ilay. The first was a soldier, the second a lawyer. Both were born in Surrey and educated at Eton, and both were very anti-Stewart and pro-Hanover – a product of the fact that they had been made to watch the execution of their grandfather in 1685 by the last Stewart king, James VII and II.

With the Scottish Parliament abolished, there was nothing for politicians north of the border to argue and fight about except for a share of the spoils. The English weren't interested in Scotland after union. Between 1727 and 1745, only nine acts of parliament were passed concerning Scotland. This meant that those put in charge of Scottish affairs were in a strong position to influence the politics of the country. After all, only 0.2 per cent of the population had the vote.

Given this situation, the Argylls used all means at their disposal to give London what it wanted. After 1725, the setting up of a series of quasi-autonomous non-governmental organisations (quangos), such as the Board of Trustees, to promote economic development in Scotland created a great deal of patronage – jobs for willing boys. In spite of this, the Argyll regime only delivered 30 of the 45 parliamentary seats before 1741 and only 19 after that. It was a system still in need of perfecting.

Part V

The Remaking of a Nation (1750–1918)

Consider Scottish women and the question of suffrage in an article at www.
dummies.com/extras/scottishhistory.

In this part . . .

✔ See how one of the poorest nations in western Europe produced great scientists and thinkers who invented the modern world.

✔ Understand the reasons behind the Industrial Revolution and how it affected the Scottish people.

✔ Examine the Highland Clearances and question the role of the landlords in replacing people with sheep.

✔ Consider the changes in the political system and see how a tiny elite of landowners gave way to a mass democracy.

✔ Identify the impact of the First World War on the people of Scotland.

Chapter 13

A Nation in Transition (1750–1832)

In This Chapter

▶ Recognising how industrialisation changed Scotland

▶ Seeing how the Highlanders were forced from their homes

▶ Supporting the British Empire

▶ Looking at Scotland's role in the Enlightenment

▶ Seeing the emergence of political radicalism

*B*etween the defeat of the Jacobites at Culloden in 1745 (see Chapter 12) to the passing of the Great Reform Act of 1832, Scotland was a nation in transition. It was evolving from a largely rural society to an industrial/urban one. The old ways were disappearing or transforming, as Scotland entered a new age.

The rapid growth of industry was accompanied by a shift of population from the countryside to the towns – in some cases voluntary (as in the Lowlands) and other cases violently (as in the Highlands). The unplanned movement of large numbers of people created appalling social problems that threatened the stability of the state itself.

On the back of these changes, groups that advocated a radical philosophy based on the rights of man emerged in the 1790s and continued into the 1820s. These groups threatened to overturn the old, corrupt political order of the landed classes.

The Scots were living through turbulent times. Nobody could predict how things would turn out.

Transitioning from an Agrarian Society to an Industrial One

Industrialisation is an area of history that is full of a tremendous amount of argument and debate. Historians disagree about the dating (when it actually began), the speed of change and the social consequences. Some historians talk about an Industrial Revolution of rapid change; others talk about evolution or slow, balanced changes. Each view has its merits. But if you view the process as regional rather than national, then it's possible to talk of an Industrial Revolution.

In Scotland, the west experienced a rapid and decisive shift from *primary production* (raw materials and agriculture) to *secondary production* (manufacturing). There was also an irreversible shift in population away from the land to towns and industry. But what caused this shift? In a word: cotton.

The cotton industry grew rapidly – from one factory in 1778, situated in Penicuik, near Edinburgh, to 198 factories in 1838. By that time, the industry was employing 36,000 workers in spinning and another 45,000 to 50,000 hand-loom weavers working in their homes or small workshops.

The rise of cotton was unexpected – in 18th-century Scotland, linen had been the main textile. But cotton showed itself more adaptable to steam power than linen was – linen's fibres snapped rather than stretched when under pressure. Prior to the application of steam power, cotton mills were situated in the countryside near fast-flowing water. One consequence of using steam to power the spinning machinery was that mills began to be situated in towns rather than in the countryside. The west of Scotland with plentiful supplies of fuel and power, and its suitably damp and wet climate, became the major centre of cotton production in Scotland.

The rapid growth of the cotton industry also encouraged growth in other industries, so there was a knock-on effect:

- ✔ **Coal was needed to supply the hungry demands of the cotton factories, so coal production had to be increased (see Figure 13-1).** The application of steam-powered machinery not only allowed for mine shafts to be sunk deeper, but also made it possible to drain water-filled coal seams.

- ✔ **Engineering experienced an expansion.** Machine tools, such as the lathe, were developed to make and maintain spinning machinery. As the industry grew, so did the ability to easily and accurately cut metal parts. This in turn made it possible to build larger and more powerful engines.

- ✔ **Iron was another industry to undergo expansion as a result of the cotton industry's spectacular growth.** The cotton mills were iron-framed, and the machinery was also made from iron. However, it wasn't until 1828 that iron production grew in line with the rapid strides being made elsewhere. James Neilson's hot blast furnace massively reduced the amount of fuel needed to smelt iron ore, and this caused production to grow enormously. It also led to a fall in the price of *pig iron* (basic material which is worked up into shapes or wrought iron in the forge), which encouraged greater use of iron (see Chapter 14).

Figure 13-1: Coal production increased during the Industrial Revolution.

© The Print Collector/Alamy

Working conditions

The first factory workers weren't men but women and children, and many of the latter were orphans. Men initially refused to enter factories because they were considered demeaning places to work, but as the machines got bigger and heavier, spinning came to be seen as a 'man's job'.

What was it like to work in these industries during the first phase of industrialisation? The short answer is: hellish. Here's an extract regarding the working conditions of women and children from a government report into the coal industry:

> in the east of Scotland, where the side roads do not exceed from twenty-two to twenty-eight inches in height, the working places are sometimes 100 and 200 yards distant from the main road; so that females have to crawl backwards and forwards with their small carts in seams in many cases not exceeding twenty-two to twenty-eight inches in height. The whole of these places, it appears, are in a most deplorable state as to ventilation. The evidence of their sufferings, as given by the young people and the old colliers themselves, is absolutely hideous.

On the main roads of some pits, the coal was carried on the backs of girls and women; in one of the pits, a sub-commissioner found a girl, only 6 years old, carrying half-a-hundredweight of coal, and making 14 journeys a day, each journey being equal to ascending to the top of St Paul's Cathedral. It was not until 1842 that these practices were outlawed.

Things were no better in the cotton industry, where long hours and low wages were the norm for women and children. Children were employed as piecers and mule scavengers, which involved crawling under machinery to pick up cotton or tying the broken threads. They worked some 14 hours a day, six days a week; on Sundays they were expected to turn up for religious instruction, so no rest, even for the innocent! The work was dirty and dangerous: some children lost hands or limbs, others were crushed under the machines and others were even decapitated.

Employers saw nothing wrong with these working conditions, and it took a number of government investigations before laws could be introduced to limit the hours of work of women and children in the 1830s and 1840s.

TECHNICAL STUFF

Was Scotland truly 'industrial'?

There is no doubting the strong evidence of progress in industries linked to cotton, such as coal and iron. But overall, the phenomenon of industrialisation in Scotland was more narrowly based on textiles. Compared to England, the industrial development that took place north of the border was not as broad based, and it didn't go as far or as fast. Here's why:

✔ As late as 1830, the majority of the Scottish population still worked in domestic service (mainly women) and agriculture. Agriculture was not just the largest employer of labour; the sector also took the biggest share of the gross national product.

✔ Industry was less developed due to the abundance of cheap labour, which held back the application of machinery. Because of this, cotton weaving was not mechanised until the 1850s.

Scotland had to wait a bit longer than England before it could claim the status of an 'industrial nation'. That had to wait until the development of the integrated heavy industrial structure of shipbuilding, engineering, and iron and steel, and that occurred after 1850.

So, rather than use the term the *Industrial Revolution* to mark the period 1780 to 1830 in Scotland, it would be better to use the word *industrialising*. This term recognises the profound changes Scotland experienced, without claiming that Scotland experienced full-scale industrialisation. The foundations of industrialisation were being laid. Industrial society was still a work in progress.

People tend to think of industrialisation as being a manly thing. They picture men shovelling coal, digging ditches and laying railway tracks, but in reality industrial Britain was built on the backs of women and children.

Urban growth and urban crisis

Historians disagree as to how many people living in a defined space constitute a *town* rather than a *village* – some say at least 1,000, some say 5,000 and some say 10,000. If we define a town as any place with 10,000 or more residents and measure urbanisation in those terms, Scotland ranked seventh out of 16 European countries in 1750, fourth in 1800 and second in 1850.

In 1750, fewer than one in ten Scots lived in towns of 10,000 or more residents; by 1850, more than one in three did. Most of this growth took place after 1780. For most of the 18th century, Scotland had lagged way behind other countries. However, when growth occurred in Scotland, it was more rapid than the growth experienced by any other European society. In the decade from 1791 to 1801, urban dwellers increased by 25 per cent over the previous decade; this figure increased by nearly 33 per cent in the decade from 1801 to 1811.

What caused this spectacular development?

✔ Because of agricultural changes, such as the enclosure of land and labour-saving machinery, the need for labour decreased, and the landless labourers flooded into the towns.

✔ Trade grew as a result of the union of 1707. The growth of ports resulted in increased demand for labour to work in services (as waiters, barbers, messengers, clerks and so on).

✔ Most importantly, due to the application of steam power to machinery, industry moved from the countryside to the towns. By 1839, 98 cotton mills were situated in Glasgow.

There is little evidence that the expansion of towns did much to immediately impact urban death rates. Indeed, it took until the 1820s and 1830s before the horrors of unplanned growth were fully apparent. From 1780 to 1815, the larger towns were generally free of epidemics. However, after 1815, the killer diseases of typhus and cholera struck with a vengeance. As a result the death rate skyrocketed. Even in the more prosperous town of Edinburgh, the death rate increased by nearly 20 per cent from the decade of 1810 to 1819 to in the decade from 1830 to 1839.

The richer society became, the higher the death rate. Here's why:

✔ Low wages meant poorer diets and a greater susceptibility to disease.

✔ Unemployment wasn't recognised by the Poor Law, so there was no relief in hard times for the unemployed and their families.

The case of Glasgow

Every county in Britain had its problems, but nowhere were they as great as in Glasgow. Fever mortality was higher than any other comparable city in Britain. The main killer was typhus (or 'Irish' fever, as it was popularly known). By 1835, more than 50 per cent of the admissions to the Glasgow Royal Infirmary were suffering from typhus, whereas in 1815 that number had been only 10 per cent.

But in the face of these appallingly high death rates, Glasgow's population continued to grow faster in times of economic distress than when the economy was doing well. As employment in agriculture fell, people had no choice but to move to the cities for work. Things weren't any better in the cities, but at least there was the prospect of work and wages. Glasgow soaked up displaced Highlanders and the Irish, both of whom had a higher birth rate than the locals.

The horrendous social circumstances didn't go unnoticed, and there is some evidence of a willingness in governing circles to address the problems. Because dirt was seen as a major cause of disease, street cleaning was made a public duty. Private companies were set up to provide clean drinking water. The problem of sanitation was also addressed – from 1814 to 1819, 6.4 kilometres (4 miles) of sewers were laid. But in spite of this, death rates continued to climb.

Not everyone was concerned about the high death rates. Some people believed that the high death rates were nature's way of bringing population in line with resources. Instead of poor relief, the middle classes offered the poor churches and schools; instead of sanitation, they were lectured on the follies of intemperance and vice. The solution to the urban crisis, which involved a sea-change in attitudes, was a long way off in Glasgow and other towns in Scotland.

✔ People were coming to Scotland from the poorest parts of the UK, including Ireland and the Scottish Highlands. Many of these people were already undernourished and highly vulnerable to diseases.

✔ Housing was in short supply, which led to overcrowding. And overcrowding allowed for the easy transmission of disease from one person to another.

The Highland Clearances: Ethnic Cleansing of the Highlands

On 16 April 1745 at Culloden Moor above Inverness, about 8,000 of the duke of Cumberland's soldiers defeated a smaller number of Highland clansmen in one hour, killing about 1,500 of them. Both sides thought history was in the making, but it was the Hanoverians who triumphed. For the Highlands, it was symbolic of radical changes already long underway (see Chapter 12), but in the next few decades the *Gàidhealtachd* (Gaeldom) would be transformed out of all recognition.

The occupation of the Highlands by Cumberland, 'the butcher of the Scots', was brutal. Invergarry Castle was razed to the ground, and lootings and indiscriminate attacks were carried out on the people. Because the Young Pretender was never captured, those suspected of harbouring him or aiding his escape were singled out for particularly harsh punishment.

There was also the suppression of Highland culture. Kilt wearing and bagpipe playing were banned. A series of Disarming Acts was aimed at destroying the warrior society. In addition, the Scottish Society for the Promotion of Christian Knowledge (SSPCK), set up in 1755, was part of a strategy to replace Gaelic with English and a Lowland mission to civilise the Highlands. By 1800, the SSPCK had established 150 schools and was educating thousands of Highland children. The government was determined that the '45 would never happen again.

However, it was not all suppression and intimidation. There was also an attempt to incorporate the Highlands into mainstream British society by the establishment of military regiments, such as the Camerons, Frasers and Seaforths. Between 1797 and 1837, the Isle of Skye alone provided 21 lieutenant generals and major generals; 48 lieutenant colonels; 600 majors, captains and ensigns; and 1,000 soldiers for the British army; plus a governor general of India and 4 other colonial governors. The Highland regiments fought with distinction during the wars against the French in such far-flung places as North America and on the battlefields of Europe. It was estimated that a quarter of Highland men of military age were serving in the armed forces between 1792 and 1815. The Highland soldier became an iconic image of the military spirit.

The drainage of Highland men into the army during the American Revolution was part of what is known as the Highland Clearances. This was supplemented by emigration – some 15,000 Highlanders left between 1770 and 1815 for British North America. But these departures were voluntary. There were also forced Clearances on the estates of men such as Alexander MacDonnell of Glengarry in the 1770s and 1780s to make way for sheep.

From the 1790s, the landlords began to oppose emigration for one very good reason: greed. Clan relations were increasingly based on commerce rather than blood. The Highland chiefs had been sucked into Lowland society and the rich life, which had to be paid for. Their clan members became a source of income rather than kin. As a result, labour-intensive communities were established in coastal areas harvesting kelp (seaweed), which was processed and then used in candle- and soap-making.

Because it brought enormous profits for the chiefs, people had to be tied to the land. In 1803, the chiefs successfully persuaded the government to pass the rather innocuous-sounding Passenger Vessel Act, but the devil is in the detail. Under the humanitarian guise of improving conditions relating to hygiene, food and comfort for passengers travelling to North America, the legislation had the effect of pushing up the cost of transatlantic passage well beyond the means of most Highlanders.

The landlords were less enthusiastic about retaining their people when the French wars came to an end with the defeat of Napoleon at Waterloo in 1815. The end of war saw the boom times disappear. Cattle and sheep prices declined, military recruitment slumped and the bottom fell out of the market for kelp. During the good times, the tenants had borrowed heavily and had run up substantial arrears; in the depression that followed, they couldn't pay their rents. As rental incomes began to fall, the landlords were facing bankruptcy. It was a case of, 'You or me, mate!'

A 'final solution' was arrived at to clear the estates of the unsupportable population. The best-known example of this was the Clearances that took place on the Sutherland estates between 1811 and 1821. Some 6,000 to 10,000 people were relocated to coastal areas and provided with a small plot of land known as a *croft,* which barely gave the *crofters* and their families enough to live on, so they had to labour at fishing and kelping for the landlord. The lands that they were evicted from in Strathnaver and the Strath of Kildonan were turned over to sheep.

The evictions were brutally carried out. People had their homes torched. At the township of Rosal, Donald Macleod, a Sutherland crofter, said: 'The conflagration lasted six days, till the whole of the dwellings were reduced to ashes or smoking ruins.'

On 13 June 1814, Patrick Sellar, estate manager for the Sutherlands, was involved in the eviction of William Chisholm and his wife from their croft. During the eviction, the roof was set on fire, with Chisholm's mother-in-law, Margaret Mackay, still inside. Margaret was rescued by her daughter, but she died five days later. Sellar was put on trial at Inverness in April 1816 for acts of gross inhumanity, including culpable homicide. Tried by a jury of landowners from outside Sutherland, he was – surprise, surprise – completely exonerated!

But Elizabeth, Countess of Sutherland, was not the only evictor. There were others, including the earl of Breadalbane in Glenorchy, Lord MacDonald on Skye and Maclean of Duart. Landlords who were moved to compassion for their tenants and who tried not to evict or offered relief projects went bankrupt – for example, Clanranald on South Uist and MacLeod of Dunvegan.

The problem for the Highland economy was that, during the French wars, it had become more firmly linked with the demands of Lowland and English markets. These markets disappeared after 1815. Falling back on the produce of their crofts, the Highlanders became increasingly dependent on the potato for survival – with disastrous results in the 1840s (see Chapter 14).

Empire and Diaspora

The Highland regiments and their fighting prowess did a lot to further British interests throughout the globe. They were the shock troops of British imperialism. But symbolically, they also demonstrated the extent to which the region had been integrated into the economy and society of Britain and its empire.

Indeed, the Highlanders' service to the empire allowed many former Jacobites to rehabilitate themselves as staunch Unionists. Fraser of Lovat, for instance, offered to raise a regiment of 2,000 men when war broke out in America in 1775. The existence of kilted regiments allowed the Scots to feel they had a distinctive identity, but one that was not incompatible with Britishness.

But, of course, the Scots didn't just make their mark as soldiers; they were also administrators, businessmen, educators and traders. The process of emigration had been well established before the '45 and Scottish settlement had been established in North America and the West Indies for many years. The profits of slavery, tobacco and sugar had made the fortunes of some incredibly wealthy Scots and continued to do so until the abolition of slavery in 1807. But by that time, the focus of Scottish emigration was shifting from what had become the United States to Canada, and also much farther afield to the Indian subcontinent.

The Scots were unknown in India before 1707, but by the end of the century they were all out of proportion to their numbers. The Scottish presence had a lot to do with the appointment of Henry Dundas, 'the uncrowned king of Scotland', as first secretary of state for India. In 1783, he was responsible for bringing the private company that ran India – the East India Company (EIC) – under the supervision of Parliament. Dundas used his office to 'Scoticise' India. By 1792, Scots made up 1 in 9 EIC civil servants, 1 in 11 common soldiers and 1 in 3 officers. The first three governors general of India were Scottish. By 1813, 19 of Calcutta's private merchant houses were dominated by them. From 1830 onward, Scots became involved as general merchants with Indian interests.

In 1821, Walter Scott observed that: 'India is the corn chest for Scotland, where we poor gentry must send our younger sons as we send our black cattle to the south.' He wasn't far off the mark! People like John Farquhar from Aberdeenshire, an explosives manufacturer in Bombay, retired to an English mansion with £1 million. Soldiers also profited; for example, James Campbell, who had risen through the ranks to colonel, was able to return to Edinburgh's New Town with a fortune of £25,000.

But it wasn't all for profit. The Scots were genuinely interested in Indian culture and history. In 1791, William Robertson, professor of history at the University of Edinburgh, wrote one of the first major histories of India; John Gilchrist produced the first English–Hindustani dictionary. The Scots also took a softer line to Anglo–Indian relations than the English. Sir Thomas Munro, Governor of Madras, was convinced that the British should try to work with the Indians rather than against them and envisaged a future in which the Indians would be self-governing.

The subcontinent also exported exotic foods and spices, porcelains and silks to Scotland and the rest of Britain. The ritual of tea drinking was a direct result of the discovery of the plant in Ceylon, a British possession from 1795. The firm of Lipton went on to dominate the trade in the 19th century.

The ever-increasing expansion of empire and the opportunities it created for advancement for the middle classes and lesser nobility formed the cement that bound the union together. It also allowed former opponents of the Hanoverian regime to become reconciled. After all, it was a Scot, James Thompson, who wrote the words to 'Rule Britannia', perhaps the greatest celebration of empire put to music.

The Enlightenment: Why Scotland?

Mr Amyat, an English physician, on a visit to Edinburgh in 1771, remarked: 'I can stand at the Market Cross of Edinburgh, and can, in a few minutes, take fifty men of genius and learning by the hand.' Tobias Smollett, the Scottish writer resident in London, described Edinburgh in his novel *Humphrey Clinker* as a 'hotbed of genius'.

Indeed, the second half of the 18th century saw Scotland gain a worldwide reputation for science, philosophy, scholarship and the arts. The country was in possession of an intellectual life of extraordinary brilliance. Its scientists and thinkers went on to create the modern world:

- **Adam Smith** became the father of political economy.
- **Adam Ferguson** became the father of sociology.
- **David Hume's** work laid the foundation of modern philosophy.
- **William Robertson** was the founder of *conjectural history* (speculation about the causes of events).
- **James Hutton** was the founder of modern geology.
- **James Watt** was the inventor of the steam engine.

In the arts, there were literary giants, such as national bard Robert Burns, as well as Allan Ramsay and Hugh Blair; painters of the stature of Henry Raeburn; and architects like Robert Adam.

What gave unity to this diverse group of intellectuals was their belief in reason, improvement and progress. Put simply, they were part of a set of beliefs whose purpose was to reform society using reason. This involved, on the one hand, challenging beliefs that were the product merely of tradition and faith, and on the other hand, advancing knowledge through the scientific method. Enlightened thinkers stressed reason, logic, criticism and freedom of thought over dogma, blind faith and superstition. They also believed that by gathering facts about the past and using them to examine human life, the truth behind human society and oneself, as well as the universe, could be revealed.

Everything was deemed to be rational and understandable. The Enlightenment took the view that the history of mankind was one of progress, something that could be continued with the right kind of thinking. Consequently, the Enlightenment also argued that human life and character could be improved through the use of education and reason. Instead of clobbering someone on the head and forcing him to accept your views, you persuaded him through the use of evidence, logic and reason.

The physical representation of these beliefs was seen in the construction of the New Town in Edinburgh, beginning in 1767. Whereas the Old Town was seen to embody chaos and disease and crime, the gridiron layout of the New Town was designed by 27-year-old James Craig and was supposed to represent order, sociability and commerce. It was also physical propaganda for the Hanoverian regime – some of the better-known streets of the New Town were called George Street, Hanover Street and Frederick Street.

The notion of progress among the Scottish literati was defined as much on English terms as Scottish. England was viewed as a far more progressive society than Scotland in all sorts of areas. In 1761, one of the clubs, the Select Society, hired an Irish actor, Thomas Sheridan, to rid their speech of 'Scotticisms' and changed its name to the Society for Promoting the Reading and Speaking of the English Language. The desire to speak correct 'English' became a passion; the old Scots language was seen as 'uncouth'.

The origins of the Enlightenment lay further back in the past (see Chapter 12), and there is little doubt that the Scots owed a great deal to major European philosophers, such as Spinoza, Locke, Voltaire and Isaac Newton. In Scotland, Frances Hutcheson, professor of moral philosophy at the University of Glasgow, was the founding father of Scotland's Enlightenment.

The Enlightenment wasn't a bolt from the blue. Like any other artistic or intellectual movement it had roots:

- ✔ **Universities:** Scotland had five universities compared to England's two. The curriculum was much more broad-based and scientific and included economics and mathematics, as well as arts subjects such as law, history and languages, particularly Latin. Specialist professorial teaching was introduced after 1707. The late 17th century had also witnessed the re-establishment of professorial chairs in mathematics. Observatories were built at St Andrews and at King's and Marischal colleges in Aberdeen. Robert Sibbald, who was appointed the first professor of medicine at Edinburgh, co-founded the Royal College of Physicians of Edinburgh in 1681. These developments helped the universities to become major centres of medical education, as well as later putting Scotland at the forefront of new thinking.

✔ **Clubs:** The abolition of the Scottish Parliament didn't kill off the public's taste for debate. It's not for nothing that the Scots have been described as a disputatious people, something that goes back to the Reformation. In the major cities, clubs were established for debating the main issues of the day and campaigning for things such as the establishment of a Scottish militia. In the absence of a parliament in Edinburgh, the clubs served as a safety valve for discontent and at the same time provided an introduction for students into this lively culture of debate and discussion.

In Edinburgh, there were the Select Society and the Cape Club; in Glasgow, the Political Economy Society; in Aberdeen, the Philosophical Society, better known as the Wise Club; in Perth, the Literary and Antiquarian Society. Perhaps the most important club was the Poker Club in Edinburgh, set up to 'stir things up'.

✔ **Politeness:** By *politeness*, I'm referring to intelligent conversation whose unwritten message was to improve morality and encourage mutual understanding. Polite culture would, in the words of the founder of the famous journal the *Spectator,* Joseph Addison, 'wear out Ignorance, Passion and Prejudice'. This would, as one historian put it, 'help to establish a new kind of society – peaceful, prosperous and pleasant'.

Lord Cockburn, speaking of the growth of polite society in Edinburgh in the 18th century, said that

> there was far more coarseness in the formal age than the free one. Two vices especially which had been banished from all respectable society were very prevalent, if not universal, among the upper ranks – swearing and drinking. Nothing was more common for gentlemen who had dined with ladies, and meant to rejoin them, to get drunk. . . . Swearing was thought the right, and mark, of a gentleman.

As part of the softening of manners women were no longer burned for murdering their husbands, nor were heretics or witches. There was also general revulsion against duelling and cruel blood sports, and a new sensitivity toward marital cruelty and infanticide. By the early 19th century, Scottish judges no longer believed that a quarrelsome wife deserved a beating.

✔ **The Church:** At the beginning of the 18th century the Scottish Church had a reputation for intolerance, fire-and-brimstone preaching, and a fierce attachment to Calvinist doctrine. In 1696, an 18-year-old student, Thomas Aikenhead, had been executed in Edinburgh's Grassmarket for blasphemy. So, the cultural atmosphere was hardly conducive to the kind of liberal intellectualism that would characterise the second half of the century. Scotland was more like a theocracy than a modern state.

Things changed after 1707 with the introduction of the Patronage Act of 1712, which placed the appointment of ministers in the hands of the landowning elites. The elites wanted their appointees to preach on stability, anti-Jacobitism and political cohesion.

Patronage wasn't welcomed by the Church, but it had little choice but to accept it. Ministers were not only defenders of the union settlement, but also more liberal in outlook, more learned and much more sophisticated than their predecessors, who were described by one Welshman in 1769 as 'furious [and] illiterate'. This new breed of minister was known as a *Moderate*. But the Moderates didn't have it all their own way. They were opposed by the Evangelicals, who were drawn to the older forms of preaching and were critical of the elites in Scottish society. However, it was the Moderates who dominated the Church in the second half of the 18th century.

The Moderates were determined to rid the Church of persecution over religious matters and to allow the unthinkable to be spoken, which was very important in allowing for the radical gains made in all fields of inquiry, from mathematics to philosophy. This meant that when the extremists among the Evangelicals attempted to try the atheist David Hume for heresy in 1755, they failed miserably.

John Calvin

John Calvin, a French reformer and theologian who died in Geneva, Switzerland, in 1564, was the most potent influence on the development of Scottish Protestantism. John Knox, the Scottish Protestant leader, called Geneva 'the most perfect school of Christ'.

Calvin had a pretty dim view of humanity, which he considered depraved and steeped in sin since the fall from grace of Adam in the Garden of Eden. He split the world into the eternally saved (the elect) and the eternally damned (the reprobates). In his view, there was nothing you could do about which category you found yourself in, even if you had lived a pious and decent life. It was all part of God's plan, even before the world began. Indeed, he argued that Christ died only to redeem those whom God had already chosen for salvation.

The problem was, who was chosen for salvation and who for damnation? There were telltale signs. The *elect* came to resemble those who had succeeded on earth. So, the better off you were, the more likely you were destined for heaven; the poorer you were, the more likely you were doomed to go to hell.

From his base in Geneva, Calvin established a *theocracy* (in which the Church controls all aspects of life). It was pretty rigid in terms of governing social life and worship. Any distraction from the worship of God was banned. This meant whitewashing church walls, removing objects like paintings and allowing singing but not music. It was pretty austere, and that also applied to social life. The ministers and the church elders policed the morals of the people.

Calvinism has been seen as responsible for turning Scotland into a dour and miserable place full of killjoy misanthropes whose greatest fear is that somewhere someone is happy! While this is an unfair caricature, the Calvinist emphasis on prayer and reflection laid the basis for the 'dreich' (dreary) Scottish Sunday where everything was shut down, including pubs and shops. It took until 1972 before pubs were allowed to open on Sunday in Scotland.

Without the open-minded and sociable Moderates' control of the Church, the flowering of the Scottish intellect may never have occurred.

Political Radicalism

As a result of the Enlightenment, by the end of the 18th century, the Scots realised that the superstitions, the dogmas of faith, and the acts of kings and queens were less important – less formative of social life – than such things as modern manufacturing, commerce and international trade. But the Enlightenment figures were close to the elite in Scottish society, too close to act politically on their liberal beliefs. Indeed, most were dependent on the patronage of the nobility. For example, Adam Smith was supported by the duke of Buccleuch while writing his *Wealth of Nations* (1776); others were given places in the universities and in public office by their noble patrons.

They were all staunch defenders of the Hanoverian state. That world would be shaken to the core both intellectually and politically by the emergence of political radicalism in the 1790s.

Political management

The political system in Britain in the 18th century was the plaything of the ruling elite. Tiny groups of men were responsible for the election of members of Parliament (MPs). Edinburgh had only 33 electors! Elections were managed through bribery and corruption (see Chapter 12).

The system of political management emerged under the duke of Argyll in the first half of the 18th century, but was perfected after 1780 with the appointment of Lord Advocate Henry Dundas (later Lord Melville), 'King Harry the Ninth', as his successor. Dundas bestowed not only political favours in Scotland on his supporters but also the spoils of empire (see 'Empire and Diaspora', earlier in this chapter). He did his job for the Tory government by delivering all 45 seats in Scotland! To the ruling class, he was a hero; others saw it differently.

Apart from the issue of delivering parliamentary seats, the English were not interested in Scotland. When they were, it was usually to complain about Scotsmen on the make in London, or Scottish politicians, such as the earl of Bute, prime minister from 1762 to 1763. In spite of ending the Seven Years' War with France and the political dominance of the Whigs, Bute proved deeply unpopular in England mainly because of his nationality. He was the subject of written, verbal and physical attacks. So fierce were these attacks that he resigned after spending only 11 months in office. 'Scotophobia' was rife in 18th-century London.

Before the 1790s, there were few challenges to the ruling power, but power could never simply be taken for granted. A number of campaigns were initiated in England against corruption in government by the radical MP John Wilkes, a noted Scotophobe. In Scotland, the Convention of Royal Burghs criticised the political system in 1784. But these organisations were only interested in shaping government policy or desiring a slight change in the franchise that would favour them. They weren't out to fundamentally change the political system in Britain by making it more democratic.

The spread of Enlightenment philosophy obviously created an enthusiasm for change, but it needed a spark to turn this growing awareness into a genuinely popular movement that could command support from across a broad spectrum of society. That came in 1789 with the revolution in France.

The impact of the French Revolution

It would be hard to minimise the impact of the events in France on Scottish/British politics in this period.

The great Edinburgh Whig lawyer Henry Cockburn recognised some years later that: 'everything was connected with the revolution in France, which for twenty years, was, or was made, all in all, everything; not this thing, but everything was soaked in this one event'.

Politics in Britain were never the same after 1789. The slogan of the Revolution – 'Liberty, Equality and Fraternity' – set the ideological battleground for reform and anti-reform for the next 60 years.

Oddly enough, the ruling classes were initially in favour of the revolution. The abolition of feudal privilege and the establishment of a constitutional monarchy in France seemed consistent with struggles fought in 17th-century Britain. The revolution, therefore, enjoyed widespread support even with the monarchy. Among the governing classes, only the arch conservative thinker Edmund Burke viewed the events in France with distaste, calling it 'abominable sedition'.

As you may expect, radicals and non-conformists were delighted at the news of the revolution – it seemed to usher in a new era of reform. Josiah Wedgwood, the pottery manufacturer, called it 'the wonderful revolution'. Robert Burns, then a customs official, sent guns to the Paris Convention. The poet William Wordsworth, in Paris at the time, revelled in: 'A time when Europe rejoiced, France standing on top of golden laws, and human nature seeming born again'.

Within a decade, all this early enthusiasm would be spent, and the cause of reform would be transformed into a dangerous and discredited thing to uphold. Samuel Coleridge wrote, in marked contrast to Wordsworth's stirring verse, that:

> There was not a city, no, not a town, in which a man suspected of holding democratic principles could move without receiving some unpleasant proof of the hatred in which his supposed opinions were held by the great majority of people.

This was a remarkable testimony as to how far support for reform had been discredited. This poses the question: why did such early promise of a glorious age of reform end in disappointment and failure? The answer lies with the events in France, particularly the Terror, and the threat posed by the radicals to the power structure in Britain.

Much of the ideological justification for reform came from the work of the American Thomas Paine. In his remarkably successful *Rights of Man,* Paine addressed the anti-reform arguments of Edmund Burke in *Reflections on the Revolution in France* (1790). Whereas Burke roundly denounced the revolution, Paine championed the cause of universal suffrage and the sovereignty of the people; he also denounced the monarchy and the aristocracy as useless archaisms. Paine's arguments made their mark, with more than 200,000 copies of his book sold; indeed, the works of Paine were found in every corner of Britain, from Cornish tin mines to the Scottish Highlands.

Although wary of Paine's ideas and their influence on the lower classes, the authorities took no steps to ban his works. However, with the publication of the second part of *The Rights of Man* in a cheap edition, they became actively hostile. In part two, Paine linked political and social grievances and his ideas were taken up by radicals the length and breadth of Britain.

Show trials

The Scottish reform movement was orchestrated by the Friends of the People, composed of Whigs, gentry and artisans, with a membership of 10,000, half of whom paid subscriptions. Its most gifted leader, the lawyer Thomas Muir, was arrested for making a seditious speech in August 1793. His arrest and subsequent trial were as much aimed at the English reform movement as the Scottish societies. Muir was sentenced to 14 years' transportation to Botany Bay in a scandalously biased trial, although he was rescued on the way by American sympathisers. Three cheers for the special relationship! Muir died in France in January 1799.

The lord chief justice clerk, Lord Braxfield, was heard whispering to a juror: 'Come awa', Mr Horner, come awa' [and] help us hang ane o' them damned scoondrels.'

A month later, the same fate befell T.F. Palmer, a Dundee Unitarian minister. Their real crime, as far as the judge was concerned, was not so much their radical beliefs and involvement in the reform movement; the issue was that they were educated men who could 'be found among the villagers, manufactories, poor . . . for the purpose of sowing sedition and discontent'.

The savage sentences given out to Muir and Palmer in no way discouraged the Scottish reformers; if anything, it made them more determined. They planned a National Convention for Edinburgh, and invitations were sent out to the English reform societies. The London radicals appointed two delegates, Margarot and Gerrald; Sheffield, the only other English society to send a delegate, appointed Browne. The Convention met briefly in October but without the English delegates. It re-formed when the English arrived in November and lasted three weeks before being broken up by the authorities.

The leaders were arrested on charges of sedition. Although the proceedings themselves were moderate, the presence of delegates from the revolutionary United Irishmen and the use of French forms of address and organisation alarmed the authorities. The minutes of the meeting had been dated the 'First year of the British Convention' and delegates had addressed each other as 'citizen'.

Skirving, the Scottish secretary, was arrested along with Margarot. At a subsequent trial, they were both sentenced to 14 years' transportation. Skirving died one year after arriving in New South Wales. The sentences were fully supported by the Pitt government, so the verdicts were as much the responsibility of the English authorities as the Scottish judges. This was the signal for an even bigger crackdown on radical activity. In May 1794, all the leaders of the main radical organisation, the London Corresponding Society, were arrested, along with important provincial leaders, with more than 800 warrants for arrest issued.

The impact of suppression was mixed. But an act suspending 'Wrongous Imprisonment' (*habeas corpus* in England) was passed by Parliament in 1794 amid rumours of an imminent French invasion. In spite of the equivocal impact of government repression on the reform movement for certain individuals, it became a load too heavy to bear. Robert Burns, a supporter of the revolution, fearing for his livelihood, rode with the Loyalist Association (in England, Church-and-King Mobs), which had been set up to terrify radicals into inactivity.

Revolution is in the air

If the repressive measures were primarily designed to check the rise of conspiratorial and revolutionary groups, they failed miserably. The government's actions forced the reform movement underground. Open organisations such as the Friends of the People were replaced by insurrectionary groups. The first sign of the new attitude were seen in Edinburgh in 1794, when Robert Watt, a former government agent, was arrested and hanged for plotting an armed uprising.

The United Scotsmen was set up under the influence of Irish immigrants. Although a national committee was established in Glasgow, it would appear that the organisation's core strength lay in Dundee, Perth and the adjacent counties of Perthshire, Forfarshire and Fife. A number of affiliated local bodies were discovered by government agents. For instance, in 1797, in Cupar, Fife, ten men, including a schoolmaster, were arrested on suspicion of plotting to overthrow the government; there were other arrests of this kind in Dundee and Dunfermline. In spite of the trials of 1797 to 1798, the United Scotsmen continued its clandestine activities, but at no time was there an armed revolt. Like all underground organisations, it failed to attract widespread support. It finally disbanded in 1802.

Nothing had been achieved. The political system was still undemocratic. Was this due to the power and resolve of the state, or was it due to the ineptitude of the reform movement itself?

Ideologically, the radicals were convinced of the 'right to resist power when abused'. In 1792, radicals proclaimed the people's natural and inalienable right of resistance to oppression and of a share in the government of the country. But in the 1790s, no one ever clarified what constituted the proper mode of resistance. Crucially, resistance was never anything more than theoretical, unless you include the activities of the United Scotsmen or its brother organisation, the United Englishmen. But there were missed opportunities to politicise the masses. In 1795, the bad harvests and the massive rise in prices of foodstuffs generated widespread discontent, but that was never channelled politically by the radicals.

Similarly, the Militia Riots of 1797 against conscription saw riots break out all over Scotland. Mobs forced local authorities to destroy conscription rolls and to sign pledges agreeing not to implement the act. The unrest was obviously political in origin, yet there was no attempt to lead it in the direction of reform. The riots were condemned by the Scottish Society of Friends of the People and the London radicals, as were the naval mutinies at Spithead and the Nore in 1797.

The radicals also seemed incapable of framing a political rhetoric that could mobilise mass support for the cause of reform. Their appeal seemed to resonate most strongly with small masters and artisans and dissident middle-class professionals. They failed to recognise the material concerns of the labouring poor. In short, they failed to use the opportunities provided by economic grievances to link them with the political struggle for the vote. Indeed, if a popular consciousness existed at all, it was to be found in the Loyalist Associations in Scotland and the Church-and-King Mobs in England. War against France seemed to be the rallying cry for men across all social classes. This patriotism was intensified by invasion scares and the propaganda of the state. As William Wilberforce said, there were 'Twenty Kings men to one Jacobin'.

It's wrong to think of the 1790s as a complete failure: it was a beginning rather than an end. It also led to a hardening of social relationships. As the reform societies developed a more radical agenda in line with the events unfolding in France, men of property – both commercial and landed – put their differences aside and joined together to defend Church and king. So, during these decades, Scotland was witnessing the birth of class society. From John o'Groats to Land's End, democratic ideas had taken root, and from that point onward the whole nature of political discussion was indelibly altered.

Popular protest: A riot for every occasion

People at this time didn't always join political organisations to make their unhappiness known to the authorities. In fact, much of the protest at this time was spontaneous and unorganised. There were various types of riots at this time, but the main ones were as follows:

- **Food riot:** This was the most common form of riot. It took place when people felt that grain prices were too high, or when in times of hunger merchants were hoarding or exporting grain to other places. The mob took possession of the grain, gave the offending merchant a kicking and then sold it at what they considered a fair price.

- **King's birthday riot:** Although designed to increase support for the Hanoverians among the common people, the celebration of the king's birthday had the opposite effect. Drunken crowds used the occasion to make fun of their betters, create mayhem and smash up the town. In Edinburgh, on 4 June 1792, the city centre was occupied by rioters for three days before soldiers brought it to an end by shooting dead six of the rioters. Three years later, a crowd of several hundred stoned the lord advocate's house. These scenes were repeated annually all over Scotland.

- **Militia riot:** Under the Militia Act of 1797, all able-bodied men between the ages of 19 and 23 were liable to be chosen by ballot to serve in the militia unless they found and could pay for a substitute. Special exemptions were available to *peers* (members of the House of Lords), clergy, teachers and those over 45 years old. The act was hugely unpopular because it was seen to favour the wealthy. Militia rolls compiled by local teachers were burned. In Tranent, near Edinburgh, rioting townspeople were indiscriminately cut down by troops. The body count ranged from around a dozen to 20 or more men, women and children dead, and more wounded.

These kinds of riots were principally engaged in by working people who were driven by hunger or other pressures from the growing commercial and industrial economy into defending their 'rights'. But even in rural areas, where conflict was more easily contained by the landlords and the law, protest developed an underground aspect, as sabotage and acts of defiance such as stealing wood, pulling down dykes, poaching and sheep stealing took place under the cover of darkness.

If we take these protests with the radical political activity, it would appear that there were a lot people unhappy in Britain at the time, and they were prepared to let the authorities know about it. We were witnessing the birth of a new political awakening, as the middle and working classes began pushing for a share of political power. Things could not remain the same, or could they?

Radicalism Reborn

The defeat of Napoleon at Waterloo in 1815 not only gave ABBA a title for a hit song, but also brought an end to the French wars, which had been going on for more than 20 years (in fact, maybe since 1763). But peace proved a curse rather than a blessing. The economic depression that followed the end of the hostilities brought mass unemployment, as thousands of demobilised soldiers and sailors joined the ranks of the unemployed. The discontent and disillusionment of the population provided the backdrop to the re-emergence of Radical activity.

But there were significant differences between this period and the 1790s:

- **Ideology:** Instead of the rights of man, the Radical attack was now directed toward corruption and the unrepresentativeness of Parliament.

- **Atmosphere:** The atmosphere in which the Radical agitation took place was also significantly different. In the 1790s, the British people were governed by a combination of force and deference, supplemented by the gallows, paternalism and patriotism. In 1816, the British people were held down by naked force as all the old restraints broke down.

- **Location:** Radicalism also relocated itself. Although London was still important, the north of England and the Celtic fringe became more important as places of action.

Agitation

The Hampden Clubs (named after 17th-century politician John Hampden) under the leadership of Major Cartwright were one of the early frontrunners of the resurgent radicalism. Cartwright had a triumphant tour of Scotland in 1816, attracting 40,000 people to a meeting just outside Glasgow in October of that year, which led to 600 petitions to Parliament in favour of reform.

But from the start, it was obvious that there was no cohesive national movement. Instead, there were leading personalities, such as Cartwright, William Cobbett and Henry 'Orator' Hunt. The authorities were naturally worried over the rising tide of agitation. Again, *habeas corpus* was suspended and a new law against seditious societies was introduced.

The crackdown provoked various insurrectionary groups into action. In March 1817, the Blanketeers (so-called because of the blankets they carried on their backs) planned to march on London from Lancashire but were attacked and turned back by Royal Dragoons. Two months later, there was a revolutionary rising at Pentrich in Derbyshire. However, their routing by Hussars led to a reassessment of strategy, and constitutionalism became the dominant means of protest.

In the depression of 1819, the radical societies moved from indoor discussions to mass open-air meetings. It was at one of these meetings that one of the most symbolic events in the history of radicalism in Britain took place. On 16 August 1819, at St Peter's Field, Manchester, a crowd of 60,000 men, women and children gathered to hear Orator Hunt. The Manchester magistrates decided that the meeting was insurrectionary and ordered the arrest of Hunt, an event that provoked a panic. The gathered crowd was literally slaughtered by the Yeomanry and the Hussars in what was known as the Peterloo Massacre (a play on Waterloo). Within 10 to 15 minutes, 11 people had been killed and 400 injured; of those wounds inflicted, 161 were by sabres and more than 100 of the casualties were women or girls.

Revolution in the air (again)

In the short term, Peterloo generated a great deal of anger and indignation; 18,000 Paisley inhabitants protested against the 'inhuman butchers of Manchester'. It radicalised people, even in areas noted for loyalist sympathies. It also shifted attention back to armed struggle. During October and November 1819, the Home Office began receiving reports of arming and drilling in Newcastle, Wigan, Bolton and Blackburn. What was even more alarming was the news that ultra-radical societies in Manchester and Glasgow were planning monster demonstrations for 13 December.

A series of acts designed to forestall further agitation were passed quickly by the legislature. The most important of the so-called 'Six Acts' was the banning of meetings of more than 50 people. The impact on the radical movement was profound. Some, like William Cobbett and Henry Hunt, abandoned reform. But as in the 1790s, government action pushed the movement underground; in London and the west of Scotland, it flourished.

In both locations, two spectacular events designed to overthrow the government took place in 1820: the Cato Street conspiracy and the Radical War.

Arthur Thistlewood and his fellow conspirators planned to assassinate Lord Liverpool's Cabinet while they were attending a dinner at Lord Harrowby's house in Grosvenor Square, London. Set up by police spies, they were apprehended and the leaders were hanged. Although often dismissed as an isolated act of desperation, the Cato Street conspirators believed that if successful it would signal a spontaneous rising in the country against Old Corruption. There were, in fact, three risings shortly after the events in London – two in Yorkshire and one in the west of Scotland.

In the weaving districts of the west of Scotland in the early months of 1820, discontent was mounting. A plan to stage a general strike on 1 April to draw attention to economic grievances was greeted with enormous enthusiasm. The strike involved the whole of Glasgow's textile workers, as well as those in Paisley, Kilsyth and a number of surrounding villages. All in all, some

60,000 workers heeded the call to cease work in an attempt to recover 'their rights'. The strike lasted only a few days. By 7 April, the weavers were said to have returned to their looms, but while the strike was in full swing it was the springboard for an audacious armed revolt.

Some 1,500 men were said to be armed and engaged in military drills with muskets and pikes. Of the armed factions, two small groups were prepared to go beyond parading:

- ✔ On 5 April, 20 men, under the leadership of James Wilson, a stocking-maker and long-serving radical, marched on Glasgow under the impression that it was in the control of rebel forces. When they discovered that this was not the case, they panicked and fled.

- ✔ Another contingent of 40 men, under the leadership of Andrew Hardie, a weaver and devout Christian, marched toward Stirling to capture the Carron ironworks, which manufactured cannons. They were intercepted by Yeomanry and a troop of Hussars at Bonnymuir, and after a brief one-sided skirmish on 5 April, they were arrested.

Between the two incidents, 88 men were charged with treason. Of these, 58 escaped; 30 were tried, of which 15 to 20 were sentenced to transportation; and 3, Wilson, Hardie and Baird, were executed.

The savagery of the execution of James Wilson, a man of 60 years, who was hung in front of a Glasgow crowd of 20,000 and then had his head cut off, was meant to shock. Two other radicals, John Baird, a 32-year-old weaver from Condorrat, and Andrew Hardie, a 28-year-old weaver from Glasgow, were executed in Stirling, watched by a crowd of 2,000. The authorities wouldn't pay the 20 guineas to have their heads severed.

The night before his execution, Hardie wrote to his girlfriend:

> I shall die firm to the cause in which I embarked, and although we were outwitted and betrayed, yet I protest, as a dying man, it was done with good intention on my part. . . . No person could have induced me to take up arms to rob or plunder; no, my dear Margaret, I took them for the restoration of those rights for which our forefathers bled, and which we have allowed shamefully to be wrested from us.

Hardie's words provide an insight into why the men took up arms, but there is no record of factory workers or coalminers being involved. Hand-loom weavers were the most disaffected group of workers in Scotland, owing to the decline in their income and status; their part in the revolt was as much an expression of distaste for changing values as it was for reform. The weavers were defending an older way of life against unplanned economic individualism. The newly formed proletariat of factory workers barely took part in the reform movement, because many of the leading lights, such as William Cobbett, had nothing to say on the issues they were affected by on a day-to-day basis.

The failure of the Cato conspirators and the Bonnymuir insurrectionists made a lasting impact on the radical movement. Failure in 1820 turned Scottish radicals away from ideas of revolution and toward constitutional and moral force. A similar situation existed south of the border. With meetings banned, most of the leaders in jail and the press under fire, the political unions fell apart. The radical cause was not helped by the upturn of the economy after 1820, which saw unemployment fall as well as food prices.

It seemed that once again nothing had been achieved. But the events of Peterloo and the 1820 risings had an impact:

- ✔ They convinced middle-class reformers, and some Whigs, of the consequences that would result from their continued loss of influence among the unrepresented masses and of the dangers of refusing to make concessions.

  As William Wilberforce put it: 'they had a duty to rescue the multitude from the hands of the Hunts and Thistlewoods'.

- ✔ Peterloo secured the right of public meetings. Never again would violence be used in such an uncontrolled way on a peaceful crowd on the British mainland.

- ✔ Peterloo fragmented relationships between workers and their social superiors. Exclusively working-class institutions began to emerge with alternative views on how to run the economy.

  With the upturn in the economy, by the mid-1820s, there was no public enthusiasm for reform. But the demand never completely died – it was just temporarily sidelined.

Enlightened Tories: An oxymoron?

The 1820s have been described as the age of 'enlightened Toryism'. Peel and other Tories were quietly reversing the most repressive legislation of the post-1815 years and embarking on a programme of reform, which included repeal of the anti-trade-union Combination laws (which had banned workers from forming trade unions), liberalisation of trade and mitigation of the most savage aspects of the penal system. Parliament also showed itself willing to reform itself on a limited basis by abolishing most of the rotten boroughs in England.

A far more important concession was the Catholic Emancipation Act of 1829, allowing Catholics to play a full role in public and political life. Major concessions on so sensitive an issue as Catholic emancipation naturally encouraged those looking for other types of reform.

The Whigs themselves were deeply divided as to what sort of parliament they wanted, but they were encouraged to step up their campaign, partly arguing out of principle, partly out of fear – fear of the masses if reform was not agreed.

By the late 1820s, popular agitation was reviving renewed economic problems. The Tories, by then deeply divided over reforms such as Catholic emancipation, hung grimly on to power until 1830. But that year proved a decisive turning point:

✔ The first event was the news of revolution in France, with the fall of the reactionary Bourbon king in a swift and bloodless coup. This inspired popular radicals – it showed that a reactionary regime could be overthrown by popular action. Many sympathisers who had held back active support from the radical movement because they feared that such action would lead to war and chaos were reassured that these outcomes were not inevitable.

✔ The second event that transformed the political situation was the death of King George IV – or rather not his death but the fact that, by law, a general election had to follow. At the election, the reform of Parliament and the attack on aristocratic privileges in general were the main issues. In spite of the increase in strength in the Commons by reforming Whigs, the outgoing Tory prime minister, the duke of Wellington, blandly stated that the existing state of representation in Parliament was perfect.

Reform or revolution

The Whigs, who came to power under Lord Grey, took a more flexible attitude to reform, although deep down they shared the same prejudices as the unreformed Tories. Grey, soon to become a national hero as Lord Grey of the Reform Bill, was an aristocrat (as were all the members of his Cabinet). Representing the most conservative section of the Whigs, Grey supported reform to 'afford some ground of resistance to further innovation' – in other words, allow for change in order for things to remain the same.

To cut a long story short, in 1831, the Whigs introduced the first reform bill, which was defeated at the committee stage. The Whigs immediately called for another general election, which further increased their strength in the Commons. A second reform bill was introduced and passed in the Commons, only to be thrown out by the Lords, an event that provoked a furious reaction throughout the country. The spectre of violent revolution seemed to be looming. Serious disturbances broke out in Nottingham and Derby, and at Bristol a mob ran riot for two days.

The question was: how could the resistance of the unelected House of Lords be overcome? The solution lay in introducing a third reform bill and creating enough new peers sympathetic to reform. The threat was clear enough, but King William refused to agree to the plan. This refusal plunged the country into confusion and panic, as the Grey administration resigned and the Tories were invited to form a new government.

The resignation of the Grey administration provoked large demonstrations orchestrated by London Radicals aimed at destabilising the Wellington government. The demonstrations proved successful, and the king was forced to consent to Grey's request for more new peers.

Faced with inevitable defeat, the diehards in the Lords allowed the third reform bill through committee. On 14 June 1832, the third reading of the bill was passed by 106 votes to 22 in the Lords. Three days later, it received royal assent. It applied only to England and Wales, but separate acts for Ireland and Scotland soon followed.

The effect of the Great Reform Act of 1832

Contemporaries spoke of the Great Reform Act and Grey became a national hero, but was such an accolade justified? How great indeed was the Great Reform Act of 1832? On the face of it, the act was a fairly moderate measure. In Scotland, eight new burgh seats were created, including additional MPs for Edinburgh and Glasgow. The old practice of only having burghs represented if they held the status of royal burgh was abandoned as meaningless; towns like Paisley and Greenock were given an MP. In England, 56 rotten boroughs were totally disenfranchised; 30 others lost one of their two members; 22 two-member constituencies were created and 20 one-member; 7 counties received a third MPs; and 26 two-member constituencies were halved, sending two MPs for each division. However, it was all a bit of a sham.

The act did nothing to reduce the power of the landed elite, but then again it wasn't meant to. It didn't really do much to increase the number of electors either. The total effect of the act was to increase the electorate of Great Britain from 478,000 to 813,000 out of a population of 24 million. Put another way, one in seven adult males over the age of 21 were enfranchised. However, there were significant national differences. In Scotland in 1820, only 4,250 males had the right to vote; after 1832, this number increased to 65,000 – an increase in the electorate of 1,400 per cent compared to only 80 per cent in England. In 1820, about 0.2 per cent of the Scottish population was qualified to vote; the Reform Act raised this to 2.7 per cent. But who was enfranchised and who remained excluded?

In urban areas a uniform franchise was introduced based on householders who could prove residence for 12 months and who had paid rates and taxes. In the countryside, it was more complex, with several categories of eligible voters, but mainly small landowners and substantial tenant farmers. So, it was property owners in the main who were enfranchised both in the towns and in the countryside. This meant that working-class males, all women regardless of social class and a host of smaller groups including, peers, paupers, lunatics, aliens, magistrates, post office workers, policemen and customs officials were all excluded.

Politically, what did this all mean? Not that much, but it did mean the Tory stranglehold on Scotland was broken. In the election after 1832, the Whigs won 43 seats in Scotland, and the Tories only 10. Everywhere, there were rejoicings, but the potential for disillusionment remained.

Parliament was still dominated by the landed elite with 342 MPs the sons of peers, baronets or near-relatives of peers. Seventy-one of the seats in Parliament and most of the seats in the Cabinet had been cornered by the landed classes. Moreover, once in power, the Whigs lost interest in further reform, seeing 1832 as a once-and-for-all change. Working-class radicals who had felt betrayed were left with a sense of bitterness, particularly as the reformed Parliament proved itself to be no more interested in address-ing social grievances than old corruption. Radical MPs elected in Glasgow opposed the introduction of factory legislation aimed at lowering the working hours of women and children. The hated New Poor Law of 1834 in England was also introduced by the new Parliament.

Many of the abuses of the old system remained: there were no secret ballots and no payment for MPs, to name but a few. Rich men could still buy their way to seats in the Commons.

So, there is little greatness to be found in the allegedly 'Great' Reform Act of 1832. However, if you think of it as a beginning that contained the promise of future reform, then perhaps you can use the term *great* in a qualified way. The door that had been effectively closed for centuries was now in the pro-cess of being wedged open. In the face of popular protest, Parliament was forced to reform itself. Might it not be placed in that position again? However, the next time the push would come not from the middle classes but from the workers.

Chapter 14

The Making of Modern Scotland (1832–1918)

....

In This Chapter

▶ Seeing the spectacular growth of industry

▶ Recognising the social consequences of industrialisation

▶ Watching the continuation of the Highland Clearances

▶ Looking at the evolving political system

▶ Understanding the growth of empire

▶ Seeing the effects of the First World War

....

The years from 1832 to 1918 witnessed the modernisation of Scotland. During the Victorian period, Scotland evolved from a country whose wealth was drawn from textiles and agriculture into an industrial powerhouse at the centre of the British Empire. The sweeping changes in the economy were accompanied by urban growth on an equally spectacular level.

These changes combined to create one of the wealthiest countries in the world, but this change was achieved at tremendous human cost. Social life in 19th-century Scotland was nothing short of miserable. The need to address social problems raised the issue of parliamentary reform; only by extending the vote to the excluded working class could its interests be represented in the corridors of power.

By the outbreak of the First World War, Scotland had been transformed into a recognisably modern country – industrialised, urbanised and part of a mass democracy – capable of fighting a total war with the rest of the UK and its allies against Germany.

The Victorian Economic Miracle

In the 18th century (and even up to 1830), Scotland lagged far behind England economically. But well before the end of the 19th century, Scotland caught up and even surpassed its southern neighbour in certain areas of production. This is why historians have labelled the achievement in this period the 'Victorian economic miracle'.

The origins of the miracle lay in one important invention – James Beaumont Neilson's hot-blast furnace of 1828. This furnace cheapened the cost of producing iron so much that costs in Scotland were lower than in the rest of Europe. Because iron was so cheap, it was used more. And on the back of this invention emerged the jewel in the country's industrial crown – iron ship-building. Clydeside, previously a minor centre of shipbuilding, became dominant in Britain and the rest of the world.

The cheapness of iron production wasn't the only thing that spurred the development of shipbuilding. There were a few other factors to consider:

- ✔ **Skill:** There were large numbers of workers skilled in metal working that shipbuilders could draw on, and their wages were lower than in England.
- ✔ **Science:** There were close links between industry and Scotland's universities, which gave the Scots an advantage in marine engineering.
- ✔ **Energy:** Scotland had large reserves of cheap, accessible coal.

It wasn't only in shipbuilding that the Scots were world leaders in. They excelled in lesser-known industries such as sugar crushing and refinery machinery, with 80 per cent of world production of these machines produced in Glasgow.

The 19th century was the great age of the steam railway, and the Scots made a major contribution. From 1870, Glasgow and its satellite towns dominated engine making, not just in Britain but in the British Empire as well. More than half of the 7,024 locomotives running on Indian railway tracks had been made in Glasgow.

Although cotton had laid the basis of industrialisation by the middle of the 19th century, it was in decline due to fierce competition from Lancashire. But its demise saw Scotland take the lead in the world production of jute and sewing thread. The largest jute factory in the world – the Cox Brothers' Camperdown Works – was in Dundee and employed 5,000 people. The thread industry of Paisley grew spectacularly after the invention of the sewing machine. The world demand for sewing thread was so great that J.P. Coats of Paisley became Britain's first multinational, with branches throughout the world; it was ranked the fifth largest company in the world.

The rewards of industry

Wages grew relative to English earnings after 1830. By the end of the century, Scotland had caught up with other cities in the UK (with the exception of London). Even the formerly very poorly paid agricultural workers of Ross and Cromarty were paid more than similar workers in Dorset and Suffolk. In spite of this, poverty and bad housing remained a feature of Scottish life and were reflected in emigration statistics.

Profits also grew and can be measured in the growth of overseas investment from Scotland. In 1870, £60 million left Scotland; in 1900, it was £300 million; in 1914, £500 million. Between 1870 and 1914, one-eighth of British foreign investment came from Scotland, with most of it going to North America, Australasia and Asia.

Slowing down

Sometimes appearances can be deceptive. On the face of it, the Scottish economy in the late 19th and early 20th centuries was booming. A few statistics bear this out:

✔ Coal production grew from 22 million tons in 1870 to 42 million in 1913.

✔ Shipbuilding output on the Clyde was 756,000 tons in 1913, more than that produced by either the United States or Germany.

But in spite of appearances to the contrary there were signs that the Victorian economic miracle had run its course and the economy was beginning to feel itself under pressure. The iron industry was in trouble, with rising costs and falling production. Within shipbuilding, profits had begun to fall in spite of the increase in output. The industry was becoming more and more reliant on naval contracts for survival, a phenomenon that created the problems for the industry discussed in Chapter 15.

One indication that something was wrong was the emigration figures. Some 282,000 people left Scotland in the first decade of the 20th century, which was roughly equivalent to over half the natural increase in the Scottish population. Many of these emigrants were skilled workers from urban areas who obviously thought that prospects looked better elsewhere.

After the 1830s, the process of transforming a backward rural society was completed. Scotland became part and parcel of the 'workshop of the world' – indeed, part of the largest global economy the world had even seen. Yet within half a century, there were signs that the boom was over.

Living in the City

The growth of industry encouraged a simultaneous increase in the numbers of people living in cities and towns. Scotland moved from fourth in the world league of urbanised countries in 1800 to second (behind England and Wales) in 1851. By 1900, Scotland was 50 per cent urbanised (on the basis of a town being 20,000 or more inhabitants), which was 10 per cent less than England and Wales but a lot more than France or Germany.

The pattern of urban growth was similar to what happened south of the border, but there were important differences. A larger proportion of the population in England and Wales remained in smaller urban settlements, while in Scotland the cities dominated to a much greater extent. By 1871, around one in five Scots lived in the four main cities (Glasgow, Edinburgh, Aberdeen and Dundee); 40 years later, it was one in three. However, Scotland had no metropolitan centre comparable to London. Glasgow was the largest, but as late as 1911 it was only two and half times bigger than Edinburgh, whereas London was nearly six times larger.

Why did cities grow? Two reasons:

- **Migration:** People came to Scottish cities, particularly from Ireland and the Scottish Highlands.
- **Legislation:** Boundary changes in 1846, 1891 and 1912 increased the size of Glasgow from 1,767 acres to 12,686.

Each of the main cities had its own distinctive economic and social structures. Glasgow was industrial, with 70 per cent of males and 65 per cent of females working in industry, as was Dundee. However, there was a major difference: after getting married, women in Glasgow left work and entered the home, while in Dundee a large proportion of married female workers found employment in the jute industry.

Although both cities could be described as industrial and working class, the same could not be said about Aberdeen and Edinburgh. They contained a number of industries within their boundaries – in Aberdeen the granite industry, and in Edinburgh extensive brewing concerns – but they were more middle class than other cities and towns in Scotland. They provided services – legal, medical, financial and retail – not only for their own inhabitants but also for the surrounding areas. Reflecting its middle-class status, Edinburgh had more domestic servants than any other city or town in Scotland.

Figure 14-1 shows a map of modern Scotland by county.

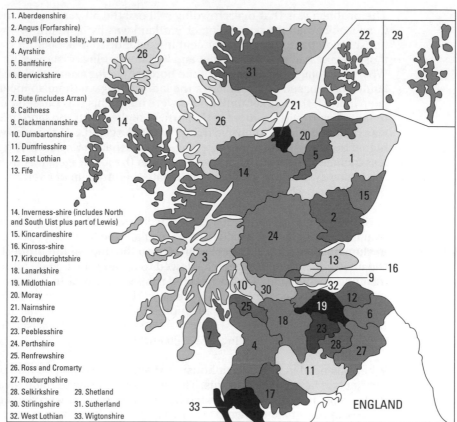

1. Aberdeenshire
2. Angus (Forfarshire)
3. Argyll (includes Islay, Jura, and Mull)
4. Ayrshire
5. Banffshire
6. Berwickshire

7. Bute (includes Arran)
8. Caithness
9. Clackmannanshire
10. Dumbartonshire
11. Dumfriesshire
12. East Lothian
13. Fife

14. Inverness-shire (includes North and South Uist plus part of Lewis)
15. Kincardineshire
16. Kinross-shire
17. Kirkcudbrightshire
18. Lanarkshire
19. Midlothian
20. Moray
21. Nairnshire
22. Orkney
23. Peeblesshire
24. Perthshire
25. Renfrewshire
26. Ross and Cromarty
27. Roxburghshire
28. Selkirkshire
29. Shetland
30. Stirlingshire
31. Sutherland
32. West Lothian
33. Wigtonshire

Figure 14-1:
Modern Scotland by county.

Squalor and overcrowding

The economic miracle and the unplanned growth of the urban environment brought with it a significant amount of human suffering. Nowhere was this better illustrated than in housing. Scotland had some of the most appalling housing in Europe, as the chief constable of Glasgow said in 1840:

> In the very centre of the city there is an accumulated mass of squalid wretchedness which is probably unequalled in any other town in the British dominions.

According to the Census of 1861, more than 1,500 single-room homes in Edinburgh were occupied by 6 to 15 persons. (A room was measured as 4.3 meters by 3.4 meters [14 feet by 11 feet].) In Dundee in 1861, 92,000 inhabitants had only five toilets between them, and three of them were in hotels!

The problem was that overcrowding still existed 50 years after the 1861 Census; over half the population of Scotland was living in one- or two-room houses, compared to only 7 per cent in England. To make matters worse, most people had to share a toilet and had no bathing or showering facilities. Why were things so bad north of the border? *Fueing* (an annual fee paid to landowners based on the value of the land sold) gave them an incentive to keep land off the market until prices were high. This was passed on to the tenants by property owners in the form of higher rents. So land in Scotland was relatively more expensive than it was in England. Also, prices were higher and real wages were lower in Scotland than in England. The Scots had less income to devote to housing. So, it was the low wages, high rents and the fueing system that combined to create the problem of overcrowding. The question was: what to do about it?

Various reforms were introduced, but they never solved the problems. One example was ticketing, which tried to regulate the number of people living in slum housing. A metal ticket was fixed to the door of the property stating the maximum number of people allowed to inhabit the house. Although well-meaning, the tenants of these ticketed properties were subject to a level of interference and control unthinkable now. Midnight raids were carried out by police and sanitary inspectors to enforce the system. But it was all to no avail because the raids were constantly frustrated by warnings passed from close to close (building to building, or tenement to tenement).

What was needed was decent housing at affordable rents, but the private market had failed to deliver this. The other option was to build local authority housing, but this was frustrated by property owners who tended to be in control of the city and town councils. They weren't likely to agree to a massive programme of public housing that would deny them an income. So, housing had to wait for the state initiatives that came after the First World War (see Chapter 15).

The following description of slum living at the end of the century shows how little progress had been made:

> Our parents established themselves in one room, with my little brother Archie. All the rest of us [four children] slept in the other room in large bunks built into a recess. The kitchen consisted of a small gas ring in the corner. The only source of water was a small basin, with a lavatory next to it. This served all the tenants on our floor.

Poor housing also had an impact on the health of the nation. The death rates among young children were scandalously high in one-room houses. Many of them died prematurely because disease spread so easily in such cramped living conditions. But many children also died in household accidents. As late as 1861, 42 per cent of all deaths in Glasgow were in the age group 1 to 10 years.

Poverty: Starving in the midst of plenty

Poverty in the 19th century was easily defined: destitution – the inability to feed, house or clothe oneself. To be classed as poor in 19th-century Scotland was to be labelled a pauper. Of course, poverty pre-dates the 19th century, but what made it such a huge social problem was that it was dramatised by being concentrated in cities and by the recurring economic slumps that put people out of work through no fault of their own.

The following is a description of the impact of unemployment on Paisley in January 1842:

> Unemployment was the rule . . . few of the workmen of Paisley were employed: they were broken up and found to be wandering about in every town in the country begging for bread.

There were no mechanisms for dealing with destitution on this level. The Old Poor Law existed, but that was only concerned with the aged, infirm and orphans, people who couldn't work. The poor law had nothing to say regarding the *able-bodied poor* (people who were able to work but for whatever reason did not). Legislation had to be introduced to deal with the new problem of mass unemployment.

On the back of the depression in Paisley, a government inquiry was set up; it recommended a new set of rules governing the provision of poor relief.

The New Poor Law of 1845

The old system had been run by the Church of Scotland, but the split known as the Disruption in 1843 led to elected parochial boards assuming control of poor relief. Rates were levied on property owners for the upkeep of the poor, but the able-bodied still had no right to statutory relief, although temporary relief could be given to them in times of emergency at the discretion of the authorities.

Among the entitled poor, the parochial boards had very clear guidelines as to which of the claimants constituted the deserving and the undeserving. As Andrew Wallace, Inspector of the Poor in Govan, explained in 1867, 'deserted wives' should be tested thoroughly because there was often collusion between the spouses. Orphans and children should be treated 'tenderly'; however, women with illegitimate children should not be taken on the pauper roll if it could be avoided because 'they have transgressed the moral law'. On the other hand, lunatics must be well cared for, although as Wallace complained, 'it is galling to think that 40 per cent of this numerous and expensive class are rendered insane through drink'.

In order to get poor relief, you had to prove that you had been resident in a parish for five years. Scottish paupers could be allowed to stay in a parish if supported by remittances from their parish of birth, but English or Irish paupers were forcibly removed. The Irish were particularly severely dealt with. Edinburgh and Dundee refused to give them relief whenever possible, and when they had to, the rates of relief were always below that given to the local population.

For the successful local claimant, rates varied across the country, but the average was between 1 shilling sixpence and 3 shillings per week. One calculation showed that for Edinburgh in 1867, 90 per cent of families on poor relief had only 1 shilling left after rent to pay for food, clothing and fuel. The rates were miserly because the poor law was intended to deter people from claiming.

But who were the poor? According to the Royal Commission on the Poor Laws of 1909, 83 per cent of those claiming poor relief in Scotland in March 1906 were women and children. Widows made up the majority of female claimants. So, the most vulnerable sections of Scottish society were the least provided for, but their ranks could be multiplied many times over during periods of economic depressions, with even skilled male workers thrown on hard times.

The Highland Clearances: The Second Wave

The speed of industrialisation and its impact on Scotland were profound, but there were equally profound changes taking place in agriculture over the course of the 19th century. These changes led to decreasing numbers of people employed on the land. In the Lowlands, the process of depopulation hardly produced any discontent, but the same could not be said of the Scottish Highlands.

The Highland Clearances had begun in the 18th century and gathered pace in the early decades of the 19th century, when peasants were forcibly removed from the land to make way for sheep (see Chapter 13). The brutality of the evictions, particularly those carried out on the Sutherland estates, are still remembered by the peoples of the Highlands and their descendants across the world. They're interpreted as an act of greed on the part of the ruling class – it acted to protect its wealth and power at the expense of the people. Thus, the whole episode is fraught with emotion and consistently provokes people to take sides.

The displaced peasantry was resettled on coastal areas on small plots of land, known as *crofts,* which were uneconomic from the start and forced crofters to find additional ways of making a living (see Chapter 13). The living was precarious and, as in Ireland, the people were highly dependent on the potato as the main source of nourishment. When the potato crop failed in the mid-1840s, the result was famine. This began what is known as the 'second wave' of Clearance.

The famine was not on the same scale as it was in Ireland, thanks to the intervention of civil society in Scotland. The free market principle upheld by the government meant that state interference was limited, but the charitable body – the Central Relief Board – averted a potential human tragedy of immense proportions.

Famine created the opportunity for the landowners to remove the surplus population from the land. The Highlands and Islands Emigration Society was set up to oversee the process of resettlement. Under the scheme, a landlord could secure a passage to Australia for a nominee at the cost of £1. Between 1846 and 1857, around 16,533 people of the poorest types, mainly young men, were assisted to emigrate. The greatest loss occurred in the islands, (particularly Skye, Mull and the Long Island), as well as the mainland parishes of the Inner Sound. But it wasn't always an agreeable affair. The brutal evictions that took place in North Uist in 1849 and those in Skye in 1853 remain a source of bitterness to this day.

The main phase of Clearance was over by the mid-1850s, but there were still unresolved issues that flamed into all-out confrontation and violence in the 1880s – popularly known as the Crofters' Wars. What caused these confrontations? In a word: desperation.

- ✔ Opportunities to earn additional income dried up with the collapse of the herring industry. In the 1870s the herring industry drew in migrants with as many as 5,000 men and women arriving in the fishing ports of Caithness and Aberdeenshire during the catching season.

- ✔ The harvests in 1881 and 1882 were poor.

- ✔ Agricultural prices were falling due to a depression in the 1870s that forced landowners to put a squeeze on rents.

- ✔ Cheaper wool and lamb imports from New Zealand and Australia were making sheep farming unprofitable in the Scottish Highlands.

The 'war' began on Skye in April 1882 when crofting families obstructed the sheriff's officer, backed by 50 Glasgow policemen, sent to enforce rent increases and carry out evictions. This became known as the 'Battle of the Braes'. From there, land raids were initiated on the Isle of Lewis. The events attracted widespread interest and support was forthcoming from the Lowlands in the form of the Highland Land Law Reform Association, which boasted a membership of 15,000 in 160 branches.

The Highland Land Law Reform Association did a lot to raise awareness of the plight of the crofters and successfully politicised the issues of land ownership. Under pressure from the public and the election of five crofting members of Parliament (MPs) in 1885, the government did two things:

✔ It sent in a boatload of marines because it feared that there would be a breakdown of law and order, as had happened in Ireland.

✔ It set up the Napier Commission to look into the 'condition of the crofters and cottars in the Highlands and Islands of Scotland'.

The Napier Commission recommendations were legislated on in 1886. The legislation provided for the three F's:

✔ Fixity of tenure

✔ Free sale

✔ Fair rents

Although between 1886 and 1950, more than 2,700 new crofts were created and a further 5,160 were enlarged, it did nothing to relieve tensions. Land raids and rent strikes continued in the Highlands well into the 1920s. It also did nothing to affect the rate of depopulation. In 1831, the population of the Highlands reached a peak of 200,955, or 8.5 per cent of the total population of Scotland; 100 years later, it was only 2.6 per cent. Education proved a far more effective way of 'clearing' people than eviction.

In Search of Democracy

Chapter 13 ends with the passing of the so-called 'Great Reform Act', which if measured in the number of new voters was a severe disappointment. But the Great Reform Act heralded the possibility of further reform, even if many people at the time thought that the franchise question was over because all property was now represented in Parliament. The 15,000 men who marched in Edinburgh in celebration at its passing watched by a crowd of 50,000 to 60,000 were of that opinion. However, that did not take into account the working class, many of whom had been active in the struggle for democracy since the 1790s.

Their disappointment was further deepened by the failure of the radical MPs in the reformed Parliament to support legislation designed to reduce the working hours of women and children in factories. In England, the introduction of the hated New Poor Law in 1834 with the workhouse as its focus also alienated the working class. In response to these developments, the first working-class movement was launched in Birmingham in 1837 to campaign through mass petitions and meetings for universal manhood suffrage. It became known as Chartism due to the fact that it had six major demands or points, including:

✔ Universal manhood suffrage for males over the age of 21

✔ Equal electoral districts to put voting in line with population

✔ Payment of MPs so that working-class men could stand for parliament and not just those who could afford it

✔ Secret ballots to stop intimidation by employers and landlords

These and a few other points seem the basis of any modern political democracy, but at the time the landowning class and the newly enfranchised middle class were alarmed by the radicalism of the Chartist demands. So, the monster petitions gathered by the Chartists in favour of reform in 1838 and 1842 were ignored by Parliament. In 1848, things got a bit nastier – hungry crowds in Glasgow called for 'Bread or Revolution', but they were never dangerous enough to overthrow the government.

The Chartist movement was a British movement, and as such it tells us something regarding how the Scots viewed themselves in the 19th century in terms of national identity. The Scots clearly had come to accept a dual identity: Scottish but at the same time British. The aim was to reform the Westminster Parliament rather than establish a separate one for Scotland. However, there were significant differences between Scottish and English Chartism.

One of the most distinctive products of Chartist activity north of the border was the setting up of Chartist churches, which were designed to combat the negativity of 'false pastors' in the Church of Scotland toward the movement. These churches performed baptisms, marriages, funerals and communion and held their own Easter, Christmas and New Year celebrations with tea drinking, concerts and dancing. There was no equivalent in England or Wales. They gave Chartism in Scotland a moral dimension missing in the latter countries.

The moralism of the movement also made it possible to adopt a more conciliatory attitude toward the middle classes than could be found in England. Chartists in Scotland were quite prepared to sign petitions in favour of the repeal of the Corn Laws. The Corn Laws were a levy on foreign imports of grain introduced in 1815 by an unreformed Parliament, which kept the price of bread artificially high; their abolition was a *cause celebre* for the middle-class supporters of free trade. When they were repealed in 1846, handloom weavers in Paisley staged a series of celebrations. The class hatred that was so apparent south of the border only really surfaced in Scotland in 1848 when young, unskilled workers and Irish in the 'Bread or Revolution' riots overwhelmed the respectable radical artisans.

The year 1848 proved a watershed for Chartism. After this, the movement collapsed, but the demand for the inclusion of the working class in the constitution did not die. It merely entered a new phase.

The Second Reform Act

The crises of the 1840s forced a number of members of the ruling class to admit that something had to be done to address the democratic deficit and to bring the respectable working class into the pale of the constitution. Lord John Russell, who in 1837 had said that electoral reform had come to an end, altered his views; by 1852, he introduced a private members' bill to widen the franchise. This sparked two decades of constitutional wrangling in Parliament, which culminated in the Second Reform Act of 1867 to 1868, an event that added around 1 million new voters (mainly urban skilled workers in the UK) and increased the size of the electorate in Scotland to 230,606.

Trade unions had argued that the denial of the vote was wrong because it 'disregarded the growing virtue and intelligence of the working class'. Their exclusion also allowed Parliament to be dominated by class interests. However, the claim this time was not for universal manhood suffrage as the Chartists demanded; instead, it was for household suffrage. This excluded slum dwellers and other undesirable elements of working-class life.

The emphasis on respectability and the moderateness of the demands of the organised working class won support within the two main parties. The surprising thing was that it was the Tories, who had opposed reform in 1832, who made the running. The Tory leader Benjamin Disraeli introduced a reform bill in 1859, arguing that if change was going to come, then it was best that the Tories should carry it out and receive the credit and, more importantly, control the extent of the changes. He didn't want a bill that would put the working class in a majority in Parliament. The application of this thinking was seen in the Second Reform Act, passed with relatively little controversy and panic compared to 1832.

The Second Reform Act had increased the size of the electorate immensely – one in three adult males could vote – but it still left a majority of men and all women without the vote. It also contained so many complicated clauses as to who did and did not have the right to vote that voter registration was placed in the hands of party agents. In certain cases, they were able to disqualify workingmen who had no party affiliations by bringing legal objections to their status as voters. Moreover, aristocratic power (read: Tory) was bolstered in rural areas by excluding agricultural labourers from the franchise.

There was also a Scottish dimension in the way that the Tories manipulated the details of the reform in their own interests. Many new constituencies were created in 1867 and 1868. On the basis of population, the number of Scottish seats should have been raised from 53 to 68, but the act only increased the number to 60. Knowing that most Scottish seats were permanently in the hands of the Liberals, the Tories wanted to limit the number of Scottish MPs. The devil is in the detail!

Where is it going to end? More reforms

It became increasingly obvious to many, especially those in the radical wing of the newly formed Liberal Party, that the enfranchisement of urban house-holders had provided the logical necessity for extending the same rights to rural householders. Radicals argued that there could be no principled objections raised toward the enfranchisement of rural inhabitants; indeed, many of them – through the redistribution of seats – had been placed in newly created boroughs and were already enjoying the vote. Another factor in their favour was the spread of literacy in rural areas, which overcame the old aristocratic objection that the labourers were too uneducated to be trusted with the vote.

The Tories were naturally suspicious and hostile to any attempts to tamper with the constitution. They were already alarmed at the spread of trade unionism among urban workers and were afraid of a similar process occurring in agriculture. When they were in trade unions, the agricultural labourers might exploit the franchise to win economic concessions from landowners. More importantly, they might try to undermine the legal power of the landed classes by demanding reform of local government, something that might lead to increased expenditure on poor relief, housing and education. The House of Lords tried to delay the bill, and that brought onto the streets of Glasgow 60,000 protesters cheered on by another 200,000 – the biggest demonstration in 19th-century Scotland.

A compromise known as the 'Arlington Street Compact' was reached, which allayed Tory fears and overcame the opposition of the House of Lords. The Third Reform Act of 1884 gave votes for the first time to lodgers and householders in the shire counties who had occupied houses or rooms for 12 months prior to registration. This increased the numbers of those eligible to vote from 2.5 million to 5 million in the UK. In Scotland, the size of the electorate doubled and, through the redistribution of seats, Glasgow had seven MPs, Edinburgh had four and Lanarkshire had six.

Was it now possible to talk of a political democracy? Well, no. Here's why:

- Forty per cent of adult males were not registered to vote.

- Domestic servants, soldiers, 'lunatics', peers, those in receipt of poor relief, prisoners and *all women* were excluded completely from the franchise.

The exclusion of all women was perhaps the greatest injustice in the electoral system, but they did not take it lying down.

Women on the march

Like the Chartists before them, the women's suffrage movement was a British movement, but there were distinctively Scottish aspects regarding tactics used to pressure the government into granting women the vote.

The women's movement came into being following the amendment of John Stuart Mill to the Second Reform Act to include the enfranchisement of women. But the immediate question that mobilised women was not the franchise but education, particularly higher education. Women were barred from the universities, which were considered male institutions. This view was challenged by Sophia Jex Blake in the late 1860s. She and other women attempted to matriculate in the medical faculty of Edinburgh University. This led to riots, opposition and intimidation by male students and staff, but eventually Parliament passed an act opening the doors to women in 1892 (although they were still banned from entering divinity and law).

The campaign for equal access to higher education radicalised women, and the focus switched from education to the suffrage question. There were women's suffrage societies in Edinburgh and Glasgow as well as in England. In 1897, they merged to form the National Union of Women's Suffrage Societies (NUWSS) under the leadership of Millicent Fawcett, wife of the Liberal MP Henry Fawcett, and the Scottish aristocrat Lady Frances Balfour, one of the daughters of the duke of Argyll. The NUWSS believed in constitutional methods of protest, such as meetings, petitions and marches.

In 1903, another society, the Women's Social and Political Union (WSPU) was set up under the leadership of Emmeline Pankhurst, wife of barrister Richard Pankhurst, and her daughters. They were committed to unconstitutional methods of protest such as attacks on property and hunger strikes.

Members of the NUWSS became known as the *Suffragists,* and members of the WPSU became known as the *Suffragettes.*

On the whole, Scottish societies favoured constitutional means of protest. Balfour argued that acts of terrorism only hardened the position of the government against granting women the vote and showed that law breakers could never become law makers. In this, she was joined by other leading suffragists such as the Scottish doctor Elsie Inglis. The Scottish movement did not enjoy the same level of support from working-class women that the movement in England did among female textile workers in Lancashire. It was more middle class in profile and more constitutional. They also resented the high-handed, autocratic leadership of Emmeline Pankhurst.

This isn't to say that there were no attacks on property in Scotland. Indeed, in 1912 and 1913, there was what the *Glasgow Herald* described as the 'outrages'. The WSPU in Scotland had members as militant as any in England.

Ethel Moorhead symbolically smashed a glass case at the Wallace monument near Stirling, threw an egg at Winston Churchill and was later imprisoned for attempted arson; Arabella Scott tried to set fire to Kelso racecourse before enduring five weeks of enforced feeding at Perth Prison; Catherine Taylor set fire to the stand at Ayr Racecourse; and, on a lighter note, Lilias Mitchell replaced the marker flags at Balmoral Golf Course with new flags painted in the colours of the WSPU.

Action in Scotland was varied and widespread, including

- Cutting telegraph and telephone wires

- Firebombing the railway station at Leuchars, near Dundee

- Setting fire to the Gatty Building at St Andrews University

- Burning Lanarkshire mansions to the ground

- Pouring corrosive acid through letter boxes across the country

- Throwing cayenne pepper at the prime minister

- Smashing shop windows

Some were arrested for their actions and when imprisoned immediately embarked on a hunger strike. This led to force feeding, with some predictably horrendous results, such as the early death of Frances Balfour's sister-in-law, Constance Lytton, largely attributed to her experiences in prison.

In 1913, the Prisoners' Temporary Discharge of Ill Health ('Cat and Mouse Act') changed government policy toward hunger strikes. Prisoners were released when they became ill. When they had recovered, they were re-arrested and taken back to prison to finish their sentences.

Things came to a head with the suicide of Emily Davison, who threw herself in front of the king's horse in the Epsom Derby in 1913. The sacrifice won the WSPU a great deal of publicity, but it had the effect of putting people off. Things had got out of hand. In any case, war was approaching and patriotism became a more important pull on women's loyalties than the vote. The main suffrage organisations suspended action during the war and, partly as a result of their contribution to the war effort, in 1918 the vote was granted to women over the age of 30.

Liberal Scotland

The franchise reforms in 1832, 1867–8 and 1884 turned Scotland into virtually a one-party state – a Liberal fiefdom. While England was largely Tory in the 19th century, Tories were conspicuous by their absence north of the border. So confident were the Liberals of their hold on the Scottish vote that they could afford to conduct intra-party squabbles in public with tremendous ferocity.

In the 1885 general election, there were rival Liberal candidates in 27 of Scotland's 72 constituencies. What exactly was the appeal of Liberalism to the Scots? Liberalism appealed to all sections of Scottish society because of

- ✔ Franchise reform
- ✔ Temperance
- ✔ Anti-landlordism
- ✔ Social justice
- ✔ Free trade
- ✔ Home rule

There was enough in the basic principles for everyone to get their teeth into – from wealthy landowners, such as the duke of Argyll (known as Whigs); to intellectuals, such as T.B. Macaulay (known as radicals); to workers (known as Lib/Labs). The great strength of Liberalism was that it was flexible – everyone had his or her own version. It was the Heinz 57 of political philosophies.

But at the end of the day, it was a coalition of different interest groups and, like all coalitions, there was an inbuilt tendency to fall apart when what divides becomes more important than what united. This happened to the Liberal Party in Scotland over the question of Irish home rule.

The attack from the right

The Tories were politically irrelevant in Scotland for most of the 19th century. The party's philosophy was seen as a 'creed for lairds and law agents' and, therefore, anathema to Scottish voters. Fortunes changed, however, with the announcement in the mid-1880s of William Gladstone, the Liberal Prime Minister's conversion to Irish home rule. This had the immediate effect of splitting the Liberal Party into two warring factions – the Liberals and the Liberal Unionists. A bit confusing, but bear with me.

The Liberal Unionists, led by Joseph Chamberlain, were implacably opposed to home rule for Ireland because they felt that it would lead to the collapse of the British Empire. Other Nationalist movements might demand the same – a sort of domino effect.

In Scotland, the Unionists had the support of the main newspapers – *The Scotsman* and the *Glasgow Herald* – as well as businessmen, lawyers and the Church of Scotland. But they could also draw on the support of some sections of the working class, particularly the Protestant Irish.

Religion and politics

Between 1841 and 1851, the Irish population of Scotland nearly doubled, which Presbyterian Scotland found very alarming. It was the industrial areas of the west of Scotland that saw the largest concentrations of Irish immigrants, with almost 29 per cent of all Irish migrants settled in Glasgow. But the smaller industrial towns of the west also had a substantial Irish presence. The population of Coatbridge in 1851 was 35.8 per cent Catholic Irish.

The Catholic Irish were discriminated against at all levels of Scottish society, from the labour market to the poor law. They were also caricatured and stereotyped as drunken and disease-ridden – typhus was known as 'Irish fever'.

Excluded from the mainstream of Scottish society, the Irish Catholics became a community within a community. This community was strengthened by the degree of intermarriage. In Greenock in 1851, 80.6 per cent of Irish men and women had married other Irish Catholics. Forty years later, the numbers were still high at 72.4 per cent.

As Catholic Irish immigrants declined in number in the late 1870s and 1880s, the Protestant Irish took up the slack. Most of these new immigrants came from the most Orange counties of the north, such as Armagh. The arrival of Ulster Protestants, with their Orange traditions, increased the tempo of sectarian rivalries. Orange lodges (local branches of the Orange Order) multiplied, with more than a quarter of them in Glasgow and Scottish membership at 25,000 in 1900.

Sectarian riots associated with the 'Glorious Twelfth parades', which commemorated the Protestant 'victory' at the Battle of the Boyne in 1690, often ended in local civil wars. For example, a violent clash between Catholics and Protestants took place in Blantyre in February 1887 and resulted in military intervention and the arrest of 51 people, including several women.

The rioting spread to Coatbridge and, after much stone throwing and window breaking, the 4th Hussars were sent in to restore order. It appeared that the whole district was under military siege, as armed soldiers and mounted constabulary were sent to Hamilton and Denny. In 1875, Catholics celebrating the centenary of Daniel O'Connell's birth in the Patrick area of Glasgow were attacked by hundreds of Orangemen, and the fighting that ensued lasted for several days.

The sectarian divisions in Scottish society also had political repercussions. The Catholic Irish were encouraged by the Catholic Church to channel their energies into home rule for Ireland, while the Protestant Irish were determined to maintain the union. So, the Liberal Unionists had the support of a large bloc of working-class Protestants in the west of Scotland. This support came into play in 1900 when, with the Boer War raging and patriotic senti-ment at a fever pitch, the Liberals failed for the first time since 1832 to win a majority of the seats in Scotland in a general election.

In 1912, the Liberal Unionists joined with the Tories to form the Conservative and Unionist Party. From that time onward, the party in Scotland was known as the Unionists.

The attack from the left

The Liberals in Scotland were under pressure not only from a resurgent right, but also from the left. The entry of the 'great unwashed' (the working class) into politics was a long-delayed phenomenon. It was only in the last few decades of the 19th century that the idea of an independent working-class party gained some credibility. Up until then, working-class men had been will-ing to give their support either to the Liberals or to the Tories.

But things were beginning to change. Why?

✔ Unskilled workers, like dockers, were becoming unionised in trade unions led by Marxists.

✔ Skilled workers were under pressure from technological change.

✔ Government intervention in industrial disputes politicised them.

Strangely enough, the politicisation of the urban working class began with concerns regarding the land. The support for the crofters in urban Scotland galvanised the left. In 1888, at a by-election in Mid-Lanark, former miner Keir Hardie stood as an independent Labour candidate. Although he was well beaten in the election, failing to win much support from the miners, the beginnings of independent labour organisation were evident. From his inter-vention, there emerged the Scottish Labour Party, which united unhappy Liberals with workers and land reformers.

Hardie realised that if the party was to succeed, the support of the trade unions was critical. As it stood, in 1889, Socialist societies had a combined membership of only around 2,000 in Scotland. In contrast, membership of the trade union movement was 750,000. A purely Scottish party was unlikely to succeed, so with the support of some trade unionists and numerous small Socialist societies, the Independent Labour Party (ILP) was formed in Bradford in January 1893. It became the forerunner of the Labour Party.

The new party was able to tap into the disappointment skilled workers had with the Liberals for failing to select working men to stand for Parliament and to protect trade unions from hostile employers and judges. The biggest ever industrial dispute in the 19th century, the engineering lockout of 1897, which was in opposition to the introduction of new technology, ended in defeat of the workers. 'Get political' – that was the message, and the trade unions did just that. Gradually, support grew and the modern Labour Party was launched in 1906.

But it should be noted that Labour made greater strides in England than it did in Scotland. The Scottish ILP had only 5,000 members in 1910. Labour organisation was said to be a shambles. The party had only three MPs and 200 councillors of all kinds – parish, town and country – and school boards by the outbreak of war in 1914.

There were two nuts Labour had to crack before they could become a major player in Scottish politics:

✔ Winning the Irish vote

✔ Destroying the Liberals

They proved unable to do this. Every time they put up Irish Catholic candidates at elections, they suffered a Protestant backlash. Moreover, the political expression of the Irish – the United Irish League – was viewed by contempt by Labour leaders. Patrick Dollan of the ILP claimed he would rather see Labour's prospects put back 30 years than form an alliance with a bunch of publicans.

Catholic attitude toward Labour was shaped by the papacy's hostility to Socialism as atheistic. There were also fears that Labour would introduce non-denominational schooling, ending the Catholic Church's control of the education of Catholic children.

Irish Catholics continued to support the Liberal Party, but then again most Scots did. Liberalism and the kind of values it stood for – such as anti-landlordism – resonated with the Scottish people, many of whom had first-hand experience of famine and Clearance. As a Labour Party inquiry in 1911 stated: 'Scotland stood by the Liberal Government so solidly because it hates the House of Lords and the landlords.'

Liberalism restored

Just when it seemed that the party was over for the Liberals, they went on to win a stunning victory in the 1906 general election. How was that possible given the squeeze on the party from both the left and the right? The answer lay in the conversion of Joseph Chamberlain to protectionism. Immediately, it split the Scottish Unionists. As representatives for many constituencies in the west of Scotland, Unionist MPs were only too aware of the necessity of the export market for Scottish goods. Imposing tariffs on imports would encourage similar action by other countries. Scottish goods might get priced out of markets because of the high duties imposed on them. Their jobs were on the line!

Another action that incensed the Scots was the decision of the House of Lords to award half the properties of the Free Church to a small minority, the Wee Frees, to merge with the United Presbyterians to form the United Free Church. As defenders of the prerogatives of the Lords, the Unionists bore the brunt of the anger. Maybe it's hard for people to understand their anger today, but people took their religion seriously.

To mend the damage, the Unionists introduced the Scottish Churches Act, but it was too late. Between 1902 and 1904, the government lost every by-election in Scotland, a fact that restored the Liberal majority north of the border. By the time of the 1906 general election, the Liberals were in good shape, standing for their core principles. A crushing victory was achieved, with the Liberals winning 58 Scottish seats against the Unionists'12. This was once again confirmed in 1910, when the elections were fought over the 'People's Budget' and reducing the powers of the House of Lords.

So, in the last election before the First World War the Liberals were restored to the position they had enjoyed for most of the 19th century. As long as morality and moral conduct were at the heart of political debate, Liberalism remained the rallying point for the political allegiances of the Scottish people. However, when class and class interests moved to the forefront of politics – as they did after 1918 – then the values that Liberalism was based on seemed out of touch with the new political realities (see Chapter 15). But in 1914, no one was in a position to predict this.

Emigration and Empire

Liberal MP Sir Charles Dilke, writing in 1888, remarked that: 'In British settlements, from Canada to Ceylon, from Dunedin to Bombay, for every Englishman that you meet who has worked himself up to wealth from small beginnings without external aid, you find ten Scotchmen.'

The Scots had made a major contribution to the expansion of the British Empire as administrators, engineers, entrepreneurs and soldiers (see Chapter 13), so much so that historians have talked about the 'Scottish Empire'. The influence of the Scots could be felt all over the globe – from North America to Australasia, from Asia to Africa. Yes, they were everywhere.

But the Scots didn't come just to exploit other peoples and resources; they also came as settlers, with their distinctive culture and religious traditions. Even today, Scottish food, culture and athletics are celebrated in the many Highland gatherings, Burns' Clubs and Caledonian Societies in North America and farther afield.

North America

In the United States, the Scots made important contributions to the development of the economy. For example, the following men were all Scottish:

- **Andrew Carnegie,** an iron and steel manufacturer
- **David Dunbar Buick,** a car manufacturer
- **William Blackie,** a tractor manufacturer

In Canada, Lord Mount Stephen was behind the creation of the great Canadian Pacific Railway, and other Scotsmen dominated the economy to the extent that one-third of the country's business elite were of Scottish origin.

Environmentally, the Scot John Muir was the driving force behind the establishment of National Parks Movement in the United States.

Culturally, American gospel music is accredited by some historians to Scottish Gaelic speakers from North Uist.

India

The Scottish presence was also strongly evident in India. The first three governors-general of India were Scots. Vast fortunes were made by imperial administrators and entrepreneurs. However, there were also scholars and scientists who made important contributions to Indian culture and society, including

- **Colin Campbell,** who completed the first geographical survey of India
- **Robert Kydd,** who created the botanic gardens in Calcutta

Even after the dissolution of the East India Company in 1857 and the introduction of competitive entry into the British administration, Scots still played a disproportionate part in the running of India. Seven of the 12 viceroys were Scottish, and many Scots served as judges, district commissioners and so on.

India became a massive market for the British economy, but more importantly for the metal industries of Scotland. Practically all the railway engines in India were built in Springburn in Glasgow. The east of Scotland was also strongly linked economically through the jute trade. Dundee became the centre of jute making in the world and the Camperdown works of the Baxter Brothers was the largest jute mill in the world.

Australasia

It was not always the pursuit of filthy lucre that was the driving force behind imperial expansion. Religious impulses were behind the desire to populate New Zealand and to create 'little Scotlands'. The Otago settlement in the South Island and the Waipu settlement in the North Island were the products of two Scottish ministers. Dunedin (Gaelic for 'Edinburgh') became the capital of the Otago settlement and already had a university by 1869. In Waipu, Gaelic was the first language in people's homes until the 1880s and many still spoke it in the 1920s.

In neighbouring Australia, the Scots were attracted like others because of the 'Gold Rush' of 1851, although prior to that, immigrants were drawn from displaced Highland peasantry and others looking for a better life. Between 1832 and 1851, around 50,000 Scots settled in Australia. Some Scots made notable contributions to Australian society. Governor Lachlan Macquarie, from Ulva, the Inner Hebrides, is seen as the father of Australia, and Catherine Helen Spence, suffragist and journalist, who arrived in 1839 from Melrose in the Scottish Borders, is considered Australia's greatest woman.

The dark side

The British Empire's growth involved the suppression of local peoples and their cultures. This was graphically illustrated in Australia with the brutal treatment of the Aborigines. The Scots were at the forefront of this assault on native peoples, showing themselves to be as ruthless as any other ethnic group when it came to land grabbing. This was also true in New Zealand were the Maori population fell from around 150,000 in 1800 to 37,000 in 1872 as a result of a protracted struggle with the settlers over land rights.

So, although the Scots distinguished themselves in many areas of cultural and economic life, the story of conquest and settlement was not always a pretty one.

Africa

Much of the justification for imperial expansion was based on the idea of the civilising mission of higher racial groups toward more backward and racially inferior peoples. Basically, we were doing them a favour. British rule was extended throughout the less-developed world through a mixture of the Bible and gunpowder. However, it was not so much as settlers that the Scots played a significant role in British expansion in Africa, but more as individuals working through the Scottish missions.

The explorer and missionary David Livingstone inspired many others to follow him to Africa, the 'dark continent'. Mary Slessor, a mill girl from Dundee, was one of them. She, like her idol, went 'literally where no white man had gone before' in her quest to save souls in the Bight of Biafra on the coast of Nigeria (formerly known as Calabar). However, by driving into the uncharted interiors of the continent and encouraging trade between the natives and British traders, they opened up the territories to further imperial expansion.

As to their mission to save souls, they were spectacularly unsuccessful. Still, men and women, such as Livingstone and Slessor, helped in the long run to change deeply entrenched notions regarding the divine right to rule 'lesser races' to a more ethical imperial policy.

Slessor, in particular, felt the native population to be only inferior to Europeans in as much as they were without God. Their desire to bring education to Africans unconsciously created national independence movements in central, eastern and southern Africa, as well as India. Moreover, it was the educational work of Presbyterian missionaries that was largely responsible for creating the widely held belief that Scottish education was the best in the world.

A Scottish Empire?

The Scots were important to the development of the British Empire in diverse ways: as businessmen, as educators, as missionaries, as imperial administrators and as soldiers. Their contribution was so substantial that it has influenced some historians refer to 'the Scottish Empire'. Although the Scots were hugely important to the growth globally of British influence, to argue that the empire was *essentially* their creation would be to ignore the role of the British state and other national groups such as the English and the Irish. The Scots may have run the empire and profited by it, but at the end of the day it was London that decided its fate. It was English laws and civil institutions that the Scots were to uphold and live by.

The War to End All Wars

The 'scramble for Africa' in the closing decades of the 19th century high-lighted the tensions that existed between the imperial powers in Europe. Britain had an empire the sun never set on, and others wanted a piece of the action. Still it took the assassination of a little-known aristocrat, Archduke Franz Ferdinand, in Sarajevo, Bosnia, in June 1914, to precipitate a war of massive proportions.

War was to affect Scotland socially, economically and politically.

The social costs of war

The onset of war saw a great deal of patriotic breast-beating. Young men couldn't wait to get out of dull, boring jobs and travel and experience adventure in a war that would be over by Christmas – or so the politicians claimed. The enthusiasm for war can be shown statistically:

- By the end of August 1914, 20,000 men had been processed by the recruiting office in the Gallowgate, Glasgow.

- By the end of 1915, the British total of volunteers was 2,466,719. Out of this, 13 per cent, or 320,589, were Scots.

- By the end of the war, the number of Scots in the armed forces had risen to 688,416.

The enthusiasm for war stalled when the horrors showed themselves in the rising numbers of dead and wounded. The government introduced conscription in 1916, which meant that all men of a certain age could be made to join up unless they were physically unable, were in restricted occupations (such as coalmining) or were conscientious objectors.

The war lasted 1,564 days. Scotland's losses during that time amounted officially to 74,000, but this was based on the arithmetic of dividing the British total by 10, because Scotland made up about 10 per cent of the British and Irish population. The losses were later revised to 100,000, or 13 per cent of the total. Even later they were upgraded to 142,218. The Scottish death rate was exceeded only by that of Serbia and Turkey.

The Black Watch regiment lost 10,000 men, as did the Highland Light Infantry. In Glasgow, 18,000, or 1 in 57, did not return from war. Of the 13,568 men who volunteered from the Scottish universities, 2,026 were killed. The majority of casualties were in the 16 to 34 age group, with 45,000 dead. There were also 150,000 men seriously wounded. Added together, it meant that 20 per cent of the active male population of Scotland was dead or injured.

Indeed, there was hardly a home in Scotland untouched by war. Husbands, fathers, brothers, uncles and cousins perished. Of those who survived, some lost limbs and others lost their minds.

The economy of war

It's often said that war is good for business, and the First World War proved to be no exception. Businesses concerned with the arming and supplying the troops made huge profits, while workers were subjected to long hours, oppressive levels of supervision and rising costs. It was said of the jute industry in Dundee that 'Jute fibres had been turned into strands of gold' –such was the huge demand for sacking and uniforms of all kinds. Workers trying to get a share of this 'gold' went on an unsuccessful 11-week strike in 1916.

The war was an economically divisive experience. Workers protested that it should not be an occasion for profiteering. In 1918, Tom Johnson, editor of the ILP weekly paper *Forward,* published a pamphlet, 'The Huns at Home', in which war profiteers were the 'Huns'. Protest slogans included 'the Prussians in Partick' and 'Fighting the Huns at Home'.

But the war brought opportunities, even if only temporary, for unskilled and semi-skilled workers, particularly women, in the munitions industry to earn higher wages. Labour shortages arose due to the numbers of men in the armed forces. Nearly half the men between the ages of 15 and 49 in Scotland were in uniform. They had to be replaced, so women were brought into the labour force in large numbers:

- ✔ In 1911, 185,442 men were employed in heavy industry on Clydeside compared to 3,758 women.

- ✔ By the end of the war, 31,500 women were employed in the munitions industry in Scotland.

The presence of untrained workers in previously skilled occupations meant that the job had to be simplified. These workers had to hit the ground running – the Shells Scandal of 1915, as the *Daily Mail* called it, showed that the boys at the front were not adequately armed as stocks of shells ran out. Production of armaments had to be ratcheted up. This led to the introduction of 'dilution' (reducing the skill content of work so that women could do work previously considered the preserve of skilled men) – the most contentious development of the war.

The industrial discontent cause by the scheme was compounded by the introduction of industrial conscription. A system of 'leaving certificates' was included in the measures, which shop steward David Kirkwood branded a 'slave's clause', because workers could leave their employment only with their employer's consent. Definitely not fair.

Red Clyde

In response to these measures, the Clyde Workers' Committee (CWC) was formed. This was a body composed mainly of shop stewards who had been well schooled in Marxist economics. They could represent the workers' complaints, because the official trade unions had signed an agreement with the government at the start of the war not to do anything to impede production. With unions' hands tied behind their backs, step forward the revolutionaries. Illegal strikes were called against the provisions of the Munitions Act of 1915.

Lloyd George, then minister of munitions, met the workers in December 1915, and they gave him a hostile reception, introducing him as 'the best paid munitions worker in Britain'. Failure to pacify the workers led to a series of measures intended to destroy the CWC. Its leading members were arrested and tried for sedition. Found guilty, some were imprisoned and others deported, normally to Edinburgh.

By these means industrial discontent was silenced. But did the shop stewards really pose that much of a threat? Were the actions of the state over the top? A couple of things to bear in mind:

✔ Skilled workers were more interested in defending their own interests than those of the working class as a whole.

✔ There was a failure by the shop stewards to link the industrial discontent with the political struggle against the war.

When tried before the court, the revolutionary chairman of the CWC, William Gallacher of the British Socialist Party, made a cringing apology, saying that he 'had no desire to impede production' and a fellow worker was called to give evidence that he had opposed strikes. Interestingly, John Maclean, a school teacher revolutionary, in his famous 'speech from the dock', condemned the leaders of the CWC for their lack of revolutionary purpose.

But there was a real dilemma even for the revolutionary elements in the CWC: to actively oppose the war ran the risk that one's own country might be defeated. Because the CWC was never prepared to take that risk, the industrial power at its disposal was never used politically to bring the war to an end.

Rent strikes

Most of the housing in Scotland was in the privately rented sector. So, even before war broke out, rents were a sensitive issue. During the war, Glasgow was flooded with munitions workers earning fairly high wages, and the housing factors decided that they could afford to pay a little more in rent. The problem with this decision was that, because it was an across-the-board increase, it penalised those families whose main breadwinner was at the front or had been invalided out of the army through injury. Their incomes were too little to afford the rise in rents. However, failure to pay the increase meant eviction. Not everyone was patriotic and doing his bit! Taking advantage of war to enrich oneself incensed the working class of Glasgow, especially when it was directed at the families of soldiers.

Attempts to evict tenants were met with mass resistance and a rent strike. These strikes were organised by the women of Clydeside. The strongholds of resistance were in the shipbuilding constituencies of Govan and Pollock. Twenty-five thousand households refused to pay rent. The pressure by the tenants forced the government to intervene. In 1915, it introduced the Rent and Mortgages Restrictions Act, which pegged rents at pre-war levels. It was the first time the state had intervened in the housing market. This brought home to the strikers and the labour movement that there untapped possibilities for social reform that a government of the people could unleash.

The politics of war

The First World War set in motion a series of political changes that would bear fruit in the peace that followed (see Chapter 15). Under the impact of war, the political landscape of Scotland began to profoundly alter. The Liberal one-party state that had been re-established in the early 1900s was seriously undermined, and a new configuration was beginning to emerge, dominated by Labour and the Unionists.

Liberals

What undermined the Liberal Party in Scotland? First, there was the war itself. Many Liberals were pacifists, and just as they had opposed the Boer War (1899–1902), they opposed the First World War when it broke out in 1914. Second, there was the introduction of conscription in 1916, which a large number of Liberals felt was a breach of civil liberties.

However, these factors faded into in significance when Herbert Asquith was replaced as prime minister by Lloyd George in 1916, an act which split the Liberal Party in two. The followers of Asquith and Lloyd George hated each other with a vengeance, feelings that carried on into the immediate post-war years (see Chapter 15).

Another factor that weakened the Liberals in Scotland was the disaffection of the Irish Nationalist community. Initially, the Catholic Irish were as enthusiastic about defending king and country; in fact, six people from Glasgow were awarded Britain's highest military honour, the Victoria Cross. But the violent Easter Rising in Dublin in 1916 to establish a Socialist republic in an independent Ireland changed attitudes. The rising was put down ferociously by the British army; its leaders, among them the Scot James Connolly, were executed. Added to this was the introduction of conscription in Ireland in the last stages of war. Because it was Liberal prime ministers who approved these actions, the Irish deserted the party in droves.

Labour

Just before war broke out in August 1914, Keir Hardie, leader of the Labour Party, called for 'No alliances, no increased armaments, no intervention in the Balkans, [and] fraternity with the workers of the world'.

The workers put country before class, and that broke Hardie's heart. He died soon after, on 26 September 1915. So at the outset, the anti-war position was an unpopular one. Of Labour's 17 town councillors in Glasgow, only two spoke out against the war, and both in Edinburgh and Glasgow the trades councils were pro-war.

What made people oppose the war? Anti-war Labour leaders saw wars as the product of the greed of arms manufacturers and financiers. They also opposed conscription because they felt the selection process was biased against the working class. So, it was the inequality of sacrifice demanded of the workers that provided the focus for opposition rather than the war itself. If we were going to have conscription, then it was for everything, including wealth. It was war Socialism!

Like the shop stewards, many of the opponents of war paid a high price for their opposition. James Maxton, a school teacher, was arrested for sedition and incarcerated in Calton Jail in Edinburgh. Conditions were brutal, with a daily diet of bread, water and porridge, combined with long hours of solitary confinement. John Maclean, the Marxist school teacher, suffered a mental breakdown, as did others.

However, the anti-war movement, due to rising casualties and disillusionment with how the war was being conducted both on the home front and the battlefield, grew in strength. The Scottish Trades Union Congress claimed that by 1917, the 'War Party is a discredited minority in nearly all the Trades and Labour Councils north of the Tweed'. On May Day 1918, 100,000 Glaswegians defied the law and stopped work to demonstrate for a negotiated peace.

Although opposed to the war, there was no thought of using it to overthrow the government. The Russian Revolution of October 1917, however, did put the idea in a few heads. Mass demonstrations were held to celebrate the establishment of the Bolshevik state, but there was no attempt to emulate it. As ILPer John Wheatley remarked, 'everyone pointed to the Russian road, but none was ready to lead the way'.

It was only John Maclean and those grouped around him who saw in the war a potentially revolutionary situation. But in spite of his popularity with the Glasgow working class (thousands turned out to welcome his release from jail in July 1917), his views were unrepresentative. At no time was he able to translate his popularity into a mass movement. However, the government, taking no chances, kept him out of the way for most of the war.

In the end, it was not the revolutionaries who gained much by the war; instead, it was the more moderate ILP that saw its support grow. There was a 300 per cent increase in ILP membership and a 50 per cent increase in the number of branches. Disillusioned Liberals, housewives, skilled workers and the Irish began an irreversible shift in allegiance away from the party of Gladstone to the party of Labour.

Unionists

The Unionists had been trounced at the polls in Scotland in 1906 and twice in 1910. Any electoral gains made since that time up to the war were due to Labour splitting the vote. In a straight contest with a Liberal, the Unionist stood no chance of victory. It was boys against men.

However, the war brought an electoral truce between the parties, and this benefited the Unionists – all they had to do was act more patriotically than Labour or the Liberals. They were pretty good at this and were well to the fore in recruitment campaigns. Moreover, they never endured the arguments, debates and splits suffered by their rivals. Thus, the Unionists were becoming, in the eyes of the Scottish people, the party of empire and patriotism, ready to stand up for king and country.

They also enjoyed the support of the Church of Scotland, which was vociferous in its support for the war and the campaign at the end to hang the kaiser. So much for the Christian value of loving your neighbour! The business community, seeing the deep divisions in the Liberal Party after 1916, and worried about the rise of Labour and the trade unions, was also moving closer to the Unionists. This signalled the class divisions that were opening up in Scottish society – divisions that would destroy the Liberal Party as a force in Scottish politics (see Chapter 15).

Interestingly, of the Unionist candidates in the 1918 general election, 46 per cent had a military prefix. Of the victorious ones, 11 were businessmen, 9 were landowners and military men, 9 were lawyers and the other 3 were from various other professions.

Putting it all together

Although the First World War did not create a revolutionary situation on Clydeside, it generated important political and social changes. Fundamental shifts in the balance of power occurred:

- ✔ The free market in housing rents was destroyed.
- ✔ The state was forced to co-operate with the trade unions in running the economy.
- ✔ The dominance of the Liberals was broken.
- ✔ The personal standing of those in the ILP who had opposed the war was raised immediately – James Maxton, John Wheatley and others became household names.

These changes would shape the social and political agenda in the immediate post-war years.

Part VI
New Beginnings (1918–2000)

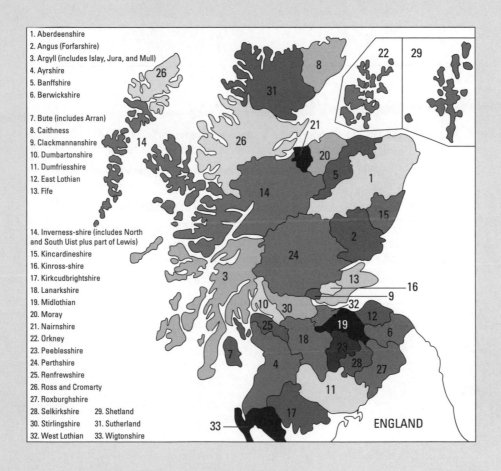

1. Aberdeenshire
2. Angus (Forfarshire)
3. Argyll (includes Islay, Jura, and Mull)
4. Ayrshire
5. Banffshire
6. Berwickshire

7. Bute (includes Arran)
8. Caithness
9. Clackmannanshire
10. Dumbartonshire
11. Dumfriesshire
12. East Lothian
13. Fife

14. Inverness-shire (includes North and South Uist plus part of Lewis)
15. Kincardineshire
16. Kinross-shire
17. Kirkcudbrightshire
18. Lanarkshire
19. Midlothian
20. Moray
21. Nairnshire
22. Orkney
23. Peeblesshire
24. Perthshire
25. Renfrewshire
26. Ross and Cromarty
27. Roxburghshire
28. Selkirkshire   29. Shetland
30. Stirlingshire   31. Sutherland
32. West Lothian   33. Wigtonshire

In this part . . .

✔ Identify the changes in the Scottish economy, particularly the collapse of heavy industry and the rise of the service sector.

✔ Consider the impact of the changes ushered in by the welfare state.

✔ Examine the political revolution after the First World War.

✔ Look at the rise of Nationalism in Scotland with the rise of the Scottish National Party in the 1970s, its collapse in the 1980s and its rebirth in the first decade of the 21st century.

✔ Consider the prospects for independence.

Chapter 15

The Devil's Decades: Politics and Poverty (1918–1945)

....

In This Chapter

▶ Uncovering the causes of mass unemployment

▶ Looking at the living conditions of the unemployed

▶ Understanding the changing political order

....

The so-called 'Great War' heralded a new beginning for Scotland and the rest of Britain. The triumphant prime minister, Lloyd George, toured the country promising a land fit for heroes. Instead, we got mass unemployment and economic depression. The changing economic fortunes of Scotland produced the backdrop not only for industrial conflict on a massive scale, but also for far-reaching political changes that saw the once all-powerful Liberal Party reduced to a rump of members of Parliament (MPs) as the new political order of Labour and Conservative asserted itself.

Toward the Depression: The Economy and Employment

During the war, Britain suffered tremendous losses – not just in men, but also in industries like merchant shipping – and the first priority of the government was to put right the deficit. This brought expectations of a post-war economic boom, which initially was more than realised. For example, shipbuilding in Britain saw the number of berths increase by more than 40 per cent above the 1914 level. Everyone was happy, profits were high, wages were good and the war had been won! Hip-hip-hooray!

But it wasn't to last. The world stumbled into depression, and unemployment grew to massive proportions everywhere in western Europe and the United States. Scotland was particularly hard hit – it became one of the unemployment black spots in the UK. The number of people on welfare grew to unprecedented proportions. The politicians were all at sea – no one had an answer that could put people back to work. Everyone was waiting for the expected upturn in trade, which never came. The onset of war in the late 1930s provided the solution to the depressed Scottish economy.

Things aren't working

Things began to go pear-shaped around the end of 1920, and the first signs of depression were seen in the growing numbers of unemployed. Demobilisation had brought thousands of extra workers into the labour market. Women who had been employed in what was described as 'men's work' (engineering, shipbuilding and munitions) were blackmailed into withdrawing into the home, because who would've wanted to stand in the way of brave men finding work? The male was still seen as the breadwinner, and women's work was undervalued and underpaid.

But the demobilised soldiers were re-entering an economy that found itself unable to meet the challenges of the post-war world. Scotland's economy was based mainly on heavy industry. We made ships, railway engines and machines of all kinds, and produced coal and steel, which were not in demand after 1920. World trade collapsed as countries tried to halt the import of foreign-made goods. To make matters worse, British/Scottish manufactures were expensive because the pound was overvalued after a return to the gold standard in 1925. As a result, Scottish exports dropped like a stone.

The reaction of employers was to cut costs, which in practice meant lowering wages and increasing hours – measures that were opposed by the trade unions. This led to massive numbers of days lost in strikes, particularly in the coal industry. Coal was the focal point of industrial conflict, and disputes there culminated in the General Strike of May 1926, when other trade unionists came out in sympathy with the miners. For nine days, Britain was paralysed, and to some it appeared that the country was on the verge of a class war. However, compromise was reached between the trade union movement and the government and employers. The Trades Union Congress called off the strike, and workers reluctantly returned to work.

Whether Britain was on the brink of revolution is much disputed by historians. Some have argued that the workers were sold out by their leaders, so 1926 was a missed revolutionary opportunity to fundamentally change British society. But on balance it would appear that the trade union leaders, who had no intention of overthrowing a democratically elected government, realised the weakness of their position – both organisationally and constitutionally – and called off the strike.

The miners carried on for another nine months, but because of hunger, they were eventually forced to return to work under worse conditions. From that point, strikes were less frequent and the number of trade unionists fell dramatically.

It's not getting any better

Many people, faced with the prospect of unemployment or, if they had work, falling wages, decided to pack their bags and head elsewhere. Half a million Scots, or 8 per cent of the population, left the country in the 1920s – a figure that more than dwarfs the Highland Clearances of the early 19th century. This was compared to 0.9 per cent for England and 4.5 per cent for Ireland. Things were obviously bad, but could they get any worse? The short answer was: yes!

The Wall Street crash of 1929 saw the world economy nosedive into depression and huge increases in unemployment. By 1932, average male unemployment was nearly 30 per cent for Scotland as a whole, and over 50 per cent in mining and shipbuilding. The young male school leavers and older workers were hardest hit. Workers in the west of Scotland, where the heavy industries were concentrated, suffered more than those in the east, with the exception of Dundee, where 37,000 people in the city were out of work in 1932. Registered unemployment in Motherwell in 1933 was 49 per cent; in nearby Wishaw, 53 per cent of the workforce was on the dole (known today as social security).

What made matters worse was the fact that many of those families that had left in the 1920s were returning in the 1930s, especially from the United States, where the depression was even worse. So, emigration, which was the safety valve for Scottish society, fell by three-quarters in the 1930s. Strangely enough, despite the poor economic conditions, the birth rate rose in Scotland – it was 30 per cent higher in Scotland than in England. Add returning immigrants to a higher birth rate and it meant there were a lot of people looking for work that wasn't there.

Hard Times

As you can imagine, social conditions were about as bad as the state of the economy. John Boyd Orr's book *Food, Health and Income* (1935) showed that the diet of the Scottish poor was insufficient to maintain health. At the high point of the depression in Dundee in the early 1930s, the staple diet was said to be 'bried [bread] and marge [margarine]'.

Diphtheria was rife among children. One-third of Glasgow children were infested with fleas and lice, and scabies was common. Shoeless children were found in large numbers in many of Scotland's towns and villages.

Many of the diseases contracted by children were due to the appalling housing conditions. Sixty per cent of Dundee's and Glasgow's populations lived in houses of one or two rooms with no toilet or bath. Housing conditions were so bad in Glasgow that one of the town councillors described the city as 'earth's nearest suburb to hell'. But even in more middle-class cities like Aberdeen, things could be equally desperate. One woman recalled that in the city's Littlejohn Street in the 1920s, 14 families had to share two toilets and had no gas or electricity and only an open fire to cook on.

The demoralisation of the adult workforce was palpable, particularly among skilled workers. Although they were no strangers to unemployment, they faced long periods of idleness. The iconic image of men in mufflers and caps standing on street corners with nothing to do was captured in prose by the Scottish poet Edwin Muir, driving in 1933 through the bleak industrial landscapes of Lanarkshire past groups of 'idle, sullen-looking young men'. He observed that 'Airdrie and Motherwell are the most improbable places imaginable in which to be left with nothing to do; for only rough work could reconcile anyone to living in them'. Most of the unemployed were resigned to their fate, schooled in the art of patience and waiting like politicians for the expected upturn in trade.

The government's treatment of the unemployed was on the harsh side. So many petty indignities were forced on the workless by a heartless bureaucracy, including the following:

- In the 1920s, the 'not genuinely seeking work test' forced the unemployed to prove to the authorities that they had sought non-existent work on a daily basis before they could receive benefit.
- The Anomalies Act of 1931 withdrew unemployment benefit from working married women and casual workers.

But these acts were nothing in terms of humiliation compared to the introduction of the household means test later that year. When statutory benefit was exhausted after 26 weeks, claimants went on the dole. They had a visit from an inspector to ascertain circumstances and to sell anything of value. Because it was household income, any children earning money, even if only delivering milk or newspapers, would be seen as contributing to that income, and the benefit would be reduced in proportion to their earnings. This forced parents to expel children over school age from the home. For this reason, the means test broke up families, and the system and those who operated it were detested by the unemployed.

The impact of the household means test and the general state of the unemployed is clear when you consider that *one-quarter* of the total population of Scotland was dependent on the dole in 1935.

For those on state aid, there was a marked change in the gender character of the claimant. In 1914, the typical claimant of poor relief was a woman, who was widowed, sick or disabled; in 1938, it was a man. Before 1914, there were few areas where more than 5 per cent of the population was claiming poor relief; in Bridgeton, Cowcaddens and the Gorbals in Glasgow, this number had increased to over two-thirds.

An expatriate Scot returning from the United States in the early 1930s remarked, 'Most of my pals are still in the Gallowgate. Some of them haven't had a job in their lives and have been living off the parish.'

Responses to unemployment

Unemployment on this kind of mass level drew a variety of responses from those affected. Some went on hunger marches; some looked for scapegoats; and others just looked for forms of escapism.

Organised opposition: The hunger marchers

Not all the unemployed took things lying down (nor did the employed; see 'Things aren't working', earlier in the chapter). Some people organised hunger marches – the first national one took place in 1922. These marches were organised by the National Unemployed Workers' Movement, a Communist front organisation viewed with distrust by the Labour Party (see 'Jerusalem Postponed: The Politics of the Interwar Years', a bit later) and the trade unions. But although they tramped the streets protesting at unemployment and government welfare policies, they had little effect. The government continued to pursue its austerity programme of cutting public expenditure.

Increasing sectarianism

In a situation of mass unemployment, some Scots looked for a scapegoat (as the Germans had done). The Catholic Irish were Scotland's equivalent of the Jews. Extremist Protestant groups were established in Edinburgh and Glasgow; they were committed to reducing Catholic participation in public life. Surprisingly, the allegedly middle-class city of Edinburgh, and not working-class Glasgow, became the scene of street battles involving thousands of people in the mid-1930s.

The Protestant Action Society, under the leadership of John Cormack, won one-third of votes cast in the 1936 local elections in Edinburgh; three years earlier in Glasgow, Alexander Ratcliffe's Scottish Protestant League won 23 per cent of the poll. This proved to be the high point of Protestant extremism; events overtook them. The prospect of war in Europe against Nazi Germany turned local politics into a mere sideshow. Moreover, if a war was to be fought for democracy, it would have been the utmost hypocrisy to support systematic discrimination against a part of the population on the basis of their ethnicity and faith.

Let's dance away our problems

Organised opposition to welfare cuts or sectarian conflict were only some of the ways the workless reacted to the depression. One way out was escapism, in the form of the following:

- **Movies:** According to some estimates, 80 per cent of the young unemployed went to the cinema at least once a week.

- **Dancing:** This was the age of the dance hall. Scotland's cities were struck by a dance craze in the 1920s and 1930s and the *palais de danse* was packed every night of the week.

- **Sport:** Dog racing and, of course, football were popular. Hillwalking and mountain climbing also became popular among the unemployed, with clubs like Craig Dhu, Ptarmigan and the Lomond emerging in the 1920s and 1930s. Cycling was another way out from the polluted cities. One cyclist from Dundee spoke of Saturday afternoons in which cycling clubs would gather at the gates of Camperdown Park like 'great flocks of colourful birds'.

Incremental improvements

Bad as things were, there were some improvements in living conditions. The fall in food prices saw living standards improve for those who had work, but advances in nutrition, better health standards and housing legislation that increased the level of public sector accommodation and improved the supply of basic amenities worked together to improve living conditions even for the unemployed.

In the 1930s, the infant mortality rate in Aberdeen fell by over one-third in the age group 0 to 5 years, which put it on a par with Dundee, but still above Edinburgh. Children in Aberdeen who survived beyond their fifth year also experienced a small increase in weight and height. In 1928–29, a typical

5-year-old in Aberdeen would have weighed 18.3 kilograms (40.3 pounds) and measured 104.6 centimetres (41.2 inches); ten years later, the respective figures were 18.5 kilograms (40.7 pounds) and 106.7 centimetres (42 inches).

The increase in public sector housing was an important factor in bringing down the infant mortality rate. Between 1919 and 1939, two-thirds of new house building was in the public sector, compared to only 26 per cent in England. A move from an overcrowded, squalid house to a council flat was a dream come true for many slum dwellers.

As one Aberdeen tenant put it, 'When we got a shift to Froghall Road we thought we were in a mansion.'

Council housing was of a much higher standard and better equipped with basic amenities, such as a bath, than that at the lower end of the private sector, but rents were higher. In Dundee, rents for council houses amounted to nearly half the average textile worker's wage. So, only the better paid could afford the new homes. For the poor, the slum was still the only option.

Getting Back to Work

International events threw a lifeline to the economy. The rise of an aggressive and confrontational Fascism in Germany and Italy created tensions with the European democracies. War became a strong possibility in the late 1930s, which drove up armament production.

War materials of all kinds – from warships to tanks to uniforms – were needed, and Scotland was well placed to take advantage of this changing economic situation. Unemployment fell to around 15 per cent in 1939, and although this was 5 per cent higher than the UK average, people were beginning to have money back in their pockets. Interestingly, the unskilled benefited more – the wage difference between unskilled and skilled workers narrowed in the 1930s.

The revival of the Scottish economy only underlines the fact that war is good for business. But was war a blessing or a curse? On the one hand, it halted a process of change away from the Victorian economic model to the new consumer-based industries; on the other hand, it brought a welcome if temporary return to prosperity. The transition of the economy was postponed, but when it arrived in the decades after the Second World War, it would make things harder to bear.

Jerusalem Postponed: The Politics of the Interwar Years

The political order underwent a peaceful revolution in the interwar years in Scotland as the once-dominant Liberal Party imploded. The once-insignificant Labour Party had become the dominant political force in Scotland in the 1920s, but that dominance was eroded by the Tories in the crisis-ridden 1930s.

Fractures within the Liberal Party

For most of the 19th century, Scotland was dominated politically by the Liberal Party (see Chapter 14), but the First World War helped put an end to that. The war created divisions within the leadership and a feud developed between H.H. Asquith and Lloyd George, which continued into the immediate post-war years.

As a result of this feud, the Liberals split into two parties, and the impact was far-reaching:

✔ **National Liberals:** They allied themselves with the Tories (known in Scotland as the Unionists) and were led by Lloyd George.

✔ **The Liberal Party:** They were the true heir to the pre-1914 party and were led by Herbert Asquith.

The impact on the Liberal Party was far-reaching – they fought the followers of Lloyd George in 1918 and again in 1922 in the general elections.

The split had a number of effects that weakened the Liberal Party in the UK generally and in Scotland in particular:

✔ Divisions led to expulsions and a loss of membership and finance.

✔ The Irish vote, which had traditionally gone to the Liberals, was transferred to the Labour Party as a result of the savage way the 1916 Easter Rising in Dublin had been put down by British forces while a Liberal government was in office. The Irish lost faith in the Liberals after that.

✔ The Liberal Party also failed to connect with those newly enfranchised by the 1918 Representation of the People Act. This legislation not only gave women over 30 the vote for the first time, but it also simplified the registration process, which in the past had been responsible for ensuring that one-third of eligible males did not vote (see Chapter 14).

The decision of the Tories in the 1922 general election to put the issue of protectionism to the electorate saw the Liberals come together to fight on the issue of free trade. Differences were forgotten as core Liberal beliefs were under threat. This began a process of healing, which was accelerated by Asquith's failure to hold on to his seat in the 1924 general election, clearing the way for Lloyd George to become party chairman. However, by the time the divisions in the Liberal ranks were healed, it was too late; the political wilderness beckoned. The party won only 40 seats in the 1924 general election.

In contrast to the failing fortunes of the Liberals, both Labour and the Tories saw their support grow dramatically in Scotland in the 1920s.

The rise and fall of Labour

Labour had benefited from the electoral changes in 1918. Most of the new voters were working class, so that meant that Labour had a bigger potential pool of voters to draw on. In particular, women and Irish Catholics flocked to Labour in large numbers. The impact was seen in the 1922 general election, when the Labour Party won 10 out of 15 parliamentary seats in Glasgow. The successful MPs were dubbed by the press as the 'Red Clydesiders'. By 1929, Labour was the largest party, winning 43.5 per cent of votes cast in Scotland; the percentage was even higher in urban areas. However, success was to bring its own set of problems.

Although popular with Scottish voters, there was growing internal strife (sound familiar?) within Labour over the role of the leadership and the political direction the party was taking, particularly when in government. The experience of being part of a minority government in 1924 and again in 1929, dependent on the support of other parties to get legislation through Parliament, only added to the dissent within the Labour ranks.

Coming from some of the most disadvantaged parts of the UK, the Clydesiders wanted to see a much more determined attack on the problem of poverty, while the Labour leadership under Ramsay MacDonald placed more emphasis on making the party part of the mainstream of the political system. In practice, MacDonald's approach meant reassuring the middle classes of the moderate nature of Labour's economic and social policies. Thus, a growing chasm between left and right began to appear within the party – a chasm that, in time, became too large to bridge.

Matters came to a head during the lifetime of the second Labour minority government. As far as the Scottish left were concerned, all Labour seemed to be doing was propping up a capitalist system that had failed (the millions of unemployed people provided eloquent testimony to this point of view).

The Labour government proved incapable of solving the economic crisis. As a result, MacDonald and Philip Snowden, the chancellor, decided to form a government of national unity with the Tories and Liberals – the great betrayal in Labour's eyes.

After this, in 1932, the Independent Labour Party (ILP) decided to disaffiliate from the Labour Party, describing it as just another party of social reform. The breakaway of the ILP meant that Labour in Scotland had to rebuild itself almost from scratch because, in many ways, it had relied on the ILP for its organisation and ideas. How much it relied on the ILP can be gauged from the fact that in 1929 out of 68 Labour candidates in Scotland all but 1 were members of the ILP.

Although the leader of the ILP, James Maxton, was optimistic about the future of the new organisation, in reality disaffiliation consigned it to political oblivion. By the end of the decade, the ILP existed pretty much in name only.

And along came the Tories

Labour was decimated in the 1931 general election, but in the mid-1930s, it staged a revival and won back some of the political ground lost in the previous election with 20 seats in Scotland. But by then it was playing second fiddle to the Tories. Indeed, the rise of the Tory vote in Scotland is as much a story of the 1920s as the phenomenal rise of the left. From only 7 Scottish seats in 1910, the Tories managed to capture 36 in 1924 and 35 in 1935. There were a number of reasons for this. The first was the collapse of the Liberal vote (see 'Fractures within the Liberal Party', earlier in this chapter). But two other factors came into play.

Reaching out: Ideological transformation

The Tories underwent an ideological makeover at the end of the war. From a party mainly appealing in Scotland to some disgruntled rural voters, it began to redirect its attention toward the urban middle class and the newly enfranchised woman. A women's organiser, Edith Baxter, was appointed to educate women in the principles of Unionism and the evils of Socialism. New organisations, such as the Junior Imperial League and the Workers' League, were set up to appeal to constituencies largely ignored in the past.

Complimenting this desire to reach out to previously ignored sections of the electorate was a shift in ideology. The party fashioned a cross-class appeal based on imperialism, patriotism and Presbyterianism, and added a good dollop of social reform to underpin these ideological tenets.

Polarisation of the electorate

The Tories also played on middle-class fears regarding Socialism. So, at a time when the Liberal Party was losing support, the Tories were able to step in and fill the vacuum and present themselves as the 'natural' party of government. That was shown in 1924 when they took 24 seats in Scotland from the Liberals. However, even in the national government, and in spite of MacDonald and Snowden occupying the leading positions, it was Tory policies that prevailed. By 1935, they were back in power.

We are all Unionists now

In the crisis-ridden 1930s, a new form of politics emerged based on a firmer commitment to a British national identity. The years before the Great War had seen demands for some form of home rule within a federal empire gain fairly wide public support and be viewed with some sympathy by senior members of the Liberal government (see Chapter 14). After the war, the demand grew louder, with the Scottish Trades Union Congress even calling for separate Scottish representation at the Versailles peace talks in 1919, and a private members' bill in 1924 that nearly succeeded in getting through Parliament.

However, as the Scottish trade unions began (under pressure from rising unemployment and falling finance) to amalgamate with English unions, the demand for home rule declined in popularity. By the late 1920s, as far as most Scottish trade unionists were concerned, home rule was 'parish pump politics'.

The depression of the 1930s further undermined support for Scottish self-government, and with the rise of Fascism in Europe, Nationalism began to be seen as a toxic political point of view. The consensus on both the left and the right in Scottish politics was that the economy was too weak for Scotland to go it alone, and its interests could be promoted only within a strong UK state committed to some form of economic planning. As such, the newly formed Scottish National Party in 1934 found it was cold-shouldered by the electorate, polling less than 1 per cent of votes cast in the 1935 general election. These feelings of Britishness would be heightened by the shared experience of hardship, suffering and loss in the Second World War.

Chapter 16

The Rebirth of a Nation (1945–2000)

*T*he victory over Fascism in 1945 almost heralded a new beginning for Britain in general and Scotland in particular. Massive strides were made in reducing inequality and promoting greater opportunity for all citizens. The state became more responsible for the welfare of the people. These reforms were made possible by an economic boom that lasted until the 1970s. During that period, Scotland underwent a major economic transformation, which ended dependence on heavy industry and encouraged the growth of a new economy based on services.

The post-war decades also witnessed an equally profound transformation in political allegiances due to the rise of Nationalism, which led to the establishment of a parliament in Scotland in 1997 and the possible breakup of Britain. By the new millennium, Scotland had changed dramatically.

Scotland and the Second World War

In most histories of the home front during the Second World War, the focal point has been London and the pounding the city received from German bombing raids. But London wasn't the only place in Britain to suffer. Industrial towns and cities proved a magnet for these raids, and among the most bombed was Clydeside, the centre of shipbuilding and engineering in the UK. But war didn't just bring death and suffering; it also held out the promise of a better tomorrow.

The blitz

It wasn't just London that was pummelled by German bombing. Other parts of Britain, like Coventry and Birmingham, were also subjected to the same treatment. But it was slow to start. There was a period known as the 'phoney war', which lasted for eight months after war was declared in September 1939. The first bomb to be dropped on Scotland, in June 1940, demolished a bungalow in Nigg on the outskirts of Aberdeen.

Things began to heat up in 1941, and industrial Clydebank became a prime target for German bombers. It was estimated that 500 tons of high explosives were dropped on Clydebank in the late winter of 1941, killing 538 people and leaving 35,000 people homeless.

Strangely enough, Aberdeen was the Scottish city most subjected to bombing, with some 40 raids. The biggest raid took place in 1943, when 25 bombers attacked the city streets, which were full of women and children, with low-flying machine-gun waves.

But Aberdeen was not the most bombed place in Scotland. That honour belongs to the fishing port of Peterhead. Why Peterhead? The answer is simple: it wasn't because of its strategic value, but because of the port's geographical position. Peterhead was the first urban settlement German bombers flying from Norway came across.

In total, there were more than 500 German air raids on Scotland, ranging from single aircraft hit-and-runs, to mass bombings by 240 planes. The last air battle in Europe was fought off the Aberdeenshire coast on 21 April 1945.

The authorities had tried to evacuate children – 30,000 of them were evacuated from the west of Scotland to rural Aberdeenshire in September 1939 – but almost all of them were home a month later.

Of 40,000 Scottish war dead, 6,000 were civilians.

The home front

The First World War had generated a great deal of discontent over not only the way the war was being run, but also issues such as dilution, conscription, pay and rents (see Chapter 15). Strikes and demonstrations occurred, and Glasgow was at the centre of this unrest, giving birth to the idea of 'Red Clydeside'. The government learned a great deal from these events and wisely put Labour in charge of running the home front. The man responsible for running the home front north of the border was the secretary of state for Scotland, Tom Johnston.

Johnston was able to use his position to introduce far-reaching reforms that benefited ordinary Scots. He set up 32 committees to deal with social and economic problems, ranging from juvenile delinquency to sheep farming. One of the most important reforms was the Clyde Basin Hospital Scheme, a forerunner of the National Health Service. This scheme was originally intended to deal with the expected huge civilian casualties from bombing raids. But although the numbers of injured were substantial, they were never huge. So, the new hospitals built to deal with this eventuality were used to treat Scottish munitions workers – brilliant! The scheme was extended to all of Scotland and wiped out a waiting list of 34,000 patients before the war had ended.

However, Johnston's most important contribution was the formation of the North of Scotland Hydro Board. Launched in 1943, it provided desperately needed electricity to the Highlands and Islands.

Rationing

In spite of these reforms, life for those on the home front was not easy. On top of the bombings, there was rationing. Rationing was introduced at the outbreak of war so that the government could control the provision and distribution of food and ensure that everyone received an equal share. Rationing was applied to basic foodstuffs like bacon and ham, butter and margarine, sugar and cheese. Ration books were issued to everyone, including children; people were required to register with a shop supplying the rationed food.

Of course, the wealthy could find ways around the restrictions; everything was available through what was known as the 'black market', if you had the money. Many ordinary Scots resented the wealthy for their ability to get what they wanted on the black market, and the situation dented the image of the 'people's war'.

Notwithstanding the discontent, the health of the population improved through access to more nutritious food. Scotland experienced the largest fall in infant mortality anywhere in Europe. The average height of Glasgow children increased by 5 centimetres during the war years.

The politics of war

The declaration of war in 1939 was not popular with everyone. Opposition came from left-wing pacifists, the Communist Party and the Scottish National Party (SNP). But it was the SNP that proved the most troublesome for the government.

The writer and poet Hugh MacDiarmid (conscripted in 1942 as a lathe turner) reckoned the Germans were bad but the British bourgeoisie was a 'far greater enemy', even suggesting that England being invaded by Nazis would amount to historical revenge. Another member of the SNP, Professor Douglas Young, who taught Greek at Aberdeen University, argued that the 1707 Treaty of Union prevented the conscription of Scots to defend 'an Empire in the government of which she has no voice'. No Scottish court agreed, and Young was sentenced to 12 months' imprisonment for refusing to be conscripted.

Although these Nationalists were depicted as trying to undermine the war effort, their political message seemed to get across to the Scottish people. In 1940, the SNP polled 37 per cent of the vote in Argyll; in the Kirkcaldy by-election in 1944, it polled 41 per cent. Dr Robert McIntyre won a parliamentary seat for the SNP at the Motherwell by-election in 1945, although he lost it in the general election later that year.

The Communist Party was also making political progress. Although the party was initially opposed to the war, after Germany attacked the Soviet Union in June 1941, it became an enthusiastic supporter. On the back of the heroic struggle of the Soviet people, the party grew in numbers to 10,000 by the end of the war. It was estimated that one in ten Scots read the party newspaper, the *Daily Worker*.

Much of the success of these fringe parties was due to the special circumstances created by the war. The main parties called a truce at the beginning of hostilities, agreeing to not to fight each other in by-elections. That agreement allowed the smaller parties to make gains.

However, when things got back to normal in the 1945 general election, it was clear that the real beneficiary of the war was the Labour Party, which won a stunning victory in the general election and went about changing the face of British society.

The Silent Social Revolution: War and Welfare (1945–2000)

The main problem for the wartime government was keeping up morale among the civilian population and those who were doing the fighting. The old world was the 1930s in which unemployment was in the millions and people went hungry. There had to be a new way forward to give people hope and reward the sacrifices the British people were making to win the war. Well, cometh the hour, cometh the man. Step forward, William Beveridge.

Fighting for a better world

The war against Germany and its allies encouraged people to think of a better world. There was little point in fighting the war if we weren't going to come out better off in the end. The publication of the Beveridge Report on National Insurance in 1942 laid out the blueprint for a new Britain, and it caught the imagination of the British people.

Beveridge, a wartime civil servant and Liberal, laid out the five great social evils:

- Want (poverty)
- Disease
- Ignorance
- Squalor
- Idleness (unemployment)

To conquer these evils, the state was to provide 'cradle to grave' coverage as a right of citizenship. In practice, this meant

- Abolishing poverty
- Creating a health service
- Expanding the provision of education, including raising the school leaving age
- Providing more and better housing
- Providing full employment

The Beveridge Report (a reaction to the problems I highlight in Chapter 15) brought Labour to power for the first time. Labour won a landslide victory in the 1945 general election because the party was more closely identified with the report than the Tories. Winston Churchill, the great war leader, was rejected in favour of the pipe-smoking, avuncular Labour leader, Clement Attlee.

Poverty

William Beveridge believed that the solution to the age-old problem of poverty was full employment. For those too old or too unfit to work, some kind of social provision would be provided through the welfare state. The Labour government of 1945 only went so far in tackling the problem because there was a fear that if benefits were too high, people might find staying at home more attractive than working in a dead-end job. The benefits from the outset were never high enough to keep people out of poverty – this has been the case regardless of which government has been in power.

Scotland has suffered more than most other parts of the UK from the problem of poverty, although even in Scotland it's worse in the west than in the east. Glasgow has some of the most deprived areas in the UK. Here are some reasons why:

- ✔ Scotland has a much smaller middle class than the UK.

- ✔ Scotland has a higher rate of unemployment than the UK average.

- ✔ Scotland has a lower level of income per head of population than the UK.

- ✔ Because of emigration, Scotland has more old and very young people.

Health

The National Health Service (NHS), set up in 1948, extended care to all citizens – young and old, rich and poor. However, in spite of the excellence of the service, Scots are among the unhealthiest people in Europe. They lead the world in heart disease and lung cancer. Why? Because of a poor diet (too many deep-fried Mars bars), cigarettes and alcohol.

In the 1990s, Scots were consuming 33 per cent more alcohol and tobacco, 48 per cent more biscuits and 50 per cent more carbonated drinks than the UK average. Again, there is a class dimension. The average age of death in some areas of Glasgow, such as Shettleston, is lower than for those living on the war-torn Gaza Strip!

Education

The 1945 Labour government's proposed changes for education did nothing to alter the fact that around 80 per cent of Scottish children left school with no qualifications in the 1950s. It also didn't make the system any more inclusive – children were divided at the age of 11 by an examination into senior and junior schools. Senior schools trained pupils for university; junior schools trained the new manual class of workers.

What changed education was the following:

- ✔ The introduction in the 1960s of what is known as the 'O level', which acted as a halfway house between nothing and the higher qualification that was necessary for entry into university

- ✔ The establishment of comprehensive education, which abolished the divisive junior and secondary schools

Higher education in Scotland has expanded. Currently, more than 50 per cent of pupils are enrolled in such institutions. But before sounding the trumpets, remember there is a way to go before the education system provides all children with equal opportunity. In Scotland, in many respects, your post code determines your opportunities.

Housing

The private market in housing (see Chapter 15) was a dismal failure in providing decent living conditions. Slums and squalor were the lot of the majority of Scots. To correct these abuses, a massive programme of council house building was initiated. By the mid-1960s, Scotland had more people living in council estates than many eastern European states did under Soviet rule!

These estates were constructed to deal with overcrowding in the inner cities. Although they provided unheard of amenities, such as indoor toilets, baths and proper cooking facilities, they failed to cater to the social needs of the residents. There were no cafes, pubs, libraries or shops; there was nowhere people could meet to chat or socialise; and public transport was dire. It's hardly surprising that after a while of living in these 'little palaces', those who could get out got out, into home ownership.

With the flight of the more enterprising and ambitious residents, most of the council estates began to literally fall apart. Nowadays, they house the elderly and the young unemployed with families. Some council estates have become a byword for alcoholism, drug use, petty crime and vandalism.

The solutions of yesterday have become today's problems. Nowhere is the divide in Scottish society more evident than in housing.

Unemployment

The Labour government of 1945–51 came to power committed to full employment. That commitment was shared by the Conservative Party. This goal was made possible by the long economic boom lasting into the 1960s.

However, from the end of the 1960s onward, unemployment has consistently been higher in Scotland than the average for the UK as a whole. In 1961, with little more than 10 per cent of the UK's population, Scotland had more than 25 per cent of the long-term unemployed. In the 1980s, the unemployment rate was running at around 15 per cent; in the 1990s, it was around 10 per cent. Men have been affected more than women, and those living in western Scotland have been harder hit than people in the eastern part of the country.

Indeed, the national figures masked a social catastrophe in some parts of Glasgow. In the 1980s, Glasgow Provan had an unemployment rate of 35 per cent for males between the age of 16 and 69; three out of five men receiving benefits had been out of work for more than six months. When unemployment reaches this level, the effects become multifaceted. People's lives become blunted and restricted on a whole series of levels.

Is it any wonder, given these figures, that people wanted to leave Scotland to find work and wages elsewhere? From 1961 to 1987, the natural increase in the population was 431,000, but those leaving amounted to 561,000. Emigrants were mainly aged 25 to 45, the most productive group for any economy.

Nationalising the utilities

The programme of welfare reform was matched by a programme of nationalisation in which coal, steel, railways, gas and electricity were taken into public ownership. The trade unions and the Labour Party had been campaigning for this for many years, and miners held street parties on hearing the news. But it was still the old private owners who dominated the new boards set up to run these industries, and public ownership didn't put an end to strikes. The coal industry was particularly militant in the 1970s and 1980s.

Sectarianism on the decline

Catholics were routinely discriminated against in Scotland (see Chapters 14 and 15), but in the aftermath of the Second World War, things began to change. This was partly due to the changes in the economy (see the next section), which destroyed the economic basis of sectarianism, but it was also due to the determination of the Churches and politicians.

There was greater interaction between Catholics and Protestants throughout Scotland. No longer did the Catholic Church insist on Catholics marrying Catholics – that signalled a massive rise in what were called 'mixed marriages'. By 2001, more than half of Scots Catholics under the age of 34 were married to non-Catholics (compared to only 2 per cent in Northern Ireland).

The labour market also became less sectarian. The old signs saying that 'Catholics need not apply' went away, and the shift from industry to services saw the jobs market become religiously blind.

Welcome as these developments are, pockets of sectarianism still exist within education and sport. Schooling is still based on religious segregation, and there is the tribalism associated with the supporters of Celtic and Rangers football clubs. But generally speaking, a person's religion plays very little part in determining voting behaviour or affecting his or her life chances.

The Scottish Economy: From Ships to Chips

The Scottish economy was largely based on heavy industry (see Chapter 15), but it was an economy that was kept alive through war – something that could not be guaranteed after 1945. Scotland badly needed to diversify into new kinds of economic activity. However, given the restocking boom that took place after the war and the emergence of the Cold War and the small wars that accompanied it, such as Korea, the old structure was in pretty robust health. Shipbuilding flourished, as did coalmining, engineering and steelmaking. Scotland was still a major player in world markets. Clyde-built still meant something.

Push the time clock on a decade or so, and things looked very different. Industry was losing 10,000 jobs a year. Shipbuilding – the jewel in the industrial crown – was being sunk by the more technologically advanced yards in Japan and Korea. The textile industries were being beaten on price and quality by competitors in places like India and Hong Kong. Coalmining, like steelmaking, was only being kept alive through government subsidies.

An unstoppable process of deindustrialisation was underway. This gathered pace under the Tory government of Margaret Thatcher in the 1980s. Many famous industrial landmarks, such as the Ravenscraig steel mill complex, the aluminium smelter at Invergordon and car making at Linwood, closed and became footnotes in Scottish industrial history.

It is possible to exaggerate the decline of manufacturing. Even as late as 2013, manufacturing accounted for nearly two-thirds of Scottish exports (although fewer than one in ten Scots work in the sector). Decline is always an uneven process, and there will always be long-established industries, like whisky, that buck the trend.

A new economy was in the process of being constructed on the corpse of the old. This economy was based on electronics, light engineering and services such as banking and retail. This shift had a profound effect on the labour market in Scotland. The old economy was based on muscle strength and craft skills; the new economy was based on brainpower. This meant that opportunities for women increased and many households became dependent on a second income. Whereas in 1911, the typical female worker was between 13 and 21 and single, from the 1970s on, the typical female worker was over 30 and married.

The increasing feminisation of the labour force has coincided with the increase in foreign ownership of industry in Scotland. The Americans (in the form of IBM,NCR, Timex and others) came in after 1945, attracted by a relatively low-paid, highly skilled workforce who could – particularly after the UK joined the European Economic Community in 1973 – allow them a backdoor into European markets. Plus, we play golf and speak English!

Has this increase in foreign ownership been a good thing for Scotland? Historians disagree. On the one hand, there are jobs today in Scotland that were not there before. On the other hand, it has meant a de-skilling of the workforce because the jobs tended to be routine assembly of parts. Plus, these companies don't stick around if there are juicier pickings elsewhere. Apart from IBM, most American multinationals, like NCR and Timex, have pulled out of Scotland.

Fighting for a way of life

The old staple industries did not go down without a fight. There were major strikes to oppose government policies toward coalmining and shipbuild-ing. The 'right to work' campaign in 1967, led by Communist shop stewards Jimmy Reid and James Airlie, was a protest against the closure of shipyards on the Clyde. The workers staged a work-in and refused to budge. Their action caught the imagination of the British people. The government was forced to nationalise the yards as Upper Clyde Shipbuilders. In the end, it did not save shipbuilding on the Clyde. When state subsidies were withdrawn, the industry all but collapsed.

Coalmining went the same way. In 1973, the National Union of Miners (NUM) won a spectacular victory over the Heath government's economic policies by restricting supplies of coal to the electricity power stations. As a result, the British people were forced to endure power cuts and spend the night hud-dling around candles! A general election was held in 1974 over the issue of who runs the country: the unions or the government? The public voted for the unions – the Tories were out, and Labour was back in power.

The victory in 1973–74 became part of the folklore of the coal industry. The miners seemed invincible, but when they tested the waters in 1984, the out-come was very different. A programme of pit closures was announced by the National Coal Board, something that hit Scotland badly because almost of all its pits were losing money and, as such, were in line for closure. The country was divided, and that was intensified by the pitch battles that took place between the miners and the police. The strike was lost, and with it the mining industry. By the end of the decade, the Association of University Teachers in Scotland had more members than the NUM!

End of an empire

Scotland's fortunes were tied to the British Empire. The empire provided markets for Scottish goods and employment opportunities in the imperial service. Some historians have argued that the Scots ran the empire, so it was quite a shock to the Scottish psyche when it all began to collapse. First, India, the jewel in the imperial crown, went in 1947, followed by Africa in the 1950s and 1960s.

Rather strangely, it was the Tories rather than Labour who presided over the dismemberment of the empire as they tried to reposition the UK economically and politically in Europe.

Running an empire had become too expensive, and the UK had been humiliated in the Suez crisis of the mid-1950s. The last appeal of empire was during the Falklands War of the early 1980s.

Scotland was the most disaffected part of the UK. Despite the deep engagement with empire, its passing left no lasting legacy unless you include the number of curry restaurants in Scotland. There are no works of art, no works of literature or even games like cricket to connect us to these formerly important ties of trade, religion and commerce.

Politics in a Changing World (1945–2000)

Just as the years following the end of the First World War saw a re-ordering of Scottish politics leading to a two-horse race between Conservatives and Labour (see Chapter 15), so the decades following the end of the Second World War witnessed another political transformation that may prove to be even more profound.

After the Labour Party's stunning victory in the 1945 general election, the 1950s saw a resurgence of the Conservative vote. However, that proved to be a false dawn, and from 1955 onward the Conservative vote began to decline – slowly at first, and then quite rapidly in the 1980s and 1990s. Another two-horse race emerged in Scotland, contested by the Labour Party and the new kids on the block, the Scottish National Party (SNP).

The SNP grew from a tiny organisation in the 1960s to one that dominates the re-founded Scottish Parliament in the 2000s. Its rise was spectacular, but the consequences this time are far greater than those experienced because of the demise of the Liberal Party in the 1920s. On the cards is the breakup of Britain should the referendum of September 2014 deliver a 'Yes' vote in favour of an independent Scotland.

I tell this amazing story of political change in this section.

The rise and fall of the Tories

In the general election of 1945, Labour won by a landslide due to its identification with the Beveridge Plan (see 'Fighting for a better world', earlier in this chapter), but by 1951 it had run out of ideas and popularity. Tory promises to end wartime rationing and the austerity programme of the Labour government struck a chord with the British people; the Tories were elected in Scotland with just under 50 per cent of the total votes cast.

What was it about the Tories that appealed to all sections of society in Scotland? Protestantism, empire and patriotism. However, these traditional rallying appeals were quickly losing their resonance with the post-war generations brought up on rock 'n' roll, consumerism and prosperity. Churchgoing had declined after the 1950s, plunged rapidly in the 1960s and failed to recover in the decades after that. The empire was rapidly disintegrating, and patriotism evaporated. Tory values were seen as old hat and reflective of a pre-war deferential society. Even the resurgence of the party during the 1980s under the leadership of Margaret Thatcher failed to connect with Scottish voters.

A massive split emerged in voting patterns north and south of the border. In 1979, over half the working class in England went Tory, while in Scotland it was under a quarter, falling to 16 per cent five years later. Why did Thatcher fail to reach Scottish voters?

- ✔ **Personality:** Scots didn't like being told how ungrateful they were.

- ✔ **Public services:** Many more Scots earned their living in the public services, and Thatcher's promise to roll back the frontier of the state threatened their livelihoods.

- ✔ **Poll Tax:** The deeply unpopular Poll Tax was introduced a year earlier in Scotland, which suggested that the Scots were being used as guinea pigs for Tory policies.

Thatcher managed to alienate all sections of Scottish society. When she gave her famous 'Sermon on the Mound' (as it was known) to the General Assembly of the Church of Scotland in May 1988, it was greeted with stony silence. Afterward, the then moderator, the Right Reverend James Whyte, politely handed her copies of the Church's reports on homelessness and the welfare system, criticising her policies and reforms. A few days later, her attendance at the Scottish Cup Final in Glasgow provoked the assembled supporters to give her the 'red card' and to roundly boo her.

The decline in the Tory vote continued until 1997, when Scotland, along with Wales, became a Tory-free zone in terms of seats in the UK Parliament. The transformation of a party from winning more than half the votes cast in the 1955 general election to zero representation in 1997 is, by any standards, one of the most remarkable political stories of the 20th century.

The rise and rise of Labour

The faltering performance of the Tory Party in Scotland was contrasted by the impressive rise in the Labour vote after 1955. Labour came to dominate parliamentary politics north of the border in spite of the rise of the Nationalist vote after 1967.

Earlier in the century, the Labour Party had benefited from two developments:

- ✔ The collapse of the Liberal Party
- ✔ The shift in the Irish vote from Liberal to Labour

However, after 1945, it was the welfare state, municipal housing and the NHS, as well as support for old industries like coalmining, that attracted Scottish voters to Labour.

The Thatcher years were, strangely enough, not the most decisive in turning Scotland into a Labour fiefdom; instead, her legacy was more important. In 1987, Labour enjoyed a 15 per cent lead over the Tories, but seven years after her leaving office, the lead had increased to around 27 per cent.

However, Labour wouldn't have it all its own way. The old two-horse race of Labour versus Tory that had dominated politics in Scotland from the 1920s onward may have disappeared, but there was a new kid on the block: the SNP.

The mercurial Scottish National Party

The story of the Scottish National Party (SNP) is one of highs and lows: from an insignificant political organisation in the 1960s, to an explosive force in the mid-1970s that threatened to shake up the party system, and back to insignificance in the 1980s and 1990s. Why has the SNP experienced such a volatile history? To answer that question, you have to look at how it made the journey from the periphery to the centre of the political system.

The story begins in 1967, when Winnie Ewing, a solicitor, captured Labour's safest seat in Scotland in the Hamilton by-election of that year. From there, a steamroller effect was evident. In May 1968, Labour was facing a rout in local elections when the SNP, with 34 per cent of the vote, outpolled all the other parties. Organisation was improved, and the SNP had 175 more branches than Labour in Scotland. A breakthrough was predicted in the 1970 general election, but in spite of polling 11 per cent of the votes cast, only one seat, the Western Isles, had been won and Labour had regained Hamilton.

Then, as if in possession of a magic lamp, the party was given two wishes:

- ✔ **The discovery of oil in the North Sea:** The discovery of oil in the North Sea allowed the SNP to undermine the arguments from the Unionist parties concerning the economic necessity of the union. The whole economic argument changed as the SNP campaigned around the slogans 'It's Scotland's Oil' and 'Rich Scots or Poor Britons'. Given that this was a period of rising inflation and unemployment, the slogans hit a raw economic nerve.

- ✔ **Britain's entry into the European Economic Community (EEC), now the European Union (EU):** At the time, the SNP opposed membership in the EEC, but joining it in 1973 raised the possibility of future European unity and suggested to some Scots that the country's interests might be better protected in the EEC than by continuing to send shed loads of Labour MPs to Westminster.

The failure of both the Labour and Conservative governments to satisfy the national aspirations of the Scottish people paved the way for the SNP's triumph in the 1974 general elections. The first election in February saw the party's support rise to 22 per cent of the vote and 7 seats; the second election in November saw support rise even further to 30 per cent of the vote and 11 seats. More worrisome was the fact that the SNP had come in a close second in most Labour seats. One more push and the door to independence would be open.

But it didn't happen. The SNP train was derailed by one spectacular event: the 1979 referendum on Scottish devolution. The Labour Party feared that if a 'Yes' vote was successful, it would lead to a reduction in the number of Scottish MPs in Parliament. Without the Scots, it was feared that Labour could never win a general election. With this in mind, and facing a revolt in the Commons, the Labour prime minister, James Callaghan, accepted a proposal from backbench Labour MP George Cunningham that those supporting devolution had to achieve 40 per cent of the vote in the referendum.

The referendum could not have taken place at a worse time:

- ✔ National confidence in Scotland was shaken by the disgraceful exit from the 1978 World Cup in Argentina.
- ✔ The Labour government was unpopular.
- ✔ The two parties nominally favouring devolution – SNP and Labour – refused to co-operate because each wanted the credit if victory was achieved.

The 'No' campaign, which included all the major players in Scottish society, with the exception of the Church of Scotland, argued that devolution would lead to higher taxes and more government. This struck a chord with many voters. As it turned out, there was a majority for devolution but not the 40 per cent needed for victory; only a third of Scots were in favour.

A vote of no confidence in the Labour government followed, and the SNP voted with the Tories to bring down the ruling party. As the outgoing prime minister, James Callaghan, said of the SNP, it 'was turkeys voting for Christmas'. In the general election of 1979, the party was routed. It was reduced to two seats in a Parliament dominated by the Tories and Mrs Thatcher.

The decades of the 1980s and 1990s were barren years for the SNP. Within the party, there was a lot of debate over which direction the party should take. Those on the left of the SNP, including current ministers in the Scottish Parliament, such as Alex Salmond, argued that it had to remake itself as an organisation capable of winning seats in urban Scotland, Labour's heartland. This meant a shift away from the centre ground of politics favoured by the party hierarchy of the then-leader Gordon Wilson, to a more determinedly Socialist agenda. This would allow the SNP to lose the 'Tartan Tory' image that Labour had successfully placed in the minds of the Scottish electorate.

With the SNP engaged in a fierce internal struggle, the baton of devolution was passed to Labour and the Liberal Democrats. As their share of the vote declined, the Tories were increasingly seen as an English party with no mandate to govern in Scotland. So, in July 1988, the Claim of Right was launched in Edinburgh. A formal declaration was signed on 30 July 1989 in the Assembly Halls of the Church of Scotland on the Mound.

The declaration was signed in the same room in which the Covenant had been signed more than 400 years before by the duke of Montrose and others before being presented to the Scottish people (see Chapter 11). The Covenant had a particular historical resonance, as did the Claim of Right. This harkened back to 1689, when the Scottish Estates presented the incoming Protestant monarch, William of Orange, with a set of demands. So, the mobilisation of the past in the service of the Scottish present and future was an important tool used by the pro-devolutionists.

The Claim was signed by 58 of Scotland's 72 MPs; 7 out of 8 members of the European Parliament (MEPs); 59 out of 65 regional, district and island councils; and numerous other political organisations, Churches and voluntary groups. The Tories and, surprisingly, the SNP did not sign the Claim, although the latter eventually did. But there was no denying that the Scottish people had spoken, and Westminster could not fail to notice.

Within eight years, another referendum to establish parliaments for Scotland and Wales with limited tax-raising powers was held by the incoming Labour government. This time, the result was a resounding 'yes'.

The Scottish Parliament

The first elections for the Scottish Parliament took place in 1999 and led to a coalition between Labour and the Liberal Democrats, but since 2007, it has been increasingly under the control of the SNP. The SNP formed a minority government after the 2007 elections, but in 2011 it actually won control of the Holyrood Parliament with 65 seats out of 129, something that the architects of devolution thought was impossible.

The stunning victory of the SNP has allowed the leader, Alex Salmond, to place the future of the union before the Scottish people. A referendum will take place in September 2014 to establish whether the Scots want to remain part of the United Kingdom.

Part VII
The Part of Tens

the
part of
tens

For a list of ten turning points in Scottish history, head to www.dummies.com/
extras/scottishhistory.

Part VI

The Part of Tens

In this part . . .

- ✔ Find ten great places to visit in Scotland.
- ✔ Get acquainted with ten little-known Scottish people who made a big difference.
- ✔ Discover ten things that Scotland has given to the world, from golf to the flushing toilet.

Chapter 17

Ten Great Places to Visit in Scotland

In This Chapter
▶ Seeing signs of Scotland's prehistoric and medieval past
▶ Closing in on castles, abbeys and even a cemetery

*T*empting though it is to send visitors to the usual tartan-clad, shortbread-tin-selling tourist attractions, such as Edinburgh Castle, Loch Ness or the 'bonnie banks of Loch Lomond', in this chapter I focus on a few places that don't always get the recognition they deserve. All the places in this chapter also play some part in the history and culture of Scotland.

The Heart of Neolithic Orkney

Want to know how our very ancient ancestors lived and died? Then make time to visit the Heart of Neolithic Orkney. It's well worth the boat trip over to one of the most northerly parts of Scotland, a barren but beautiful archipelago. Situated in the western part of the main island of Orkney, this UNESCO World Heritage Site comprises the following:

- ✔ Skara Brae, a domestic settlement
- ✔ Maes Howe, a chambered tomb
- ✔ The Ring of Brodgar and the Standing Stones of Stenness, stone circles that date back to between 3,000 and 2,500 BC

Recently, there have been archaeological excavations at the Ness of Brodgar, a 6-acre site that lies between the Ring of Brodgar and the Standing Stones of Stenness. Discoveries at this site have led archaeologists and historians to think that this area and, in particular, the Ness of Brodgar could be the centre of ancient Britain. Techniques used here may have been copied at later sites, such as Stonehenge, which was constructed almost 1,000 years later!

Excavations at the site have also uncovered evidence of a large temple complex, housing, large walled enclosures and many artefacts, which have led them to think that this was a place for rituals to link the land of the living to the land of the dead. Creepy, but fascinating!

Eilean Donan Castle

Okay, this one *is* the shortbread-tin Scottish castle of a thousand advertising campaigns, but that makes it no less worthy of a visit, not least because it lies in the Kintail National Scenic Area in the northwest of Scotland. Thought to have been the site of a monastic cell dedicated to Donnánof Eigg, an Irish saint martyred on the island of Eigg in the seventh century (after whom it was named), there is evidence of earlier Iron Age fortifications at the site.

The castle began the development of its main fortifications in the 13th century. Its position on an island made it a stronghold against the Norse invaders, and it became the seat of the Mackenzies of Kintail for many years. It stood up to the Scottish Wars of Independence, bitter clan feuding and the civil wars of the 17th century. However, in 1719, the castle was mostly destroyed by three royal navy gunships over a three-day period during a time of unrest following the third Jacobite uprising.

The castle was rebuilt in the early 20th century and has been the set of many film and television series, as well as being on those shortbread tins!

Glencoe

Visit Glencoe to get a real sense of the majesty of the Scottish Highlands. Best approached from the south, on a drive up across the bleakness of Rannoch Moor, the gateway to this impressive U-shaped volcanic glen is marked by the distinctive shape of the mountain, Buachaille Etive Mòr.

Glencoe has everything a Scottish glen should have: the towering mountainsides (a haven for walkers, climbers and skiers), a rushing river that cascades over rocks on its way down to open out at Loch Leven, as well as some bloodthirsty history.

The infamous Massacre of Glencoe in 1692 saw the deaths of 38 male members of the MacDonald clan, murdered in their homes by a troop of soldiers who were staying with them. Forty women and children died of exposure when their homes were burned and they were forced to flee into the unforgiving Highland winter.

A visitor centre at the Loch Leven end of the Glen tells this story. You can still sense the sadness and bleakness if you visit the Glen on a grey, misty day.

Bannockburn

The site of Bannockburn may just be a boring old field to the south of Stirling, but in June 1314, an army of Scots led by Robert the Bruce faced the mighty army of King Edward II of England here. Although outnumbered almost three to one, the Scots used the advantage of the terrain to defeat the English over two days of bloody battle. This was the decisive victory in the Wars of Scottish Independence, leading to King Edward and his army retreating back south, 'sending him homeward to think again'.

The 700th anniversary of the battle has seen the construction of a state-of-the-art visitor centre employing all the latest technology to offer a 3-D look at the battle and its combatants. It celebrates the achievements of Scottish army and goes some way to explaining why the Scots still sing about the battle with pride and why the song 'Flower of Scotland' is considered Scotland's unofficial national anthem.

St Andrews

St Andrews isn't a large town, but it has so much to offer a tourist. It's not just the home of Scotland's oldest and most venerated university (and where Will and Kate met) or the birthplace of golf; St Andrews also has a rich and varied history that can be discovered on a walk round its bustling tourist-filled streets.

In fact, St Andrews has always been a tourist attraction. In medieval times, it housed the relics of Scotland's national saint – St Andrew – and that drew in pilgrims by the hundreds. Today they come by the thousands to play the most historic golf course in the world, the Old Course.

However, in spite of its prosperous facade, St Andrews declined in national importance from the 17th century. Once it was the centre of Christendom in Scotland, but the Reformation led to its decline. The wars over faith led to the ruination of the town's famed cathedral and its castle. They also led to the burning of Protestant heretics – make sure you look for the marked spot outside the chapel where Patrick Hamilton was burned alive.

The university continued but was reduced to a tiny, insignificant seat of learning well into the 19th century. It's only in the last 30 years or so that St Andrews has once again regained its place as one of the premier universities not just in Scotland but in the entire United Kingdom.

So, if you want to relive the tempestuous times of religious controversy and struggle that made up what we call the Reformation (see Chapter 10) then this is the place to come. History is literally on the doorstep!

Falkland Palace

Situated in the heart of the Kingdom of Fife, Falkland Palace was one of the royal residences of the Stewart monarchs – in fact, you could say it was their holiday home. It was acquired from the MacDuffs of Fife in the 14th century by the Scottish crown, but was remodelled in the 16th century by two Stewart kings, James IV and James V. The two Jameses transformed the old castle into a beautiful Renaissance palace, one of only two in Scotland. James V also commissioned the setting out of the gardens and park, which were then in a poor state.

The Stewarts used Falkland as a retreat, with more kingly business happening at either Edinburgh Castle or Stirling Castle. Here, at Falkland, they entertained guests, hunted deer or wild boar in the park and surrounding area, practised falconry and played tennis – Falkland has the oldest tennis court (built in 1539) that is still used for play today. It was here that James V died in December 1542, after learning that his wife had given birth to a daughter, Mary, Queen of Scots, at Edinburgh Castle.

Mary loved Falkland, and her descendants, James VI, Charles I and Charles II, all enjoyed visiting here. A fire destroyed much of the palace during a time of occupation by Cromwell's troops in the Civil War years, but careful restoration work, started in the late 19thcentury, has returned Falkland to its glory days.

Remember to bring your tennis whites!

The Necropolis

The Victorian era was one of huge importance to the city of Glasgow. It grew in size as engineering and manufacturing sprang up along the River Clyde – the population nearly tripled in just a couple of decades. With the trade pouring into the port towns of the west of Scotland, Glasgow was undoubtedly the 'Second City of the British Empire'. How did the great and the good celebrate their new wealth? How did they let future generations know they had done well? They left monuments behind. In 1833, the Glasgow middle class decided to build a Necropolis, or City of the Dead, in true Victorian Gothic style, and many were said to be dying to get in it!

The tombs were elaborate, huge visible markers of material success. Many of them were designed and crafted by the renowned architects and artists of the time. Alexander 'Greek' Thomson and Charles Rennie Mackintosh both created monuments and architecture that make up that part of the Necropolis clustered around the 1825 memorial to John Knox.

At the time, Glasgow was witness to some examples of extreme poverty. Some people have claimed that the Victorians took better care of the dead than the living – you can visit the Necropolis and make up your own mind about that.

Melrose Abbey

At the request of King David I, in 1136, St Mary's Abbey, Melrose, was founded by the Cistercian Order of monks near a bend on the banks of the River Tweed in the Scottish Borders. It was built in the shape of St John's Cross and took ten years to be completed. Further construction work continued for 50 years, adding more buildings to the abbey complex. The location and importance of St Mary's Abbey led to it being the recipient of much unwelcome attention, particularly from invading English armies.

A destructive attack (and there were many) by Edward II in 1322 led Robert the Bruce to order its rebuilding. The pattern of destruction and rebuilding lasted more than 300 years. In the end, much of the main abbey was left in ruins. What was left intact was handed over as the parish church in 1610, the last Cistercian monk having died in the mid-16th century.

What makes this mostly ruined abbey worth a visit? First, the abbey is the well-documented site of the burial place of Robert the Bruce's heart, as per his dying wishes (his body was buried at Dunfermline Abbey). Second, the abbey, even in its ruined state, is considered one of the most beautiful examples of medieval architecture. It has some ornate and elaborate stone carvings, including cooks with ladles, dragons, demons, angels and a bagpipe-playing pig!

Alloway

Alloway, in southwest Scotland, is to Scots what Stratford-upon-Avon is to the English. Scotland's most celebrated poet and lyricist, Robert Burns, was born in a cottage built by his father, William Burnes, in the village on 25 January 1759. Responsible for a huge body of work, mainly in the Scots' tongue, 'Rabbie' Burns is known the world over. Alloway is an essential place to visit, with a collection of places of interest situated in a small area, all part of the Robert Burns Birthplace Museum.

Burns Cottage is maintained to show what life was like for the Burnes family at the time of Rabbie's birth. A short walk along Poet's Path, past sculptures linked to some of his works, brings visitors to the recently built museum, which not only tells Burns's story, but also houses the world's largest and most important collection of his works and artefacts.

Across the road from Alloway Church lies Auld Alloway Kirk, which, in addition to being where Burns's family worshipped when he was a child and the final resting place of his parents, is used as a scene in 'Tam O' Shanter', one of his most famous poems. Make sure you have a copy of the poem handy when you visit, so you can picture the scene.

Burns Monument Gardens lie another short walk away, where the monument, designed by Thomas Hamilton, overlooks the River Doon and the Brig o' Doon, where Tam O' Shanter's fleeing horse lost her tail in the poem. Look for the telling of the tale of Tam O' Shanter along the Poet's Path and watch out for *cutty sarks* (naked dancers)!

Alloway is a must-see for all those who love the poetry of Burns.

Whithorn

Whithorn, in the southwest of Scotland, developed after St Ninian, a fourth-century Christian missionary, built a church here around 397 AD. This church was known as the 'Candida Casa', or 'White House', because, unusually for the time, it was built of stone. This is the first recorded Christian church in Scotland, established more than a hundred years before St Columba came to Iona. A settlement grew up around it, with trade links to Gaul (France). By the end of the fifth century, Whithorn was importing fine wines and pottery and had an established port at the nearby peninsula, the Isle of Whithorn, making it, very possibly, the first town in Scotland.

The now ruined priory and the shrine of St Ninian, which it contained, made Whithorn one of the most popular pilgrimage destinations in Scotland. Many notables – including Robert the Bruce and Mary, Queen of Scots – visited here.

The area around Whithorn also has many ancient sites and places of interest to visit, including castles, tower houses, standing stones with cup and ring markings, Iron Age forts, farm steadings and medieval churches. The area also appeals to film buffs because many of the scenes in the classic horror movie *The Wicker Man* (1973) were filmed in the area, including the climactic final scene.

Beware of giant straw men!

Chapter 18

Ten Little-Known Scottish People Who Are Worth Knowing About

In This Chapter

▶ Identifying people who made a difference

▶ Admiring people who stood up for human rights

▶ Considering people who enriched our understanding of the world

*T*he people covered in this chapter aren't as famous as the usual suspects of Scottish history – William Wallace; Robert the Bruce; Mary, Queen of Scots; and so on – but they deserve their place in the national story. Who knows? When their contribution is put before the Scottish public, they may become as well known as these more illustrious figures!

Bridei, King of the Picts (616/628?–693)

We know very little about Bridei, but it appears that he became over-king of the Picts in 672 and reigned until his death in 693. He is believed to have been buried in Iona and was remembered as the man who freed his kingdom and for being a friend of Adomnán, the biographer of St Columba. For more on the Picts head to Chapters 2 and 3.

St Ninian

Most people see St Columba as the first apostle to the Scots, but today some historians are coming around to the view that St Ninian was more important or at least as important in bringing Christianity to Scotland. We don't know a great deal about Ninian's life, except that he was a bishop and a Briton by birth, who had studied in Rome. He came to Whithorn, Galloway, around

500 AD, where he built the famous Candida Casa (White House) in which he was later buried. He was said to have restored the sight of King Tudwal, who had become blind after harassing the saint.

Ninian's fame was based on his bringing Christianity to the southern Picts. There is some doubt regarding that story, but one thing we know for sure is that his cult spread throughout Scotland and into the Northern Isles. Due to Ninian's celebrity and cult following, Whithorn became a place of special pilgrimage for Scots. Among the more famous of countless pilgrims was Robert the Bruce, during his last illness, and after him, James IV. If you want to know more about the coming of Christianity to Scotland, dip into Chapter 3.

Andrew de Moray (?–1297)

Many people have heard of the exploits of William Wallace in his struggle to free Scotland from English domination, but equally important was the contribution of another hero and patriot, Andrew de Moray. De Moray was a descendant of a Flemish family that had been invited to Scotland in the mid-12th century by David I. His father, Andrew, was part of the Scottish aristocracy as the king's chief law officer in northern Scotland; he also held lands near Inverness and the Black Isle. De Moray fought in support of King John Balliol and against English interference in Scotland. In 1296, he was captured and taken prisoner along with his father and uncle at the Battle of Dunbar.

In the winter of 1297, de Moray somehow managed to escape from captivity in Chester Castle and returned north to Morayshire. With his father still a prisoner in the Tower of London, de Moray led the northern rebellion against English rule in 1297. By the end of 1297, his guerrilla tactics had loosened English control in Morayshire, and his forces had taken possession of the principal castles of the region, including Elgin, Banff and Inverness.

Some of de Moray's deeds were apparently appropriated by Blind Harry in his epic poem, 'The Wallace', and attributed to William Wallace. One example was Wallace's alleged attack on the port of Aberdeen, in which, according to Blind Harry, he burned English ships moored in the harbour. There is no evidence that Wallace was ever in Aberdeen, which means that the action was probably the work of de Moray.

De Moray's success in the north was matched by William Wallace in the south. In September 1297, the two joined forces and inflicted a crushing defeat on the English at Stirling Bridge. De Moray was named in letters along with Wallace as 'the leaders of the army and of the realm of Scotland'. However, victory came at a price: de Moray was wounded at Stirling and died, it is believed, sometime in November 1297.

By the Battle of Stirling, English control of Scotland was in tatters. Some historians have argued that too much credit for this has gone to Wallace and that the successful campaign of 1297 owed more to de Moray than it did to his more celebrated contemporary. If you want to learn more about the wars of independence, turn to Chapter 7.

Patrick Hamilton (1504–1528)

Patrick Hamilton was Scotland's first Protestant martyr and his execution by burning at the stake was one of the first signs that winds of change were blowing through the aisles of the churches north of the border.

There was nothing in Hamilton's privileged childhood that would have indicated martyrdom in later life. He was the son of Sir Patrick Hamilton of Kincavel and Catherine Stewart, daughter of the duke of Albany, the second son of James II. At the age of 13, Patrick was titular abbot of Fearn Abbey, Ross-shire, and the income he received from it allowed him to study in Paris. Although he graduated in 1520, it was in Paris that young Patrick began to go astray, when he was introduced to the writings of the German reformer Martin Luther. After further study in Louvain, Holland, Hamilton became a student at the University of St Andrews and, later, a member of the teaching staff.

Hamilton was bursting with enthusiasm to spread the so-called heretical ideas of Luther and other Protestant reformers. This brought him to the attention of the odious Archbishop James Beaton of St Andrews (also chancellor of Scotland), who decided to summon Hamilton in 1527 to stand trial on a charge of heresy. Not being eager to attain martyrdom at the age of 23, Hamilton escaped to Germany, where he enrolled as a student in the newly opened University of Marburg. But after a short stay, he returned to the family home in Kincavel in the autumn of that year. There he got married – we don't know whom he married, but the marriage did produce a child, Isobel.

Marriage and a pregnant wife didn't stop Patrick's preaching. Beaton hatched a plot to incriminate the naive young abbot. He invited Hamilton to a conference in St Andrews, where for a month he was given free rein to preach and debate his ideas. This allowed Beaton and his spies to gather material that would later be used to accuse Hamilton of spreading heretical doctrines.

Hamilton was arrested during the night of 28 February 1528 and charged with13 counts of heresy. The following morning, he was tried before a council made up of 13 bishops and clergy. The trial was a sham – the verdict was already written before it began: guilty as charged! Under cross-examination, Hamilton stood by his beliefs, which made execution a certainty. Found guilty of being an 'obstinate heretic', he was handed over to the town council for sentence to be carried out in front of St Salvator's Chapel. The burning at the stake took place as soon as the trial was over, which made a rescue attempt by his friends impossible. The weather was damp, and this drew out the execution for six hours – it was said he was roasted rather than burned. His last words were said to be, 'Lord Jesus, receive my spirit.' Hamilton's daughter was born after his death.

Beaton's planned attempt to silence Hamilton and his ideas forever backfired spectacularly. The execution drew even more attention to the doctrines Hamilton had been preaching. This helped to spread the Reformation throughout Scotland, and Beaton was warned by a colleague that the 'reek of Master Patrick Hamilton infected as many as it blew on'. If you want to know more about the Reformation, go straight to Chapter 10.

The memory of Hamilton lives on in a rather odd, superstitious way. Traditionally, during exam time St Andrews University students avoid standing on the monogram of Hamilton's initials on the cobblestones outside St Salvator's Chapel for fear of failing!

Sir William Paterson (1658–1719)

Scottish history is littered with countless knaves, rogues and scoundrels, who have taken advantage of situations and people, but very few of them have demonstrated the ability to con a whole nation – that is, with the exception of one William Paterson, banker and trader. So, this is a story about an exceptional, but delusional, visionary whose career was testament to J.M. Barrie's view that, 'There are few more impressive sights in the world than a Scotsman on the make.'

Born in 1658 in a farmhouse in Dumfries-shire, Paterson emigrated to the Bahamas at the age of 17. It was in the Bahamas that he first conceived the idea of establishing a colony on the Isthmus of Darien, Panama, which would be a centre for trade with the Far East. Paterson returned to England after the Revolution of 1688 and made a fortune in foreign trade, which gained him a reputation as a trader and financier of some standing in London.

The public first began to hear of him when, along with a group of London merchants, he set up the Bank of England in 1694. Fortunately for the bank, Paterson soon fell out with his fellow directors, sold his stock and left. Unfortunately for the Scots, it gave Paterson more time to concentrate on his plan to establish a colony in Panama, known as the Darien Scheme.

In 1695, he convinced the Scottish government to set up the Company of Scotland with the intention of sending a fleet and settlers to Panama. The Company's aim was to raise finance from both English and Scottish merchants, but opposition in the English Parliament quashed any hope of investment from that area. The Scots had to go it alone. They raised £400,000 in a couple of weeks (roughly equivalent to £42million today). This was a quarter of the total amount of money in Scotland (think about that!), and it was lost along with the lives of the majority of settlers in two ill-fated expeditions. Paterson himself lost a great deal of money and his wife and child to disease.

The collapse of the Darien Scheme was one of the factors that led to the Union of Parliaments in 1707. If they voted for union, the investors were promised compensation for their losses through a scheme called the Equivalent (see Chapter 12 for more on the Darien Scheme and the Union of Parliaments). Paterson got his money back in 1715 but died soon after, in 1719, and is buried in Sweetheart Abbey, Kirkcudbright.

Thomas Muir the Younger of Huntershill (1765–1799)

Thomas Muir was a lawyer and political reformer who tried to change the corrupt political system in Britain and make it more representative of the people. Like many people of the day, he was inspired by the French Revolution of 1789. The ideas of liberty, fraternity and equality hit a nerve. Soon various societies were set up across Britain to campaign for democracy or the 'rights of man' (no one talked about women's rights).

Muir and others set up the Friends of the People in 1792, but the government, fearing that the 'terror' in France might be exported across the English Channel, began a general crackdown on radical groups. As one of the leading Scottish radicals, Muir was singled out and arrested in January 1793 on a charge of sedition. He was released on bail and went to France to plead with the Jacobin leaders to spare the life of the French king, Louis XVI. Muir realised that if Louis was executed, the support of those among the upper classes in favour of reform would evaporate. The king was executed, leading to an even greater crackdown on radical groups and a declaration of war against France.

Muir returned to Scotland in August 1793 and was immediately arrested. At a sham trial, he was sentenced to 14 years of transportation to Botany Bay, Australia.

Thomas Muir had become democracy's first martyr in Scotland. The radical movement in Scotland suffered another blow when more of its leaders were also sentenced to transportation and joined Muir on the convict transport ship *Surprise,* reaching Sydney in October 1794.

Two years later, Muir escaped onboard an American ship and returned to Europe via California, Mexico and Cuba, arriving in Spain in the spring of 1797. His entry to Spain was far from easy – a British man-of-war engaged the ship carrying him in battle, and Muir was severely wounded, with his left cheekbone blown off. From Spain, Muir made it to Paris, where he was hailed as a hero of the French Republic. But by this time, he was very weak and half-blind.

While in Paris, Muir called on the French government to intervene militarily on behalf of the Scottish people and help them establish a republic. But he didn't live long enough to see this come to pass. Indeed, it never happened, and Muir died on 26 January 1799. However, his struggle to change the political system bore fruit in the long run. Think of him and the other political martyrs the next time you decide you can't go out to vote because it's raining!

Lachlan Macquarie (1762–1824)

Although Lachlan Macquarie is seen as the 'father of Australia', he is virtually unknown in the land of his birth. Born on the island of Ulva, off the coast of Mull, he was a crucial presence in the transition of New South Wales from a penal colony to a free settlement. Before he was governor, Macquarie was a soldier, joining the British army at the age of 14, taking part in the American War of Independence and earning a commission as a lieutenant. From there, he served in India and Egypt, where he was present at the capture of Alexandria and the final expulsion of the French army from Egypt, attaining the rank of adjutant general.

Macquarie was appointed governor of New South Wales in 1807 and arrived at the end of 1809 in a colony renowned for disorderly government; indeed, there was a rebellion against his predecessor the year before he arrived.

To restore order and provide good government Macquarie set about reforming the justice system, setting up new courts and restraining the excessive use of corporal punishment by magistrates. His administration reduced the average annual expenditure per convict by about two-thirds, even though the number of prisoners increased about tenfold after the end of the French Wars in 1815.

Macquarie's reforms provoked opposition from vested interests, particularly from army officers who had been running the colony since the overthrow of the last governor. Macquarie quickly realised that he had to break the power of these officers if law and order was to be maintained. He had no choice but to run the colony as an 'enlightened despot'.

He also tried to improve the situation of the convict population of New South Wales. Those who had served their time or been granted a pardon were known as 'emancipists', and Macquarie appointed some of them to government positions: two were made magistrates! In exchange, he demanded that the ex-convicts live reformed (that is, Christian) lives.

On top of this, he encouraged greater exploration of the continent. This exploration was crucial in opening up new lands for settlement. In July 1813, the colony at last obtained a coinage in place of the notes of hand and barter previously used. At the end of 1816, despite the opposition of the British government, he encouraged the creation of the colony's first bank.

Macquarie also flouted the British government's ban on building expensive public buildings in the colony, overseeing the construction of the Sydney Conservatorium of Music. In fact, he listed 265 works of varying scale that had been carried out during his time as governor. It was clear that Macquarie had gone past viewing New South Wales as simply a dumping ground for British criminals.

Macquarie's attitude to the Aborigines was ambiguous: he ordered punitive missions against them, but at the same time he showed sympathy for them, opening an institution for the education of Aboriginal children in 1814. In spite of some of his enlightened policies, the (free) settler community opposed his autocratic form of government. An adverse report on the running of the colony led to his resignation in 1821. Macquarie returned to Britain and died in London three years later, after successfully negotiating with the government for a pension in recognition of his service in New South Wales. His body was laid to rest on the Isle of Mull.

Since his death, Macquarie's reputation has grown, and he is now seen as the most enlightened and progressive of the early colonial governors who sought to establish Australia as a country, rather than as a prison camp. The name of Australia was first used in an official dispatch by Macquarie in 1817. So three cheers, cobber!

Mary Somerville (1780–1872)

By any stretch of the imagination, Mary Somerville was a truly remarkable woman who proved to Victorian society that women could understand science! Born in Jedburgh, as a child she developed an interest in mathematics, but for girls of her background and age, finding a husband was considered more important than studying. Besides, the seats of higher learning were for males only. Mary married her cousin, Samuel Grieg, and when he died in 1807, she married another cousin, William Somerville, an army doctor, in 1812. (Nothing like keeping it in the family!)

It wasn't until her late 40s that Mary embarked on a career as a science writer. Her first task was to translate a book by the French astronomer Pierre-Simon Laplace in 1831. Her next task was her own work on the physical sciences, which ran to nine editions. This was followed by other publications on science and geography. She wrote her last book – *On Molecular and Microscopic Science* (1869) – when she was in her 89th year!

The press gave Somerville the title 'the Queen of Science' and she more than lived up to the accolade. She proved that male fears that scientific education was too much for a woman's brain to cope with were unfounded. In 1826, she became the first woman to read a paper to the Royal Society and to have it published in its *Philosophical Transactions.* In 1835, she and Caroline Herschel became the first women members of the Royal Astronomical Society. In 1869, she was awarded the Victoria Medal of the Royal Geographical Society.

Somerville lived much of her later life in Italy (she died in Naples and is buried there in the English Cemetery) because of her husband's ill health. But she was rewarded with numerous honours in Britain; perhaps the greatest of these was Somerville College in Oxford, which was opened in 1879 and named after her. Somerville did much to popularise science among women, but she also tried to improve their social and political position. Indeed, four years before her death at age 91, she signed John Stuart Mill's unsuccessful petition for women's suffrage.

Eliza Wigham (1820–1899)

Eliza Wigham is one of the least known but most important women of 19th-century Scotland. Her family were Quakers and had been involved in the struggles to end slavery in the British Empire. By the time Wigham reached adulthood, the focus had shifted to the United States. Anti-slavery movements sprang up both in Scotland and in America, and Eliza and her whole family were at the forefront of the struggle to free the slaves. This brought her into contact with the leading American abolitionists, including the radical William Lloyd Garrison, who also favoured promoting the rights of women. Garrison convinced Wigham and other women that they were as unfree as slaves.

This linkage of abolition and women's rights divided the anti-slavery movement in the United States and Britain; indeed, Wigham found herself in opposition to her father, John, leader of the Edinburgh Emancipation Society, over the issue of women's rights. But this family disagreement didn't stop her fighting to link freedom for slaves with freedom for women.

Slavery came to an end after the American Civil War, but Wigham didn't put her feet up and think the job done. There were other causes to attend to, and she worked tirelessly to improve the position of women in the UK. She was prominent in all the important campaigns:

✔ She opposed the Contagious Diseases Act, which allowed for any woman to be arrested as a prostitute on the suspicion of a police officer.

✔ She fought for women to gain access to higher education.

✔ She was a passionate advocate of women's right to vote.

As a Quaker, she was also fundamentally opposed to war and argued for the setting up of a High Court of Nations to settle all international disputes. On top of her international activities, Wigham worked continuously to improve the condition of poor working women in Edinburgh. If ever a person deserves a plaque or a statue, Eliza Wigham does – but you won't find one, not even outside the house in the street in Edinburgh where she lived!

Roland Eugene Muirhead (1868–1964)

It's hard to believe today when there is a parliament in Edinburgh that Nationalism was once a political view held by only a tiny minority of Scots. It was men like Roland Muirhead and their commitment that kept the idea of an independent Scotland alive. Without him and his fellow Nationalists, the Scottish National Party would never have emerged, far less grown into a party of government.

Muirhead was the son of a prosperous businessman in Lochwinnoch, Renfrewshire, but in spite of a privileged upbringing, he became a Socialist due to the influence of his elder brother, Robert. While working in Latin America in the late 1880s, Roland became a convinced Nationalist, reasoning that if a country like Paraguay, with a population less than 100,000, was able to run its own affairs, why couldn't Scotland? On his return to Scotland, Muirhead became involved in local politics and took over the running of his father's tannery business at the Bridge of Weir. He was a model employer: he arranged for workers to have a share in the ownership of the business and introduced a 40-hour workweek.

Although a shrewd and capable businessman, Muirhead was not interested in acquiring surplus capital for his own personal consumption. Instead, he used his money to finance any political organisation or radical cause that he felt warranted his support. From the 1890s onward, this meant supporting Scottish home rule. In 1901, he joined the Liberal-orientated Young Scots Society, whose aim was to encourage home rule legislation. But as Parliament turned down one home rule bill after another, Muirhead grew disillusioned with the Liberals.

In 1918, he became a member of the Independent Labour Party. With the help of some of its leading members, he revived the waning Scottish Home Rule Association (SHRA). But he soon tired of Labour's lukewarm support for the cause of home rule, and in 1928, he resigned from the party and the SHRA. With likeminded Nationalists, Muirhead formed the National Party of Scotland and was its first chairman. He stood for Parliament as a Nationalist candidate a number of times in the 1930s, convinced that 'English rule in Scotland had been a failure', but he received only a tiny number of votes.

The National Party joined with other groups in 1934 to form the Scottish National Party. And in 1936, Muirhead was elected honorary president. As part of his opposition to the British state, he refused to support the call for king and country in both world wars and opposed conscription as contrary to the Treaty of Union. Later, he was active in the Campaign for Nuclear Disarmament in the 1960s. Although he failed to see the Scottish National Party take off as a popular political party in Scotland, the 'Grand Old Man of Scottish Patriotism', as he was known, was one of a number of stalwarts who built the platform, and he should be remembered for it.

Chapter 19

Ten Things Scotland Has Given to the World

In This Chapter

▶ Looking at advances in science, technology and medicine

▶ Considering religion and sport

▶ Focusing on the all-important whisky

For a small country, Scotland has had its share of ground-breaking inventions, covering all areas of human life. Okay, so the Scots didn't invent the wheel, but they invented or discovered pretty much everything else! Penicillin, the telephone, the steam engine, paved roads and television all originated here. In this chapter, I cover just a few of the many things that you may or may not have realised were invented in Scotland.

The Flushing Toilet

Archaeologists at Skara Brae on Orkney have discovered evidence that Neolithic man used a system of hydraulic technology involving a nearby river and drainage channels to wash away their waste as early as 3,000 BC. However, one of the most crucial developments in the history of the flushing toilet was patented in 1775 by Alexander Cummings, a watchmaker from Edinburgh, when he invented the S-bend. His design uses standing water in a valve system to prevent nasty smells and waste from backing up out of the sewer. The design is still in use today. Phew! Thanks, Alex!

The King James Bible

The King James Bible of 1611 has been described as the most important book in English culture and religion. Although there had been translations of the Bible and parts of the Bible into English dating back to the 15th century, none was as ambitious in scale or coverage as the King James Bible. Its birth was due to King James VI of Scotland, who, since 1601, had expressed a desire to have the Bible translated into everyday English.

When James became king of England and Scotland two years later, one of his first acts was to commission a new translation of the Bible into English, one that he insisted would adhere to the character of the Church of England. The translation was carried out by 47 scholars working in Oxford, Cambridge and Westminster. Their work was finished in 1611, and the new printed bible sold at 10 shillings loose-leaf or 12 shillings bound. The translation wasn't plain sailing, and it took time to be accepted, but it eventually became the authorised version used by Protestants all over the world.

The importance of the King James Bible is not just spiritual – it's also literary. It has contributed more sayings to the English language than any other single source, including Shakespeare. Examples include 'feet of clay' and 'reap the whirlwind'.

Criminal Fingerprinting

We've all seen countless examples in TV shows and movies when the criminal leaves a fingerprint at the scene of the crime and because of this gets convicted. Each fingerprint is unique – the chances of two different people having the same fingerprint are thought to be 1 in 64 billion!

The uniqueness of the fingerprint has been long recognised. It was used in India by Sir James Herschel in 1877 to prevent the relatives of deceased government pensioners from fraudulently collecting their pensions after their death. However, it was a Scottish surgeon and medical missionary, Henry Faulds, working in a Tokyo hospital, who in 1880 first proposed using printing ink to record them. He also worked out a system for fingerprint classification.

Faulds returned to Britain in 1886 and immediately offered his invention to Scotland Yard, but the police authorities dismissed it. Undaunted, he approached Charles Darwin, but because Darwin was getting on a bit and not in the best of health, he passed Faulds's letter to his half-cousin, Francis Galton. Unscrupulously, Galton used Faulds's invention and methods without attribution in his book *Finger Prints.* But there is no doubt that Faulds published the first paper on the subject in the scientific journal *Nature* in 1880. So, the honour of having been the inventor of criminal fingerprinting goes to him.

Unfortunately, Faulds resented the lack of recognition he received for his work during his life. He died in March 1930 at the age of 86, a very embittered man.

Whisky: Water of Life

Although Scotch whisky is enjoyed in more than 200 countries today and is a multi-billion-pound export industry, it was not the drink of choice of Scots until the 17th century. Before then, Scots drank wine and porter, a kind of ale. The first record of whisky distillation was in 1494 by Friar John Cor of Lindores, Fife. Because it was cheap to produce and didn't need much scientific knowledge (practically anybody could do it), the production of whisky soon grew.

The Scottish government – never short of new methods of raising taxes – introduced the first duty on whisky in 1644. This led to widespread evasion, and the number of illegal whisky stills multiplied. By 1780, there were reckoned to be 8 legal distilleries and 400 illegal ones!

Many bloody encounters occurred between the *excisemen* (government officials empowered to shut down illegal stills) and whisky smugglers. The former weren't too successful – about half of all the whisky distilled in Scotland never resulted in any duty being paid. However, step by step, the government drove the illegal distillers out of business, and by 1840, the industry was in the hands of the legal distilleries licensed by government order.

The invention of the column still by Aeneas Coffey in 1830 cheapened the production even more and produced a smoother-tasting spirit. In 1850, Andrew Usher introduced blended whisky, which combined grain (made from wheat, rye and so on) with malt (made from malted barley). Its cheapness increased the spirit's popularity. However, what crowned whisky as the number-one spirit of choice was the phylloxera bug, which destroyed wine and cognac production in France in 1880. So, when you raise a dram in a toast, remember that it's the most fought-over alcoholic beverage ever produced!

Colour Photography

One thing you can say about Victorian Scots is that they were an inventive lot, and none more so than James Clerk Maxwell. Although better known for his work on electromagnetism, Maxwell presented the world's first demonstration of colour photography to the Royal Institution in 1861. He had been interested in colour theory all his adult life and had written scientific papers on colour blindness. His research led him to the conclusion that if you took three black-and-white photographs of an object or a scene through red, green and blue filters – the primary colours seen by the eye – and projected those onto a screen using three projectors with similar filters, the eye would be deceived into thinking that it was a composite of all the colours in the scene.

For the 1861 presentation, a tartan ribbon was used and the photograph was taken by Thomas Sutton, the inventor of the single lens reflex (SLR) camera. (No, he wasn't Scottish.) From that point onward, the three-colour method became the foundation of all colour processes, whether chemical or electronic. Say cheese, everyone!

Anaesthetic

Can you imagine what it must have been like to have surgery before the introduction of anaesthetics? Think of the agony! We have a lot to thank James Young Simpson for. Simpson, an obstetrician who was born in Bathgate, West Lothian, was responsible for the discovery of the anaesthetic properties of chloroform. He discovered it one evening in 1847 during an experiment with his friends, in which he learned chloroform could be used to put people to sleep. His friends didn't wake up until the next morning! Then he tried it out on his niece, who fell asleep after inhaling it while singing. Happy first, sleepy later!

Within weeks of the publication of his 'Account of a New Anaesthetic Agent', chloroform had almost completely replaced ether as an anaesthetic. However, it was not universally accepted until Dr John Snow administered chloroform to Queen Victoria when she gave birth to the last two of her nine children, Leopold in 1853 and Beatrice in 1857. When Simpson died in 1870 at the age of 53, a grateful nation turned out in their thousands to bid him farewell.

Raincoats

Outside the Amazonian rainforest, there is only one part of the world where you would be in greater need of something to keep you dry – the west of Scotland! Like most inventions, the waterproof coat was the result of an accident. In 1823, as he was experimenting with rubber, Charles MacIntosh from Glasgow (where else!) created the world's first waterproof material. He called this material 'rubberised cloth' and initially used it to produce waterproof versions of British riding coats. The coats had two qualities never before experienced: dryness and comfort.

There were early teething problems connected to smell, stiffness and a tendency to melt in hot weather! But these difficulties were later overcome by his business partner, Thomas Hancock. 'Macs', as they were known, became the height of fashion when a waterproof military cloak of blue cloth, lined with crimson silk, was made for the duke of York. The demand increased, and these rubberised coats became standard issue for the British army, the railway staff and the police. When his patent ran out, hundreds of firms began to manufacture versions of the MacIntosh raincoat. It's still keeping the world dry today!

Golf

You may think of golf as a good walk spoiled, but it's clearly one of the most popular sports in the world. There is some debate about its origins: the Dutch claim to have invented it, and so do the French. However, while there was something like golf played with ball and stick in these places, there was one thing missing: the hole. The object of the game as it evolved in Scotland was to get the ball in the hole! That simple task has broken a million hearts, destroyed countless marriages and led to many a nervous breakdown.

The game seems to have started in Scotland in the late medieval period. The earliest reference to it was in 1502, when James IV, who had previously banned golf in favour of archery, purchased a set of golf clubs from a bow-maker in St Johnston (Perth). When James VI became king of England and Scotland, he introduced the English court to the game. Emigrants took the game to America in the 18th century. In 1786, Scottish merchants established the South Carolina Golf Club in Charleston, the first golf club in the United States.

It was still a far cry from the game we know today with its many rules and regulations. However, golf was evolving: on 7 March 1744, the Gentlemen Golfers of Leith produced the first set of written rules; stroke play was introduced in 1759; and the 18-hole course made its appearance in 1764. Over the years, new innovations in equipment appeared, and the first Open Championship was held at Prestwick in 1860.

Although professionals began to emerge later in the 19th century, in Scotland it was still the people's game. Unlike in England, where golf was snobby and revolved round the clubhouse, it was the course that counted in Scotland. Many of Scotland's most famous courses – like the Old Course of St Andrews – are still owned by local councils. Today, the Royal and Ancient Golf Club of St Andrews is the governing body of world golf, responsible for legislation on the rules – but don't ask them to allow women members!

Dolly the Sheep

Dolly was the first mammal to be successfully cloned from an adult cell. The cloning was carried out by scientists at the Roslin Institute in Edinburgh by inserting DNA from a single sheep cell into an egg and implanting it in a surrogate mother. When the ewe was born on 5 July 1996, she was given the name Dolly after the American country-and-western singer Dolly Parton, due to the fact that she was cloned from a mammary cell. (If you know Dolly Parton, you'll understand why!)

Dolly's birth was heralded as one of the most significant scientific break-throughs of the late 20th century. Subsequent DNA tests revealed that Dolly was identical to the ewe who donated the mammary cell and not the surrogate mother. After cloning was successfully demonstrated through the production of Dolly, many other large mammals were cloned, including pigs, deer, horses and bulls.

Dolly's arrival sparked ethical concerns regarding its application to human beings – the idea of a Hitler-type 'master race' was much discussed in the media. All this concern proved unfounded. Today, cloning is helping scientists understand genetic diseases and the aging process. Dolly lived only six years; on 14 February 2003, she was put down because of an incurable lung disease and severe arthritis. She was given to the National Museums Scotland, and her remains are conserved as an exhibit. Dolly is now on display in the Museum's Connect Gallery. Pop in and say, 'Hello, Dolly!'

For Auld Lang Syne

The song 'Auld Lang Syne' is one of Scotland's great gifts to the world. It's traditionally sung at midnight on Hogmanay (New Year's Eve) from Tokyo to New York to celebrate the start of the New Year. But it's also used at many gatherings from *ceilidhs* (traditional parties with music and dancing), to *Burns suppers* (celebrations of the life of the poet Robert Burns), to Boy Scout jamborees and more, to bring the proceedings to a glorious end. The song has been recorded by countless recording artists, including Jimi Hendrix and Elvis Presley!

Written by the national bard, Robert Burns, in 1788, 'Auld Lang Syne' recalls the love and kindness of days gone by, but by taking our neighbours' hands during the singing, it also points to a future based on community and friendship. The universality of these sentiments is the reason for its popularity and longevity.

The literal translation of the song's title into English is 'old long since'.

Index

• F •

About the Author

William Knox is a senior lecturer at the Institute of Scottish Historical Research, University of St Andrews. He was educated at Edinburgh city schools and read history at the University of Edinburgh, where he completed his PhD in 1980. He has been teaching history to undergraduates and postgraduates at the University of Edinburgh for over 20 years. Much of his published work has focused on social and labour history, but he has also written on gender and cultural history. Bill is the author of six books and over 30 articles covering the last 300 years of Scottish history. Among his major publications are *Industrial Nation: Work, Culture and Society in Scotland, 1800–Present* (1999) and *The Lives of Scottish Women: Women and Scottish Society, 1800–1980* (2006).

Dedication

For Joyce

Author's Acknowledgments

This book is a synthesis of the work of other historians working in the field of Scottish history; without their knowledge and scholarship, it could not have been written, so many thanks to them.

On a personal note, I would like to acknowledge the support of my partner, Joyce Carson, whose assistance and feedback during the writing of the book was most appreciated. I also appreciated the brainstorming moments spent with Susan Kerr. Thanks also to the book's technical editor, Richard Finlay of the University of Strathclyde. This book is stronger because of his input. Thanks also to my editor, Elizabeth Kuball, for her professionalism and efficiency; she knows how to get the ball rolling and, more importantly, keep it going in the right direction.

Finally, a word to all my family and friends and those who buy and read the book: this is us; this is our story; this is where we come from.

Publisher's Acknowledgments

Executive Commissioning Editor: Mike Baker

Project Editor: Elizabeth Kuball

Copy Editor: Elizabeth Kuball

Technical Editor: Richard Finlay

Project Coordinator: Melissa Cossell

Cover Image: © iStockphoto.com/bkindler